FAITH, FREEDOM AND THE FUTURE

FAITH, FREEDOM AND THE FUTURE:

Challenges for the 21st Century

Michael Nazir-Ali

Wilberforce Publications

WIPF & STOCK · Eugene, Oregon

First published in Great Britain by Wilberforce Publications Limited.

www.wipfandstock.com

PAPERBACK ISBN: 978-1-5326-0024-1
HARDCOVER ISBN: 978-1-5326-0025-8

Contents

Preface: Spiritual Renewal and the Defence of Freedom   7

Part 1: Faith, Hope and Love   9
1. Faith Working through Love   13
2. Love and Law in Christianity and Islam   25
3. Is there a Gospel for the 21st century?   37

Part 2: Christians and Society   55
4. Why Christians should be Involved in Public Life   59
5. Calling all Christians: Should we be Prepared for Exile?   67
6. The Constitutional and Sacramental Significance of the Coronation   81
7. Why Can't the Voice of Christians be Heard?   87

Part 3: Freedom and Responsibility   91
8. Freedoms we Risk Losing   95
9. Women and the Veil (what should we do with the veil?)   109
10. How to Save Marriage from Hitting the Rocks   113
11. Boys, the Family and the Need for a Father   125
12. Designer Babies are a Disaster for Society   131
13. Three-parent Babies: an Ethical Boundary has been Crossed   135
14. A Christian View of the Donation and Transplantation of Organs   139
15. Let us Help People to Live rather than to Die   145

Part 4: Islamism's Challenge to a Christian Future   149
16. Arab Spring, Islamist Summer   153
17. Radical Islam and its Invisible Victims   159
18. Protect the Christians   169
19. Freedom in the Face of Resurgent Islam   173
20. We Cannot Avoid the Battle over Blasphemy   185
21. The Global Resurgence of Islamism   191
22. Resources for Christian Leadership in the Middle East   195

Part 5: Church in Crisis   213
23. The Nature and Future of the Anglican Communion   217
24. Jesus, Lord of his Church and of the Church's Mission   231
25. The Anglican Communion and Ecumenical Relations   243
26. Thinking and Acting Morally   269
27. A Dumbed-down Christening: Culture and the Church of England   287

Epilogue: Working in the Light of the Gospel   291
Bibliography   295
Index   301
Acknowledgements   327

PREFACE

Spiritual Renewal and the Defence of Freedom

So many wars have been fought to protect freedom and there has been so much struggle to achieve it and yet today we are faced with unprecedented challenges to it, both globally and locally, from without and within.

Anyone reasonably self-aware will ask how we are to be free as persons, not in terms of licence, selfishness or greed, but in the fuller and untrammelled expression of our true nature. The Christian faith answers this in terms of our minds being transformed through faith in Jesus Christ and of our being conformed, more and more, to the image of God in which we have been created and which has been perfectly revealed to us in Christ and declared in the apostolic preaching (Rom. 12:1–2, Col. 1:15–23, 1 Thess. 1:6, Heb. 13:13–15). Any attempt to bring good news to this century must answer the question: "*how am I to be free?*"

The question about freedom is certainly an existential question, but it is also a political and social one. How is the freedom of persons, families and communities to be guaranteed against the power of an ever-encroaching state? How will the growing challenge of totalitarian ideologies, secular and religious, be met? Will the informed conscience of the citizen be respected or trodden down? This is then the ever-present problem of how freedom is to be balanced by personal and social responsibility.

The challenges posed for both freedom and responsibility are discussed in relation to a number of issues, many to do with belief and its expression, with the dignity of the personal at every stage of life, with the nature of marriage and the importance of the family and with the use of medical technology.

Radical Islamist ideologies are becoming a particular threat not only to world peace and to national security but to the very survival of Christian, Yazidi, Jewish and other minorities throughout the Islamic world and beyond. Some attention is given as to how such a threat is to be met, how minorities can be protected and freedom protected even, perhaps especially, in such situations.

The West's preparedness in meeting these challenges has to do, of course, with military resources, effective intelligence and informed diplomacy but it also has to do with spiritual and moral preparedness. Here the abandoning of the Christian faith by large numbers of people, the continual secularising of the state, partly as a consequence of loss of faith in the population and partly leading it, and the large-scale rejection of Christian teaching in the mainline churches themselves has left the West unprepared to understand and meet the challenge from a religiously-inspired ideology.

It is only through a renewal (or revival) of the vision of the Bible that the West will be able to strengthen its own moral and social basis and to counter the challenges being posed from outside. It may be that God, in his mercy, will renew and revive the existing denominations (this has happened before) or, if not, it may be in fresh ways that the Spirit will blow over parched lands and dry bones. Whichever it is, we must pray urgently for the Spirit's refreshment and for not only spiritual but moral renewal. The one must lead to the other.

+Michael Nazir-Ali

Part One

FAITH, HOPE AND LOVE

In this section, we consider the fundamentals of the Christian faith and ask what they mean in our contemporary world. How are these basics to be communicated in a world of many faiths and of an increasingly confident secularism, as well as one with a desire to return to primal paganism in many parts of the West?

We ask how the Gospel responds to the felt needs of our day and how it can provide freedom, integration and direction for individuals alongside a moral and spiritual framework for society. Christianity is not only a faith but a world view which helps us to make sense of our lives and of the universe.

We consider how we come to be right with God and what implications this has not only for right believing but right living. We affirm that our friendship with God is re-established *only* because of Christ's work on our behalf, but that the grace which does this also enables us to recognise and act on what God commands in his Word and in the preaching and teaching of the Church. Notions of 'super-grace' can so quickly become those of 'cheap-grace'. By grace, we gradually become what we have been declared to be.

Is there some recognition of the ways of God in other faiths and of the demands he makes on us? If so, how can we see and use this as *praeparatio evangelica?* How is the Gospel distinctive in what it claims to provide for human beings and the world in which they live? In what ways are the perspectives of other faiths different and how does this lead to different personal and social values? These are not just abstract questions but a great deal of human welfare, both personal and social, depends on the answers that are given.

1

FAITH WORKING THROUGH LOVE: ORIENTATING THE CHURCH'S TEACHING AND PRACTICE TO CHRIST

In his influential and comparative work *The Christian Understanding of Atonement*, the Oxford scholar F W Dillistone has noted the idea of an original universal harmony which is found within many cultures and religious traditions. This harmony, however, is often seen to have been disrupted and must be put right through some kind of cosmic or eternal sacrifice. The sacrificial rituals of different civilisations, which he examines in some detail, attempt to portray and to participate in such a sacrifice. By the offering of a sacrificial victim, those who offer the sacrifice become involved in the business of cosmic death and renewal. Dillistone allows that in many ancient cultures such rituals had become cults of 'dying and rising gods' closely associated with the cycle of nature and the fertility both of the earth and of human beings.[1]

When we come to the Bible, we enter a different world altogether. It is true that the ideas of life renewal and life enhancement are present in the Jewish sacrificial cultus, but the emphasis is very much either on celebrating God's mighty acts of deliverance – we might say, God putting right the injustice and the oppression suffered by his people – or on the expiation of sin. As far as the latter is concerned, the terms often used for the sacrifices, e.g. *ashám* and *hattá't* also stand for the sins for which the sacrifices are being offered. What is important here to note is that notions of a sacrifice 'representing' and 'substituting' for the offerer are already to the fore – and without these it would be difficult to make sense of the Bible's provision of sacrifice.[2] By the offering of the victim, the person or the community is, in some sense, being put right with God.

The system of sacrifice is to be understood then in the wider background of the just God who wills justice in the world which he has created. This justice has been disrupted by human wilfulness and rebellion and needs to be restored. The notion of animal and other sacrifices was, however, the subject of a severe critique by the prophets who saw an over-reliance on its mechanical observance as obscuring the necessity for a change of heart and a need to honour God with the whole of our lives. The former Chief Rabbi, Lord Jakobovits, has pointed out that the writing prophets are not wanting to do away with sacrifice altogether but to emphasise, rather, its spiritual and moral aspect. It is this which leads them, and the Psalmist, to exalt self-sacrifice over and against mere ritual as a surer way of restoring a relationship with God.[3]

There is also a growing recognition in the Old Testament that the suffering of representative people – prophets and martyrs, for example – can and does lead to the fulfilment of God's saving purposes. The themes of the Son of Man in Daniel and of the Suffering Servant in Isaiah show how a representative figure recapitulates in himself both the suffering of God's people as well as their vindication by God. All of this is brought to a head in Psalm 40 where a representative figure steps forward in obedience and this brings about communal deliverance. The writer of the letter to the Hebrews, in his commentary on this passage, encapsulates the entire purpose of the sacrificial system and sees in the coming of Jesus the fulfilment of the hope for a messianic figure who, by his work of suffering for the people, finds vindication by God. By his freely-willed obedience the eternal and incarnate Son offers up himself as a final, unrepeatable and unique sacrifice. As so often in the Bible the speculation, myths and wistful longings of humanity are brought to the bar of a historical event, a person in whom God is himself acting in a saving and sacrificial way (Psalm 40:6–8, cf Hebrews 10:5–7).[4]

As Peter Toon pointed out in his *Justification and Sanctification*, the keywords here are the Hebrew ṣdq and the Greek *dikaioō*. According to him, in the Old Testament the term has a forensic meaning i.e. the verdict of a judge in favour of one party, thus declaring it to be just or righteous. But this also carries ethical overtones, meaning that someone has remained within the Covenant of Faith. The key to understanding the meaning of ṣdq is to think of relationships and their right ordering whether with God, the very source of our being, our fellow human beings or, indeed, with the natural world. The Hebrew, as the Arabic today, also has the sense of personal integrity or character. The story of the Old Testament, however, is that of God's faithfulness but also of the faithlessness of humans, even of his chosen people. So how is God's 'saving justice' to come about? One answer in the Old Testament is that it will come about through the Messianic King who will bring God's justice to the world, freeing people from oppression and bringing prosperity to them (Ps 72:1–4, Ps 146:7–9).

The words related to *dikaioō* in the New Testament, in spite of their etymology, certainly have a declarative intent – not then so much to make righteous as to declare righteous. And yet, as John Piper points out in his response to Tom Wright, such a declaration also accomplishes something. Taking Romans 5:1 as his point of departure: "Therefore, since we have been justified by faith, we have peace with God through our Lord Jesus Christ," that it is to say, alongside God's calling and the awakening of faith, God does something which makes that person's standing right with God. Such a declaration of acquittal, on the basis of faith, which unites us with Christ, also makes us members of his body and thus of the covenant community.[5]

In this way, we become part of God's single-plan-through-Israel-for-the-world, as Tom Wright has pointed out, and which has long been understood by biblical theologians as the meaning of Salvation History.[6] The big picture, important as it is, should not crowd out the personal. Membership of the covenant community must hinge on the individual's God-given faith that his or her sins have been dealt with by Christ standing in his or her place and by Christ's faithfulness, even bearing the ultimate punishment for sin *viz* death, thus averting God's anger from the sins of the individual. My sin and his and hers is no longer reckoned or imputed to us but the righteousness of the obedient Christ is. He, as our representative head and sacrificial substitute, reconciles us to God, thus ending the enmity (2 Cor 5:19, 20; Eph 2:15, 16). The all-important word here is *logidzomai* and its cognates in Romans 4:3 and Galatians 3:6 (the usage in James 2:23 is, admittedly, somewhat different): Abraham had faith in God and it was *reckoned* (or *imputed*) to him as righteousness (cf Gen 15:6 where a cognate of ṣdq is, in fact, used). What is true of Abraham, the father of the faithful must also be true of every believer. We must then, along with St. Paul, insist on the justification and forgiveness for all those in Christ without forgetting that each one of us has to be justified and forgiven. It is not enough to say that we are part of the corporate body. The Bible is full of people, in both the Old and New Testaments, who claimed such membership but who could not be 'reckoned' righteous as Abraham was.

Both Tom Wright and his opponents agree that in Ephesians, the two (or several?) perspectives come together: if Ephesians 2:1–10 is about sinners saved by grace through faith, the rest of the chapter is about the breaking down of the dividing wall of hostility between Jews and Gentiles. We might add, for good measure, that chapters 1 and 3 reveal to us God's cosmic plan "to unite all things in Christ, things in heaven and on earth (1:10)".[7]

In the Anglican tradition there have been those, like Richard Hooker, who have attempted to understand justification in ecclesiological terms, for example, in seeing baptism as the sacrament of justifying righteousness and the Lord's Supper as the sacrament of sanctification (the sacraments being, as it were, the external forum for inward grace).[8] Equally, there have been others, such as JC Ryle, the first Bishop of Liverpool, who have emphasised, rather, the individual in the transaction that takes place. For Ryle, justification is the *counting* of a person to be righteous because of what Jesus Christ has done, whereas sanctification is *making* a person righteous. The first righteousness is not ours but is Christ's and is perfect; the second, which is imparted to us by the Holy Spirit, is ours but it is imperfect. The first is always complete whereas in the second there is room for growth – indeed, there must be growth until the resurrection. In holding such a view, although differing in emphasis, Ryle's position is not all that different from the one set out in Hooker's famous sermon *A Learned Discourse of Justification*. Against this, however, there developed another view, characterised by some of the so-called Caroline Divines of the 17th century, that although justification was made possible for us by the righteousness of Christ, it was made actual by our faith which God accepted as the basis of our justification. (It was said that Abraham *believed* God and it was counted to him for righteousness – Gen 15:6 and related verses in the New Testament.) Such faith, for them, is not merely believing (which even demons do – Jas 2:19) but actively trusting in God resulting in a new attitude and good works which flow from this. These Caroline Divines were clearly trying to meet the dangers of antinomianism but the question arises 'faith in what?' Can it not be fairly said that it must be in what Christ, our leader, representative, substitute and head, has done so that we may be acceptable because of our own union with him? Of course, it can be said that a changed attitude and good works are a sign that we have been justified, but justification cannot be made to depend on them or even on faith itself but, rather, on God's grace given in what Christ has done for us.[9] This does not mean that we have to know what a correct doctrine of justification is but it must mean that we accept that forgiveness of sins is through who Jesus is and what he has done (Acts 13:38, 39).

From the earliest period, there has been debate about how the initial event of justification relates to the growing sanctification of the believer. St. Augustine of Hippo is quoted on every side of the matter and whether he believed in the imputation of Christ's righteousness to the believer or not, he certainly believed that it is the righteousness of God alone brought to us through Christ which avails to salvation. For Augustine, however, and for the whole of the Latin tradition after him, *justificare* tended to mean 'to make righteous', and so justification was seen not simply as an event but as a process by which we increase in holiness and love.[10] The passage often quoted here, Galatians 5:6: 'faith working through love', became an important point of debate and polemics at the time of the Reformation. The Reformers, relying on Erasmus' edition of the Greek Testament and its Latin translation, taught that faith was primary and love its necessary result against medieval attempts to make the verse mean that it was our love that brought about faith.[11] How far we have come, partly because of biblical scholarship, is shown by Pope Benedict in his work *Paul of Tarsus*, where he translates the passage as 'faith that works through love' in a way that the Reform-minded would have approved.[12]

As the Anglican-Roman Catholic agreement *Salvation and the Church* recognises:

> The theologians of the Reformation tended to follow the predominant usage of the New Testament, in which the verb *dikaioun* usually means to 'pronounce righteous'. The Catholic theologians, and notably the Council of Trent, tended to follow the usage of patristic and mediaeval Latin writers, for whom *justificare* (the traditional translation of *dikaioun*) signified 'to make righteous'. Thus the Catholic understanding of the process of justification, following Latin usage, tended to include elements of salvation which the Reformers would describe as belonging to sanctification rather than justification. As a consequence, Protestants took Catholics to be emphasising sanctification in such a way that the absolute gratuitousness of salvation was threatened. On the other side, Catholics feared that Protestants were so stressing the justifying action of God that sanctification and human responsibility were gravely depreciated.[13]

The Reformers certainly held that we were counted right with God because of Christ's obedience being imputed to us. This 'justifying righteousness' is not ours, it is alien to us, but is given to us as a gracious gift. It results in a work of the Holy Spirit which brings about a righteousness which *is* ours. The former is perfect as Hooker saw, whilst the latter, in this life at any rate, is imperfect. This means, among other things, that the justified believer is *simul justus et peccator* (at the same time righteous and a sinner). The Reformers saw this teaching as denied by the Council of Trent. The imparting of Christ's righteousness at baptism was held by this (Roman Catholic) doctrine to have expelled all sin. Any lapse from such post-baptismal purity could only be treated through the sacrament of penance which would restore the Christian to purity.[14]

Peter Toon has pointed out that even in the heat of controversy at the Reformation, agreement on this matter was possible between the Reformers and at least some Catholic theologians. To illustrate the extent of what was even then possible, he published Article 5 of the Regensburg Agreement of 1541 which spoke of justification in terms of 'righteousness which is imputed to us on account of Christ and his merit, not on account of the worthiness or perfection of the righteousness imparted to us in Christ.'[15] At Trent also, there were those, like Cardinal Pole, the Englishman, later to be Papal Legate and Archbishop of Canterbury under Mary Tudor, and Cardinal Seripando, the head of the Augustinians, who wanted to maintain a position which would have permitted imperfection and the existence of sin in the justified believer but their views did not prevail. The Anglican Newman too had insisted on the presence of Christ in us, in addition to inherent righteousness, as that which makes us right with God.[16]

Hans Küng, in his work *Justification* claims that the liturgy of the Roman Catholic Church since Trent, assumes believers to be *simul justus et peccator*. *Salvation and the Church* notes that *Lumen Gentium*, the Dogmatic Constitution on the Church, of the Second Vatican Council, states that the Church is at once holy and in need of purification, constantly following the path of penance and renewal.[17] This seems to echo Karl Rahner's teaching that the Church is sinful both as a matter of doctrine and of experience. The Lutheran-Roman Catholic declaration on justification claims that Lutheran and Catholic views of the remaining sinfulness of believers can be expressed in *simul justus et peccator* language in spite of the differences between Trent and the Lutheran confessions.[18] *Salvation and the Church*, similarly, uses the expression, pointing out that it is of Augustinian inspiration.[19] If all of this means that sinners are justified by the righteousness of Christ alone and that any imparted righteousness remains imperfect and coexists with sinfulness (however that is understood), then this is to be welcomed so long as there is no ambiguity. As Toon remarks in his exposition of the work of Michael Schmaus, a Roman Catholic theologian, it would have been better for all concerned if Trent had been able to distinguish between justification and sanctification.[20]

The great Reformation Confessions repeatedly affirm that justification comes about through faith alone – *ex sola fide Jesu Christi* – and we are accounted just before God *propter meritum Domini* (by the merit of the Lord). However, although we are justified by faith alone, faith is never alone for it is always accompanied by love and operates through love. Good works are the necessary fruit of faith and reveal its genuineness. Here there has been an unusual intervention: Pope Benedict, in his addresses *Paul of Tarsus,* tells us that for St. Paul, after his conversion, saving justification through faith in Jesus Christ became a dominant theme that runs through his letters. Referring to Romans 3:23–24, he repeats that all have sinned and fallen short of the glory of God and are now justified by grace as a gift, through the redemption which is in Christ. In going on to Rom 3:28, he tells us that though the text reads: "We hold that a man is justified by faith apart from works", Luther translated this as "justified by faith alone", even if 'alone' is not in the text. He goes on to say, remarkably, and against the thrust of much post-Reformation Roman Catholic exegesis, that Luther was correct in doing this as it is Christ who makes us just so further observances are unnecessary. Later on, he goes on to explore the relationship between faith and love in ways to which even Tyndale could not have taken exception![21]

The Lutheran-Roman Catholic joint declaration states that "the doctrine of justification is that measure or touchstone for the Christian faith". No teaching may contradict this criterion. In this sense, the doctrine of justification is "an indispensable criterion that consistently serves to orient all the teaching and practice of our churches to Christ."[22] Would that the Council of Trent had listened to those Protestants who attended some of its sessions! We would certainly have been spared much division and suffering. This is not to say that what Hooker called the 'grand question' that hangs between Rome and the Reformation has been resolved. Toon himself points to a whole host of remaining issues but, because of the renewal of biblical scholarship, perhaps, the rules about the discussion have changed and some Catholics are at least willing to consider the issues raised by the Reformers.

The joint declaration tackles head-on the question of assurance; we should look away from our own weakness, as the Reformers taught, and look only to Christ and trust solely in him. It is constantly by looking to Christ that we are preserved in grace.[23] As a result of the debate between John Piper and Tom Wright, it is important to reiterate that our final justification is as much a matter of our faith in Christ as our initial justification. The works produced by the sanctifying work of the Holy Spirit are, to be sure, signs and tokens that we have been justified by faith in all that Jesus has done for us but they should not be taken, in any way, as contributing to our final justification. To do this would be to unravel the whole force of the Reformation view that we are saved by trusting in what God has done for us rather than our own efforts.[24]

One of the criticisms of the doctrine of justification has been that it is well-nigh impossible to make it intelligible to present-day society, at least in the Western world (Tillich).[25]

One of the ways in which we can begin to communicate this essential doctrine is to point to the experienced alienation of modern human beings: from others, from their work, even from themselves and, ultimately, from the very source and ground of their being, God. Another aspect of contemporary life is anxiety: there is a crisis about existence itself, its fragility and its meaning. There is also a sense of guilt about our past in what has gone wrong: the betrayals, the deceptions and self-deceptions, the misuse of power, the wrong acquisition of wealth and so much else. People are fearful about the state of the world, the threat of war, the breakdown of family and of civil society, radical environmental degradation and nuclear holocaust.

In order to mask the loneliness and the anxiety, men, women and even children have given themselves over to addictions of various sorts: endless entertainment, consumerism, drugs, alcohol and pornography. They seek refuge in these from the stresses and strains of life but, of course, these addictions produce new problems of health, of relationships, or mental well-being.

In such a context, the Gospel of being forgiven because of what Christ has done for us, of being accepted and pronounced to be right with God can lead to the reunification of divided personalities, the renewal of relationships, the freeing from anxiety about our immediate or ultimate fate, in short to what the Bible calls the fruit of the Spirit (Gal 5:22f). We are rescued from our constant need to hide our fears and to live with our heads held high because we have been declared to be God's children through the grace of adoption (Rom 8:12–17; Gal 4:6–7). Such a realisation of acceptance, of true freedom, of being part of God's covenant people throughout history and across the world, and of a personal relationship with Christ as the friend who is always for us, can make a proclamation of justification by grace and through faith just what is needed today.

Peter Toon comments that Paul's teaching on justification by faith, hammered out in the context of Jesus' own critique of works-oriented religion, came to life at the time of the Reformation as the Reformers confronted a distortion of the

Gospel by an over-reliance on works.[26]

As I have experienced, Paul's teaching on justification also comes alive in the context of Islamist revivalism with its emphasis on strict enforcement of the *Sharī'a* (Islamic Law), on minute rules for daily living and on ritual prayer, etc. To understand, in such a situation, that we are accepted by God not because of what we are able to do, which is always radically inadequate, but because of what Christ has done for us is, indeed, to be liberated from the law of sin and death and to find ourselves free children of the promise. In both mission and in teaching, this doctrine then remains at the fore and at the core of our identity as Christians and of the Church's identity as the Bride of Christ who is made perfect by and for the Bridegroom.

Notes

[1] F.W. Dillistone, *The Christian Understanding of Atonement*, Welwyn, Nisbet, 1968, pp29ff.

[2] See Michael Nazir-Ali, *The Unique and Universal Christ: Jesus in a Plural World*, Milton Keynes, Paternoster Press, 2008, pp45ff and R.J. Thompson's article on Sacrifice in the Old Testament, *The Illustrated Bible Dictionary*, Leicester, IVP, 1980, vol 3, pp1358ff.

[3] Immanuel Jakobovits in *The Authorised Daily Prayer Book*, St Ives, Singers, 1992, pp918ff.

[4] Nazir-Ali, *The Unique and Universal Christ*, Paternoster, 2008, pp46ff.

[5] John Piper, *The Future of Justification: A response to N.T. Wright*, Nottingham, IVP, 2008, pp40ff.

[6] N.T. Wright, *Justification: God's Plan and Paul's Vision*, London, SPCK 2009, pp18f, 212f etc.

[7] Wright, ibid, pp144, 150f.

[8] Peter Toon, *Justification and Sanctification*, London, Marshall, Morgan & Scott, 1983, pp94f.

[9] Toon, ibid, 97f.

[10] Toon, ibid, pp45f.

[11] See, for example, William Tyndale's invective against the Bishop of Rochester, John Fisher, in *The Obedience of the Christian Man*, London,

Penguin, 2000, pp80f.

[12] Benedict XVI, *Paul of Tarsus*, London, Catholic Truth Society, 2009, p101.

[13] London, CTS and Anglican Consultative Council, 1987, p17.

[14] C. Fitzsimmons Allison, *The Pastoral and Biblical Implications of Trent on Justification*, SLJT, June 1988, Vol XXXI, No 3.

[15] Peter Toon in *Justification and Sanctification* ([ed.] Susan Harris), Charlottetown, Canada, 2008, p88f and 105f.

[16] Allison, op cit.

[17] Lumen Gentium 8 in A. Flannery (ed), Vatican Council II, *The Conciliar and Post Conciliar Documents*, New York, Costello, 1988, p358, *Salvation and the Church*, p21.

[18] *Joint Declaration on the Doctrine of Justification*, Grand Rapids, Eerdmans, 2000, p44.

[19] *Salvation and the Church*, p21.

[20] Toon, op. cit. p122.

[21] Benedict XVI, op. cit., pp98ff.

[22] op. cit., pp46f.

[23] Ibid pp23f, 35f.

[24] John Piper, *The Future of Justification: A response to N.T. Wright*, op. cit, pp117ff.

[25] Toon, op. cit., pp126f, Paul Tillich, *New Being,* Scribner, New York City 1955 and *Systematic Theology* vol 3, University of Chicago Press, 1976.

[26] Toon, ibid, pp135ff.

2

LOVE AND LAW IN CHRISTIANITY AND ISLAM

Both Christianity and Islam emphasise a personal experience of the divine; what in Islam is sometimes known as *ibtighā' wajh Allah* and in Christianity as the vision of God. The implications of this experience have, however, to be worked out for the whole of life and in terms of structures and institutions which sustain such a vision.[1]

Love and law are intimately related in the Hebrew Bible. The best known injunction 'to love the Lord your God with all your heart, soul and might' is found in the Book of Deuteronomy or 'the book of the second law' found in the Temple during the reign of Josiah in the seventh century BC (Deuteronomy 6:5). Its usual companion 'and your neighbour as yourself' is found in the Book of Leviticus, once again in the context of legislation (Leviticus 19:18). It has been said about Leviticus that its underlying aim is to ensure that God's holiness will be able to regulate and direct every area of human activity.[2] Where else have we heard this sentiment?

It is, perhaps, worth remarking at this point that the Hebrew word for love is *aheb* which seems etymologically related to the Arabic *habba*. In trying to find common ground between Abrahamic faiths, it is worth investigating their Semitic background, in terms of language and culture, a little more thoroughly, though we should avoid the temptation of seeing every aspect of Semitic life today as illuminating the biblical material!

In his teaching, Jesus was not abolishing the law but interiorising it. It is not the letter of the law that is most important but its spirit and the change that it brings into our lives and attitudes. Thus it is not only murder that is forbidden but any desire to destroy or even ridicule another human being. Similarly, it is not only committing adultery which is wrong but every evil desire which looks on other human beings as objects which exist only for the fulfilment of my appetite (Matt 5:21–30).

Jesus, moreover, combined the two precepts about loving God and loving one's neighbour in a highly original way. According to him, these two commandments are the ones from which all others derive. They are, therefore, the basis of the Mosaic Law and also the inspiration of the prophetic books (Mark 12:29–31; Matt 22:37–40; Luke 10:25–8). Leviticus had foreseen the question of the lawyer: 'And who is my neighbour?' The injunction 'to love your neighbour as yourself' is followed rapidly by the command 'to love the stranger as yourself' (Leviticus 19:34). In the parable of the Good Samaritan, Jesus removes any possibility of misunderstanding and teaches that even those furthest removed from us in terms of creed, culture or class are to be regarded as our neighbours (Luke 10:29–37).[3]

St. Paul too, continuing the moral teaching of Jesus, tells us quite clearly that 'love is the fulfilling of the law' (Romans 13:10b). The Augustinian maxim 'love and do what you will' is also to be understood in this sense. For Augustine, of course, the possibility of loving is itself a divine gift: *Da quod iubes et iubes quod vis,* 'Give what you command and command what you will' (*Confessions,* Book X, xxix [40]).

In the Christian tradition, therefore, there is the basic understanding that even the possibility of our loving God and our neighbour depends on God's prior love. It is because God loves us and we respond to his love that we are able to love. A central feature of the Gospel is God's love of sinners (brought out beautifully in the parable of the Prodigal Son – Luke 15:11–32).

We are not able to love in the strength of our own nature for that is vitiated by selfishness and rebellion. It is as we open ourselves to God's love that it transforms not only our own lives but also flows out to others. A parallel to God's love for sinners is the teaching to love even our enemies, to pray for them and to meet their basic needs (Matt 5:44; Romans 12:17–21).

Maulana Jalāluddīn Rūmī, in the preface to the second book of the *Mathnawi,* claims that in Islam also God's love is primary whereas our love is derivative. It is only the grace of God which makes it possible for us to love God. He refers to Q 5.54 where it is said that God loves the believers, *yuḥibbuhum,* and they, in turn, love him, *yuḥibbūnahu.* Louis Massignon was convinced that Islamic mysticism, was deeply rooted in the Qur'ān itself, and certainly the ubiquity and popularity of Sufīsm in the Muslim world cannot be accounted for except in this way.

The earliest *Ṣūfīs* were profoundly aware of Qur'ānic teaching in this respect, and their word for love was derived from Qur'ānic usage. It was the term *maḥabba* that was used for speaking of our love for God or of God's love for us. The term *'ishq,* with its overtones of sensual passion, was not used at first and came to be accepted as suitable in this context only gradually. At first, the *Ṣaḥw,* or 'sober' school of mysticism was characterised by *maḥabba,* and the *Sukr* or 'ecstatic' school was characterised by the use of *'ishq.* Eventually, however, *'ishq* gained respectability and even the more orthodox began to use it.

Both Muḥammad Iqbāl and Margaret Smith have drawn our attention to the contact and dialogue between the early *Ṣūfīs* and the Christian monks of the deserts of Syria and Egypt. Iqbāl goes so far as to say that the presence of this kind of monasticism as 'a working ideal of life' was one of the causes of the rise of Sufism towards the end of the eighth century AD.[4] Metropolitan Anthony of Sourozh tells us that God's infinite love and condescension and the response of love which they elicit was ever a concern of the Desert Fathers.[5] We certainly see it among the early *Ṣūfīs.*

The *Ṣūfīs* regarded love as the great tendency towards unification in the world. The striving for the ideal is a movement of love, according to Ibn Sīnā (Avicenna), and it is this which drives forward the evolution of forms. Everything is moving towards the Divine Beloved and will be fulfilled when all is united to the Beloved. This last sentiment is both characteristic of Sufism and the most frequent cause of division within it.

There are some who, under the influence of Neo-Platonism, and perhaps of Indian monism, began to speak of this unity as absorption and assimilation, *istighrāq*, into the Beloved such that no individuality remained. Such a position came to be known as *wahdat al-wujūd* or essential monism. Its leading metaphors were the river flowing into the ocean and the drop of water lost at sea. In various ways, it spoke of the soul's identity with God.

Referring to the famous *Ṣūfī* martyr Manṣūr al-Hallāj, Rūmī puts it like this:

> *Dar qulzum-i-nīstī-i-khud ghauta bekhurd,*
> *Anke pas azān durr-i-Anā'l Haqq mīsuft.*

> He dived into the sea of his non-entity,
> And won for me and you this pearl: 'I am the truth'.[6]

Athough elements of monistic thought are sometimes discernible in Rumi's work (particularly in the *Diwān-i Shams-i Tabrīzī*), it has to be said that the tenor of the *Mathnawī* is, on the whole, orthodox. The mystic takes on the characteristics of God in the same way as iron takes on the qualities of fire when it has been in it long enough. It does not lose its own properties but takes on the heat and the glow of the fire.[7] Even with al-Hallāj, Massignon has attempted to show that his cry of *Anā al-Haqq*, 'I am the truth', can be interpreted in a theistic light. It is worth remembering that Iqbāl in his lectures interprets it in the light of the tradition: *takhallaqū bi-akhlāqi Allāhi*, 'Create in yourselves the attributes of God'.[8]

Iqbāl is himself a leading representative of the *wahdat al-shuhūd*, or testimonial monism, school (along with others such as Shaykh Ahmad Sirhindī). Although in one place he does say *Ishq-I Haqq ākhir sarā pā Haqq būd*, 'Love of God at last becomes wholly God', his basic position is reflected in a *Ṣūfī* verse:

> *Mardan-i-Khudī nabāshand,*
> *Laikin zi Khuda judā nabāshand.*

> The people of God do not become God,
> But nor are they ever separated from God.[9]

Love for God makes us more and more conformed to God's will, but we do not lose our personalities thereby. Rather we are more sharply defined and enriched by this encounter. Like Shaykh Ahmad Sirhindī, Iqbāl believed that the experience of absorption into the Divine or even of annihilation, *fanā*, is only the beginning of mystical experience and that the mystic must go on in the spiritual path before the ultimate experience is reached. This experience is the realisation that the Divine is the ground of our being and the one in whom we live and move. It is in this experience that we realise both our unity with the Divine and our own immortality, *baqā ba'd al-fanā*.

Iqbāl does not favour the common tendency to see in God only the beautiful Divine Beloved. Islam teaches that God is angry with sin and its consequences. Love for God must include love of this wrathful aspect as well which destroys all that is not according to the Divine purpose:

> *Dilbarī bī qāhiri jādūgarī ast,*
> *Dilbarī bā qāhiri paighambarī ast.*

> The fascinating Divine Beauty without the tremendous
> Divine Majesty is merely magic,
> The fascinating Divine Beauty with the tremendous Divine
> Majesty is apostleship.[10]

In another verse he puts it in terms of Otto's *'mysterium tremendum et fascinans'*:

Ibtidā-i-'ishq-o-mastī qāhirī ast
Intihā-i-'ishq-o-mastī dilbarī ast.

The beginning of the intoxication of love is an experience of the tremendum.
The climax of this intoxication is an experience of the fascinans.[11]

Among the *Ṣūfīs*, love and fear are very closely related. It is worth noting that al-Ghazzālī's conversion had come about as a result of realising afresh the holiness of God and the great fear this had brought upon him. Yet he speaks of God's love as well and, commenting on the mystic Rābi'a al-'Adawiyya, he points out that she distinguished between a 'selfish' love for God so that we may gain temporary blessings and a 'worthy' love which is for his sake alone.[12] The Bible also tells us: 'The fear of the Lord is the beginning of Wisdom' (Proverbs 9:10).

Iqbāl is typical of *Ṣūfī* attitudes when he holds that love is the true test of faith and the criterion for distinguishing true believers from false. Those who adhere to the formal aspects of Islam are not necessarily Muslims. On the other hand, there may be some who, even though they are outside the formal community, are true believers:

Agar hō'ishq to hai kufr bhī Musulmānī,
Nā hō to mard-i-Musulmān bhī kāfir-o-zindīq.

If there is love even the unbeliever is a Muslim,
without love even the Muslim is an infidel and heretic![13]

This kind of attitude led *Ṣūfīs* to a positive view of people of other faith. The important thing was love of God; everything else was transcient.

Rūmī puts it like this:

Na Tarsā na Yahūdam man na Gabram na Musulmān am,

Baajuz 'ya Hu' o 'ya man Hu' kasi digar namidānam,
Zi Jām-i-'ishq sar mastam do ālam rafte az dastam.

I am neither Christian, nor Jew, nor Gabr, nor Muslim,
I have no other than 'O He' and 'O He who is',
I am intoxicated with Love's cup, the two worlds have passed
from me! [14]

In his theological work Rūmī tells us that love for the Creator
is latent in all, be they Zoroastrians, Jews or Christians. How
can anyone not love the author of their own being? When the
impediments are removed, the love becomes manifest:

'Ijl bā ān nūr shud qibla-i-karam,
Qibla bī ān nūr shud kufr-o-sanam.

The calf with the Divine Light became a sanctuary of grace,
The sanctuary without the Divine Light became infidelity
and an idol.[15]

The allusion is, of course, to the golden calf.

For Iqbāl also God is not exclusively worshipped in any
religious system but reveals himself to all those who desire him
ardently:

Na tu andar haram gunjī, na dar but khanehe mīā'i,
Wa laikin sūī mushtāqāna chē mushtāqāna mīā'i.

You are not contained in the sanctuary, nor are you limited
to the idol-temple,
But how lovingly you come towards those who desire you
fervently![16]

He emphasises the importance of a worshipper's sincerity rather than the formal religious system in which the worship is offered:

Kāfir-i-bīdār dil pesh-i-sanam
Bih zi dīndāri ke khuft andar haram.

The infidel with wakeful heart before an idol
Is better than a believer asleep in the sanctuary.[17]

In most *Ṣūfī* literature, it is perhaps fair to say, love means either the love of God or the love for God. There are instances, however, where it could also refer to the love of our fellows. There is a verse, for example, where Iqbāl claims that love is the summary of the *Sharī'a*, the Muslim Law:

Zi rasm o rāh-i-Sharī'at nakardeam tahqīq,
Juz inke munkir-i-'ishq ast kāfir o zandīq.

I have not researched into the custom and the way of the Law, except to find that the denier of love is an infidel and a heretic.[18]

It was Iqbāl's conviction that the *Sharī'a* is primarily a law of love and should produce loving Muslims, which made him a follower of Shah Walīullāh of Delhi, the eighteenth-century Muslim theologian and reformer. For Iqbāl, he is both the last great theologian of Islam and also the first to have felt a new spirit within him.

Walīullāh was much exercised by the problem of relating the *Sharī'a* to the modern world. According to him, when a law is revealed to a prophet it takes special notice of the culture to which the prophet is sent. The law enumerates universal principles of right and wrong and the prophet applies them to concrete cases, keeping in mind the culture in which the prophet is placed. The penal code of Islam, for example, enumerates universal principles of what is right or wrong, but the punishments it prescribes are culturally conditioned and may or may not be appropriate for every situation, culture or generation.

Iqbāl argues, of course, for a thorough re-interpretation of the fundamental principles of Islamic Law. The exercise of primary *ijtihād* (free enquiry into the bases of the *Sharī'a* in the light of contemporary conditions and knowledge) is advocated so that the *Sharī'a* may appear as a progressive force which fosters the true welfare of those under its protection.

Apart from *ijtihād*, Iqbāl held that *ijmā'* (or consensus of the community) can also limit or extend the application of Islamic law. In classical jurisprudence, such a power could only be exercised by those who had been Companions of the Prophet of Islam. Iqbāl was interested, however, in the development of institutions which could exercise this power in the context of a modern state. A limitation of law might take the form of specifying the conditions under which it might be enforced (a nomadic society, widespread ignorance, the lack of an adequate penal system, etc.). If such conditions did not exist, the scope for applying such a law would naturally be restricted.[19]

I have pointed out elsewhere that even a number of classical schools of law make some provision for the extension or limitation of the application of law. The different principles of *istiḥsān, istiṣlāḥ and istiṣḥāb* in the various schools of law are crucial if the development of Islamic law is to be taken seriously, and if such development is to be seen as emerging from within the tradition rather than being imposed upon it from outside.[20]

Islam is not, of course, a stranger to adaptation nor is it unique in having to address the context of a post-modern world. All the major religions are faced with this question and have to address it in one way or another.

For Iqbāl, love is most important for the whole of life and it cannot be compartmentalised:

Bī muhabbat zindigī mātam hameh,
Kāro bāresh zisht o na-muhkam hameh.

Without love life is all mourning,
All its affairs ugly and unstable.[21]

Love must be primary in society. Such love includes both love of God and love of one's neighbour. It is love of God which leads to religion having an important place in society. Religion is not, however, merely dry-as-dust ritual, law and theology; it is devotion to the living God. Religion itself, moreover, recognises that our love of God is shown by our love for fellow human beings. This is why, according to Iqbāl, the *Sharī'a* includes both our duty to God and our duty to our neighbour. Perceptions of our duty to our neighbour, furthermore, are changing rapidly. This is why *ijtihād* must constantly be exercised. The law must take into account new and better ways of caring for our neighbours; only then will the promulgation of law mean also the service of love. As the New Testament has it, 'If anyone says, "I love God", and hates his brother, he is a liar; for he who does not love his brother whom he has seen, cannot love God whom he has not seen' (1 John 4:20). And as St. Paul put it, 'If I speak in the tongues of men and of angels, but have not love, I am a noisy gong or a clanging cymbal' (1 Corinthians 13:1).

Notes

[1] See further, Kenneth Cragg, *The Mind of the Qur'ān*, London, 1973, pp165ff, and also Q 2.272, 13.22, 92.20.

[2] R. K. Harrison, *Leviticus: an Introduction and Commentary,* Leicester, 1980, p32.

[3] On the question of the sense in which Jesus was original at this point, see further C. E. B. Cranfield, *The Gospel According to St Mark,* Cambridge, 1966, pp376ff, and D. E. Nineham, *St. Mark,* Harmondsworth, 1969, pp323ff.

[4] M. Iqbal, *The Development of Metaphysics in Persia*, Lahore, 1964, pp76ff; Margaret Smith, *Studies in Early Mysticism in the Near and Middle East,* London, 1931.

[5] *The Sayings of the Desert Fathers,* ed. Benedicta Ward SLG, London, 1981, pp viif.

[6] *Kulliyyāt-I Shams-I Tabrīzī,* ed. M. Dervish, vol III, Tehran, 1341, p76.

[7] *Mathnawī-i Ma'anawī,* Cambridge, 1925-40, Vol. II, 1345-51, 53.

[8] *The Reconstruction of Religious Thought in Islam,* Lahore, p. 110.

[9] See A Schimmel, *Gabriel's Wing,* Leiden, 1963, p376.

[10] *Zabūr-I 'Ajam,* Lahore, 1970, p264.

[11] *Pas che Bāyad Kard Ay Aqwām-i Sharq,* Lahore, 1936, p15.

[12] See further M. Smith, *Rabi'a the Mystic and her Fellow-Saints in Islam,* Cambridge, 1928.

[13] 'If there is Love, then infidelity is Muslimhood. No love, and even the Muslim is an infidel and heretic', *Bāl-i Jibrīl,* Lahore, 1936, p54.

[14] *Diwān,* ed. Tabriz, 1280, pp124, 126.

[15] *Fihi mā fihi,* Tehran, 1959, pp240-1; and *Mathanawī,* vol. VI, 2073, 2075.

[16] *Payām-i Mashriq,* Lahore, 1969, p207.

[17] *Jāvīdnāme,* Lahore, 1974, p39.

[18] *Zabūr,* p160.

[19] *Reconstruction,* pp. 168ff. For Walīullāh's thought see his *Hujjatullāh al-bāligha,* Lahore, 1979, and G. N. Jalbani, *The Teachings of Shah Waliullah,* Lahore, 1967.

[20] See *Islam: A Christian Perspective,* Exeter, 1983, pp. 48ff; and see further Wael B. Hallaq, *Authority, Continuity and Change in Islamic Law,* Cambridge, 2001, for a nuanced discussion of development in Islamic law.

[21] *Zabūr,* p. 264.

3

IS THERE A GOSPEL FOR THE 21st CENTURY?

What is the Gospel?
I think it is first useful to say what I believe the Gospel to be, and in this I don't want to go much further than our Lord himself when he began his ministry in Luke 4, and we have something called the Nazareth Manifesto, when Jesus got up in the Synagogue and read from Isaiah 61. What did he say? He said that his ministry was about the good news coming to the poor, or to the afflicted, the release of captives, so that the blind may see and the deaf hear, and so that the oppressed may be freed from their oppression. That is what he believed the good news he was bringing to be and I think that is as good a point of departure as any that we could have.[1] So if that is the Gospel, and in the end it is of course Jesus himself who is the Gospel, what is the situation today to which this Gospel is addressed?

What is the Problem?
The first thing that strikes us as we look at the human situation in the light of the Gospel, is that of *alienation* – that people are alienated from the very source of their existence – they are alienated from God and they are out of sorts with one another. Wherever you go, whichever country, whichever community, whichever neighbourhood, people are to some extent alienated from one another, even within families; sometimes sadly we find this. And then there is also an alienation from what is within, that

is to say, in many different ways we are strangers to ourselves and many different thinkers down the ages have noticed this: our alienation from the very source of our existence – a subject which Hegel addressed – and also from the rest of creation.

Karl Marx said many things that were completely mistaken, but I think his analysis of how workers are alienated from work is still useful for us: that what we produce we do not own, not just in the physical sense but being in tune with it. We are alienated from the product of our work. I am experiencing this, by the way, with the publication of another book. When you write a book, up to a certain point you own the book; you've got the manuscript and everything. Once you give it to the publisher, they take over. The whole thing is out of your hands and in the hands of technical experts so you experience this kind of alienation from the product of your labour. We are also alienated from our fellow workers because the kind of division of labour that suits the techniques of mass production does not give a sense of making and owning the whole product. The developing disciplines of psychiatry, of psychotherapy, and their different modes, have shown us how we are alienated within ourselves, and how such alienation can be overcome. This loneliness and aloneness that we experience in the world in which we live, even in our communities and in our families, must be addressed in our sharing of the Gospel today.[2]

The second aspect of the human condition which the Gospel addresses very urgently is that of *anxiety*. There is a basic anxiety about our existence throughout our lives and this is particularly true of people in the modern world, that people are unsure about why they are here at all. So they question the meaning of their very being, as it were, and the question of non-existence is always there; the fear of death – not spoken about but it is there. There is guilt about what people feel they have done wrong, and they are not able to deal with the guilt that has flowed from that. I find there is more and more anxiety about the future of the world – well you may say the state of the world justifies that anxiety. I was thinking the other day (and I don't always think like this): I have some knowledge of a country like Iran and some knowledge of the Holy Land and the countries surrounding it, and it struck me suddenly out of the blue that Iran, by proxy in the form of Hizbullah, is now within forty miles, if that, and it may be less than forty miles, of the site of Armageddon. Now that made me very anxious indeed. So alienation and anxiety certainly characterise our lives today and the Gospel addresses it, as we shall see.[3]

The third is *addiction*. Now modern life is characterised by addiction. That may be with drugs. I am amazed in university settings how many people actually use drugs, whether it's the so-called soft drugs or the harder variety. It can be alcohol. The amount of alcohol that some undergraduates drink now is absolutely astonishing. How they do any work having drunk so much alcohol is a mystery to me. But, of course, addiction can be about other things. It can be about possessions, motor cars; people are addicted to all sorts of things as if somehow they provide a balm in the stresses and strains of modern living. They can also be addicted, as Tim Keller says, to power, success or sex. These addictions take the place of worshipping the one, true God and what is desired by the addict becomes an idol.[4]

What can the Gospel do about it?
Now, as we, on the one hand, have the Gospel and, on the other, this alienation, anxiety and addiction, what can we say about the Gospel in terms of how it addresses the situation? I think the first thing (and you won't be surprised by this) is to say that the Gospel is about *forgiveness*. The Gospel is about being forgiven ourselves; the need to know that we are forgiven because one of the things about anxiety is a sense of guilt. Alienation comes about because we've made enemies with somebody or because they have made enemies of us. Knowing that we are loved and forgiven is absolutely basic to the Christian faith, and to the story of restoration and wholeness, which is the meaning of salvation in the Gospels (Mark 2:3–12). Of course, it is not only that we are forgiven but are able to forgive. That's very hard. I find it very difficult – let's be up front about it – to forgive those who,

I perceive, to have wronged me. If we are going to allow the Gospel to work in our lives, then we must experience not only the forgiveness that God brings, this good news that Jesus has brought, but also the possibility of forgiving (Matthew 5:23–24, 18:21–22).

Now you may ask, how can this happen? It happens really because of what you might call *friendship*. Friendship first of all with God. You see the basic problem is that friendship with God, which was one of the main reasons for our being created, was broken by us, by our turning away from that relationship with God; by our wilfulness, our rebellion, our waywardness, whatever you want to call it. And the message of the Good News of Jesus is that he has come to re-establish that friendship. We know in what a costly way that friendship was re-established by Jesus on the Cross. The Cross means many different things and there is a richness about the Cross that I certainly cannot exhaust, but at the very least I think we should say that Jesus did on the Cross what we could not do ourselves; what we were unable to do and also what we were unwilling to do.

Our state of rebellion was such that we could not see what needed to be done. Have you ever come across a person like that? A son or a daughter who has taken a path which you as a parent can quite clearly see isn't leading to anywhere good, but they can't see it. Well, all of humanity is like that - unable and unwilling. And so God himself, Father, Son and Holy Spirit, provides a way out of this damning impasse: Jesus on the Cross, by returning us to that friendship with God, did for us what we could not do, and were unwilling to do, and thus turned away God's anger from our waywardness and our rebellion.

Bishop John Robinson, in a very fine commentary on the letter to the Romans, once said God is only love. Those who turn to him in love, experience it as love; those who turn away from it experience it as anger.[5] And so Jesus turned that experience of wrath back again into an experience of love by re-establishing that friendship with God, by opening up a way once again for it to be real for us, and of course that friendship doesn't then end

40

in our friendship with God but flows out into friendship as such. I mean, friendship should be something that the Christian Church talks about all the time. I believe we don't talk about it enough. The world would understand more of what we mean if we talked about friendship. We live in a world in which friendship has been greatly impoverished. People don't have time for friends and at a younger and younger age (it seems to me anyway, but perhaps I am getting older!) people pair off. You know, sometimes I see boys and girls having paired off and I think, are they old enough for this kind of thing? But of course, they think they are, but what this means is that same-sex friendships now are not as lasting or deep as they used to be because they are just not given that attention. Perhaps if they were, we wouldn't then have the problems that we are facing in other respects. So, you see, friendship is very important for us to talk about; how friendship is established by God and with God. It is this friendship that spills over into our relationships which enables us to be friends with our families and communities.

Faithfulness

Now one of the things to do with friendship, as you know, has to do with *faithfulness*. God is faithful. That is one of the reasons for the coming of Jesus, the coming of the Gospel, to demonstrate God's faithfulness. When we had completely mucked up the human project God did not give up, and he persisted in his faithfulness and so he called us, therefore, also to be faithful: faithful to him, faithful in our relationships. Again, faithfulness is a fundamental virtue that society needs. Look at the world of business. I think – contradict me if I am wrong – the best of British life used to be characterised by things like accountability, responsibility, 'my word is my bond', a sense of vocation, of faithfulness in other words, to our work, to our colleagues, to the organisation that employed us. There was an expectation of trustworthiness with other people with whom we were dealing, and then what happened in the 1980s? There was the 'Big Bang' – you know the 'Big Bang' didn't just occur 14 billion years ago, it also occurred in London in the 1980s when we were all urged, or at least those in business were urged, to give all this up and to substitute for it slogans like "Greed is Good". Boris Johnson is Mayor of London and the *enfant terrible* of British politics. I was with him on 'Any Questions' on one occasion. He was sitting next to me and he turned to me and said, "Bishop, greed is good isn't it?" So I said to him, or words to this effect, "Why do you say that? I know you'd expect me to contradict you, but why do you say it?" He said, "Well, it makes people rich and then it makes the country rich." I said, "Boris, I don't think there is really any evidence for this. What greed has done is to have put us all into debt and a debt that we will not be able to pay ourselves but that our children will have to and our children's children will have to." The point is that this kind of keeping faith was given up by these silly slogans that made a few people rich, it is true, but have left a lot of us, and indeed the nation, in a great deal of difficulty.

Family

The term 'faithfulness' leads to thinking about where that faithfulness is seen, not only in business, not only in friendship but particularly in the *family*. The Gospel, the Good News of Jesus Christ, is received in homes, it is lived in homes and it is passed on in homes. This is what Callum Brown says in his book, *The Death of Christian Britain* – that Christianity ceased to be of public importance in this country, according to him, when it stopped being passed on in the home: not in the Church, not in the school, but at home. On the same theme, but from a different perspective, Mary Eberstadt has shown how the fortunes of faith and family are firmly linked.[6] So we must be attentive to faithfulness in the family, that is, faithfulness in the sense of keeping faith with the God who has revealed himself to us and who calls us to discipleship to follow him, but also faithfulness to one another. In this context, of course, that faithfulness to one another is of a particular kind.

It goes back to the 'one flesh union' that the book of Genesis talks about: that coming together of a man and a woman in a particular way, both having been created in God's image, both having been given a common mission to fulfil, which they fulfil of course each in their own way; a coming together that is for the sake of their own security and well-being, but also for the sake of the children (Genesis 1:26–31, 2:24). One reason why marriage has to be lifelong is because the human child takes an awfully long time to grow up! The faithfulness then has to do not just with the coming together but with the staying together. It is not just contractual for the bringing up of children or for that commitment that a husband and wife have for one another, but it is as St. Augustine (of Hippo not of Canterbury) called it – a sacramental union where it is no longer two but one (that's what one flesh union means) and the Christian Church must continue to uphold this teaching; it is absolutely vital to the Gospel. You may ask, "why?" Of course marriage is something given in creation, that is true, and that is why we say it is for the good of society, but it also has to do with the coming of Jesus and our relationship to Jesus. What does St Paul say about marriage? Marriage is the only thing that is called a sacrament in the New Testament. In Ephesians 5:32 he says that the union of a man and a woman in marriage is a sacrament (in Greek, *mysterion*) of the relationship between Christ and his Church. So it is not just something to do with creation but also with redemption: marriage is a sacrament of our redemption, of the relationship of Christ to his Church.[7]

So the Gospel addresses us concretely in terms of our everyday experience, whether that is of forgiveness, of being forgiven, or forgiving; it addresses us in terms of our friendships and our relationships, our family, our faithfulness at work – all of those things.

The Spiritual

But secondly, the Gospel addresses us as *spiritual beings*. We are not just super-monkeys with large brains. We are spiritual beings and we have spiritual awareness. David Hay and Kate Hunt, who are academics in the University of Nottingham, did some wide-ranging research on people who do not belong to any organised religion and they discovered a deep awareness of the spiritual among them.[8] The Alistair Hardy Research Institute in Oxford also, many years ago, similarly established that many ordinary English people (particularly men – they concentrated on men) have spiritual experiences.[9] We are aware of ourselves as spiritual beings, even if in our worst moments we deny it. But not only is there awareness, there is also aspiration. There is spiritual aspiration in human beings; they want somehow to develop the spiritual side of their character if they are allowed to by culture and by custom.

In the course of my work I often meet people who have come to Christian faith from another faith tradition – whether that's Islam, or Hinduism, sometimes Buddhism – and one of the things I have found is that they do realise when they come to Christian faith that many of the things they have done or believed have been mistaken and they need to give them up. But I have never met anyone who believed that everything they had spiritually aspired to before they became a Christian was mistaken. I've never met anyone like that. In fact, they nearly always say that what Christ has done for them is to fulfil their authentic spiritual aspirations. And that you could also say about people who come to Christ from no particular faith background, perhaps a secular background, that Jesus Christ fulfils their deepest spiritual aspirations. So then, when we present the Gospel we must do so in such a way that Jesus Christ can fulfil people's authentic spiritual aspirations, however deeply buried they may be.[10]

Meaning

There is then, as spiritual beings, the necessity for the discovery of *meaning*. Human beings are unique in demanding that this universe should mean something and that our lives here should mean something. No other creature on earth, as far as we know, demands such meaning from the world and about their own lives, and the Gospel tells us what that meaning is. It is not that we are simply mistaken about this need for meaning, nor is it absurd for us to ask for meaning in a meaningless universe. The Bible tells us that the deep structures of the universe and of our own lives answer to this quest for significance and intelligibility. There was a psychiatrist saying the other day on the radio, "Well I can prescribe pills for depression but I can't give people meaning in their lives." But, you see, the Gospel can.

The Gospel can provide you with the reason for why you are here: why God has put you here, why God loves you and why his Son has redeemed you. And that discovery of meaning, of course, has to do with *direction*; how we direct our lives. It is not just self-direction. The Gospel provides a direction for our lives and we submit to that good news that God has provided for us. And in this the Church can help us in many different ways; by its teaching, by the help of the sacraments, through pastoral counselling, we can be given direction in our lives by the Gospel. This is so important for us as spiritual beings. Whether that direction is given to you by your confessor or your spiritual director or your pastor, whatever you call such a person, you must make sure that the *Gospel* is able to direct you in this way, and that it is not just an amorphous something-or-other that sits outside you and with which you just come into contact from time to time, maybe on a Sunday morning for an hour or so.

At the same time, pastors can certainly take account of secular theories of human development and of social functioning. After all, all truth is God's truth, but their fundamental orientation in their pastoral counselling must be drawn from the Gospel's understanding of the human condition and its cure for what is wrong with it. This should also enable them to critique various secular theories, and their assumptions, from an evangelical point of view.

Destiny

It is so important for us to allow the Gospel to direct our lives. So of course the Gospel is about our *destiny*: where we are going. We desperately want to know where we are headed. What is the outcome of this life, this short span of life that we have, this 'episode of consciousness', that somebody called it. Well, again, Easter is so significant here because Easter shows us what our destiny is. The rising again of Jesus Christ from the dead was God's great vindication of him and the work that he has done and who he is. But it also reveals to us our own destiny, where we are heading and God's plan for us, and not only for us but for humanity, indeed, for the universe as a whole.

The Gospel and the Mind

The Gospel should also capture the *mind*. We should be unapologetic about this. There is an intellectual side to Christianity. People often ask me why aggressive secularists are so hostile, in particular to Christianity. Have you ever noticed that? They're quite friendly with all sorts of other things but not with Christians. The reason is that Christianity is the only really seriously intellectual rival to aggressive secularism; that's the reason for the hostility. They see that; we should see it.

I was once on the television in a programme on the BBC chaired by Michael Buerk called 'The Soul of Britain'. It was very interesting because he brought together a lot of people: there were astrologers there, 'new agers' of different kinds, and so on, and then there was Peter Atkins, who is a very militant atheist and myself as the Christian. What happened was that Peter Atkins and I teamed up to see off the astrologers and the 'new agers', because we had a lot in common. We were both committed to the use of reason, for example, and it was fairly easy to see them all off and then we were left to fight it out. We must not neglect the intellectual side of how the Gospel provides us with a world view – a view of the world which is distinctive and based on Creation, that is to say, God's reason (that is what *Logos* means) has made the world and this is why the world is open to us, to reasonable investigation. John Polkinghorne is continually marvelling at this, and I marvel at him as a distinguished scientist when he says that the amazing thing is why science is possible at all; why the universe has these laws, why physical events are predictable in principle, even if there is randomness, openness and spontaneity; why a complex universe is patient of explanation by our minds, and why there are laws which govern the existence of our universe. Without any of these things, science would not be possible. This view of the world has arisen from the Bible.[11]

I used to know a very eminent man called Sir Joseph Needham who was Master of Caius College in Cambridge and, at that time, and perhaps in the whole of the last century, the leading expert on China. He wrote volumes about Chinese science and civilisation and so on. He used to ask this question: "At the beginning of the Middle Ages, China was far more advanced civilisationally than Western Europe (gunpowder, paper, stirrups that made horses war machines, and so forth – China had all of that), so what was it that made Western Europe leap forward in scientific and technological progress?" Needham very reluctantly came to the conclusion that it was Christianity because Christianity provided for a world view of an ordered universe where there was predictability, where there were laws of nature that could be investigated and where human and divine freedom to act could be affirmed.[12] It is very interesting because things have come round full circle and now the Department of Culture in the People's Republic of China is very interested in talking to Christian leaders precisely for this reason, because they know what it was that triggered scientific and technological development in the West, and they want to know what they can do about it.

Science and Faith

So worldview is very important, but science as it developed in Europe also had a downside to it, and the downside was that scientists got more and more interested in *what* things were – and this is a proper activity for the human person; Adam was after all called to name the creatures – *what* things were and how they worked. But what has been neglected in the last five hundred years or so of scientific development is the *why?* of things. Why is there anything? Why is there this thing or that, or this animal or that? And then the *what for?* question: not just *what* things are, how they work, but *what are they for?* This is in theological language what we call the teleological question. What are things for? What am I for? What are you for? What is the world for? These are hugely important things for us to know and to answer.

There were some enormously positive developments in the nineteenth century as far as science was concerned; I do not in any way deny that. But one of the things that the nineteenth century did was to give people the impression that science had arisen from nowhere, a great leap forward of the mind without reference to the past. But this is not actually true. The origins of scientific and technological development are to be found in Christian thinkers down the ages and without them it would not have occurred, as indeed it did not in other parts of the world. James Hannam, a Kent scientist, has written a very fine book from the scientific point of view called *God's Philosophers* which traces the origin of modern science to medieval Christian thinkers.[13]

Biblical Time and its Significance

Another effect of scientific development was what you might call the flattening of time. The Bible is the only sacred book in the world that has a view of time that is open and progressive; all other ancient religions, or indeed modern ones, are cyclical – things go round and round and repeat themselves or else they are spasmodic and occasionalist. Our modern view of time comes from the Bible: open, progressive, leading to what is absolutely, or at least relatively, new.[14] As Christians lived in this time of the Bible, there was of course ordinary time when people did mundane things like washing up or hanging out the clothes, or ploughing the field or whatever it was, but within this time there were moments when people were taken out of themselves. Sunday, of course, was one such. This is the pity of the loss of the traditional Sunday.

I was once sitting next to a very interesting person who was one of those who guided the Sunday Trading Bill through the House of Commons, and in the course of our lunch he said, "Bishop, I have a confession to make." So I said "Well I'm always ready to hear confession," and he said that the biggest mistake of his political life that he had ever made was to pilot the Sunday Trading Bill through Parliament. Well, I agreed with him because it was that special day that took people out of themselves that has been destroyed for so many now. But it wasn't just the Sundays, it was the festivals: the great festivals of the Church – sometimes even little festivals that had local significance – and I often say that this is signalled by a change in the meaning of a word. You know what that word is? Yes, holy days became holidays!

Sacred Space
And just as time was flattened, so was space. This is all part of the secularising disenchantment that has taken place around us, so no space is more special than any other space. The Holy Land used to be called the fifth Gospel, because if people wanted to understand the first four Gospels they went to the Holy Land to understand them, and anyone who has been to the Holy Land will realise what a special place it is – whatever preconceptions you have, whatever the commercialisation, it makes an impact when you get there. I was once leading a pilgrimage to the site of the Sermon on the Mount and I noticed that in a garden there were two of my party, including a rather hardened businessman, so I went up to talk to them and I found that they were weeping. So I said, "What is wrong?", and they said, "Nothing, Bishop,

it's just the place, the atmosphere here has overtaken us."[15] So space can be special, time can be special, but this is what we have to restore if we are to allow the Gospel to make an impact on people's lives: a new way of living in time, a new way of treating space.[16]

The Gospel in Public Life

So the intellectual side of the Gospel is very important and then we come to what you might call the impact of the Gospel in *public* life. Very reluctantly, I keep getting involved in this, but I just want to mention three or four areas where this is hugely important today. First, we hear a great deal about the dignity of the human person. All the great declarations talk about it, that *human dignity* is inalienable. But it is only the Bible that gives you the answer as to why this is so: why is human dignity such that it cannot be taken away from human beings? It is because we are made in God's image. That is how this belief in human dignity arose. There are other religious systems that could not give birth to such a view: Buddhism, for instance – a lot of Western people flirt with it, but the Dalai Lama has said that there is no conception of the self in Buddhism. In fact, if you believe that there is a permanent self, that is an obstacle to achieving enlightenment in Buddhism. Such a religious system is not going to produce a belief in inalienable human dignity because there is no self to which such dignity would attach. This belief has arisen from a particular way of thought and of life and, unless that is recognised, it will wither away.[17]

Secondly, *equality*: there is a huge equality industry in Britain. I was invited a few years ago to address what was then the new Equality Commission and I said to my secretary, "there must be some mistake, I'm not the sort of bishop they would invite." So she checked and said to me, "Bishop, there is no mistake; they really do want you." So I went and they were lovely and very sincere people beavering away at equality, but do they know why human beings are equal? I mean, on the face of it human beings are not equal. They are differently mentally endowed, differently physically endowed – as we discover at the Olympics – they are rich and they are poor, all sorts of differences. Why do we believe they are equal? Because of the Bible's teaching of common origin: that human beings have a common origin in God's Creation.

When I was at the Church Mission Society (CMS) I used to read what CMS missionaries did in the past – also in the present but in the past too – and I remember reading about CMS and other missionaries in Australia who went from place to place preaching in these little frontier towns, and quite often I discovered that they would study and preach on this verse from The Acts of the Apostles, about St. Paul in Athens where he says, in the old translation, speaking about Creation to the Greeks, "Out of one blood hath he made all the nations of men" (Acts 17:26), and quite often these missionaries were driven out of these towns because the settlers did not want to believe that they were of the same origin as the Aboriginals. Such a radical view of equality would be difficult to achieve in classical, caste-based Hinduism. Indeed, Hindu reformers sometimes explicitly acknowledge their debt to Christianity in their struggle against the caste system.[18] There is common origin, inalienable dignity, equality based on common origin, and then there is liberty.

Liberty belongs to the very nature of the Gospel. You cannot be forced to respond to the good news of Jesus Christ; you have to respond to it freely. Pope Benedict XVI was asked by a reasonably hostile journalist, "For centuries the Roman Catholic Church has been saying that error has no rights. Now you have started talking about religious freedom. Why have you changed your mind?" And the Pope said, "In this we have gone back to the earliest form of the tradition, which is the teaching of Jesus himself." Well, I thought that was a good answer to give, but it takes us back to the time of the Reformation because that is what the Reformers were wanting, when even the ploughboy should be free to read God's Word for himself. That is what Tyndale's hope was in his translation of the Bible.[19] So liberty is, again, a precious value that comes to us from the Bible and which is hugely necessary in the public space today.

Some of the difficulties that we have experienced in this country with the segregation of communities from one another (I've drawn attention to this myself), which gives an opportunity for extremists to use people for their own ends, have arisen because of the failure of Christian hospitality. When people began to come to this country to live and to work, they should have been welcomed here on the basis of Christian hospitality. To say, look, this is who we are, this is how we have become a nation; the Christian faith is absolutely central to our institutions and our values. Now you are welcome to live here and to work here and to make your own contribution on this basis. Hospitality would have led to engagement and to dialogue. In turn, these could have led to common values and commitments. Instead of which what happened was the invention of multiculturalism, which was basically saying, "Well we really don't know who we are, we certainly don't know who you are, so let us continue living our own lives as best we can." So there was no communication, there was segregation, as I say, with people living their own lives, no common view of citizenship, no *lingua franca*, no sense of common values, and that has led us to where we are now.[20] So the bringing of the Gospel to the public space also remains important.

We have seen, therefore, how the Gospel bears on our experience as individuals and as communities. We have seen what the Gospel has to do with our spiritual nature which defines us as human beings. We have seen that it engages the mind and renews the mind, and we have seen what the Gospel has to do with our public life together. Whether existentially or socially the Gospel remains crucial for men, women and societies as much as it ever has, if not more. This Gospel remains good news for us today as it has always been for human beings down the ages. It is for us and those around us, as it always has been and always will be. The challenge is for the Church to share it in ways which make sense for people today.

Notes

[1] On the importance of the Nazareth Manifesto and the Galilean Option in the ministry of Jesus, see Norberto Saracco, *The Liberating Options of Jesus*, in Vinay Samuel and Chris Sugden (eds), *Sharing Jesus in the Two-Thirds World*, Bangalore, Partnership in Mission, Asia, 1983, pp49ff.

[2] See Michael Nazir-Ali, *The Unique and Universal Christ: Jesus in a Plural World*, Milton Keynes, Paternoster, pp44ff.

[3] For an analysis of the cumulative impact of this 'aloneness' and anxiety, see Martin Buber's *Between Man and Man*, London, Collins, 1971, pp199ff.

[4] Tim Keller, *Counterfeit Gods*, London, Hodder, 2010.

[5] John Robinson, *Wrestling with Romans*, London, SCM, 1979.

[6] Callum Brown, *The Death of Christian Britain*, London, Routledge, 2001, and Mary Eberstadt, *How the West Really Lost God*, Conshohocken, PA, Templeton Press, 2013.

[7] On this see further, Michael Banner, *Christian Ethics and Contemporary Moral Problems*, Cambridge, CUP, 1999, pp21ff.

[8] *Understanding the Spirituality of People Who Don't Go to Church*, Centre for the Study of Human Relations, Nottingham, University of Nottingham, 2000.

[9] See further the Church of England report, *The Search for Faith and the Witness of the Church*, London, CHP, 1996.

[10] Michael Nazir-Ali, *The Unique and Universal Christ*, op. cit, pp119f.

[11] See John Polkinghorne's trilogy, *One World, The Interaction of Science and Theology,* London, SPCK, 1986, *Science and Providence*, London, SPCK, 1989, and *Searching for Truth: A Scientist looks at the Bible*, Oxford, BRF, 1996.

[12] Rodney Stark, *The Triumph of Christianity*, New York, Harper Collins, 2011, p286.

[13] James Hannam, *God's Philosophers: How the Medieval World Laid the Foundations of Modern Science*, London, ICON, 2009.

[14] On all of this, see Thomas Cahill, *The Gifts of the Jews*, Oxford, Lion, 1998, pp25.

[15] For the growing importance of pilgrimage to the Holy Land, see Steven Runciman, *A History of the Crusades*, London, Penguin, 1991, Vol 1, pp38ff.

[16] On the question of sacred space see the Church of England report, *Communities and Buildings*, London, CHP, 1996, pp32ff.

[17] See Roger Ruston, 'Theologians, Humanists and Natural Rights' in Mark Hill (ed), *Religious Liberty and Human Rights*, Cardiff, University of Wales Press, 2002, pp14ff. For a sympathetic account of what Buddhists believe about the 'no-self' or 'no-soul' see Elizabeth Harris, *What Buddhists Believe*, Oxford, One World, pp38f.

[18] John Harris, *One Blood*, Sutherland, NSW, 1990. For a Christian critique of caste and its influence on leading Hindu reformers see M.M. Thomas, *The Acknowledged Christ of The Indian Renaissance*, London, SCM, 1969.

[19] David Daniell, *William Tyndale: A Biography (Yale Nota Bene)*, Yale University Press, 2001.

[20] See Michael Nazir-Ali, *Triple Jeopardy for the West*, London, Bloomsbury, 2012, pp11f.

Part Two

CHRISTIANS AND SOCIETY

In rapidly changing societies the assumption of a Christian basis to our common life is being challenged and rejected. How should Christians respond in such a situation? Some are advocating withdrawal from social and political engagement so that churches can better concentrate on their core tasks of evangelism, discipling of believers and the enabling of worship honouring to God. Others wish to engage in a 'prophetic' ministry of simply denouncing what is going wrong because of godlessness. Yet others yearn nostalgically for the old Christendom.

The chapters which follow indicate a different line of approach which emphasises critical engagement: affirming what is good in culture, strengthening civil society where we can, but also resisting what does not lead to the common good. The question of respect for the consciences of Christians and others will be to the fore as will that of the reasonable accommodation of belief and the manifestation of belief in the workplace.

There should be a reiteration of the need for the Judeo-Christian tradition informing the legislation and the policies of the nation and serving as a basis for guaranteeing the freedoms which have arisen from it and which are necessary in a plural (but not pluralist) society. This is not about nostalgia but is a necessity precisely in the sort of world we now find ourselves inhabiting. Even in 'exile' Christians and the Church will want to continue, as did St. Paul in Athens, arguing the Christian case in both marketplace and academia.

4

WHY SHOULD CHRISTIANS BE INVOLVED IN PUBLIC LIFE?

During a General Election campaign in Britain some of us decided to organise meetings of Christians with those who were standing for Parliament. These meetings I found very helpful indeed because they showed me first of all what those people, who wanted to be our political masters, actually knew and believed. That was quite revealing. But also it showed them what Christian concerns were. And for some of them this was the first time they had seen a body of Christians expressing themselves. This is very important. However, the point is that many large, particularly evangelical, churches did not take part in this campaign and the reasoning that they gave was this – they said, "Look, our business is to make new Christians and to nurture them. Our business is not to interfere in politics." Now you may recognise that. I was very sorry about it but it has made me think what should be the basis for Christian involvement in civic affairs and in national, political, social and economic life. What is the basis? If you think about it, the basis goes back to the story of Creation itself.

Created in Community
When God created man and woman he created them together. He created them together in his own image. You know if you read the Genesis account, it is quite clear. He gave them common work to do, a common mission, which each was to do in his or her own

way. This is the basis of biblical thinking about community. We are not socially contracted in the sense that individuals somehow got together to decide how they were to protect themselves and agreed to a contract for mutual protection. Human beings are inherently communal, inherently social. This is not something that has happened to them because of external circumstances.[1] Of course, we realise that human rebellion and sinfulness - fallen-ness if you like - has affected God's purposes for human community. We do understand that, but God has not given up on us. His election of Israel was an election as a people. Here was a whole group – wandering nomadic tribes in the Middle East despised by their neighbours. All of the evidence we have of the early Hebrews is that they were despised by those around them – Egyptians, Assyrians, Syrians and so on. And yet God chose them, and made them a nation.[2] Sometimes I think that about Britain – warring tribes, invasions from Vikings and Danes and goodness knows who else, petty kingdoms, and mutual hostility. What made Britain a nation? And the answer is quite clear what made it a nation; it is the Christian faith.[3]

Israel and the Nations
It was God who made Israel a nation and he did this for many purposes, some of which we know. But one of those, I think, was to reveal his plan for how people were to live together as nation and as community. David Phillips has pointed out in some of his writings how already from early times there was a distinction made between priesthood and monarchy, between temple and crown. They were not mixed up.[4] And this is quite important when we are thinking about Islam where there is no distinction between the political and the religious. In the Bible's worldview there is. But not just concerning the nation of Israel; the Bible also tells us that God has a concern for all the different nations of the world. Just as He has been working with Israel so He's been working even among Israel's enemies. Amos 9 is about God's providential ordering of the nations. I was in Egypt recently and one of the things that Christian Egyptians – but also some

Muslims – are very proud of is that the Bible says "Blessed be Egypt, my people". Do you know where it says that? Isaiah 19: "Blessed be Egypt my people, Assyria the work of my hands, and Israel my heritage."

So we can be clear from our reading of the Bible that God is working in nations. And He calls us also to engage with the nations where we find ourselves. This may be a nation that is not ours, where we may have been sent as exiles or refugees or immigrants or whatever it may be. A very aggressive interviewer on the BBC described me as an immigrant; I think it was a way to score on his part. But so be it. Wherever God puts us we have a responsibility for that society and you will all know what Jeremiah said to the exiles who were going to Babylon. In terrible circumstances with the destruction of their national life, with the deprivation that they were suffering of their property and relationships – in that situation where they were singing that Psalm "How shall we sing the Lord's song in a foreign land" (Ps 137:4) – even in that terrible situation what did Jeremiah say to them? He said, "Go and live in this city. Plant gardens and eat the produce of those gardens. Get married and get your sons and daughters to be married and to have children and to work and to pray for the peace and the wholeness and the welfare and the prosperity of that city" (Jer 29: 4–10). Even in such adverse situations we are not excused. We cannot simply stick to our faith and ignore the rest of society. That is not an option for Christians.

Give to God – Give to Caesar
And that is what I was telling these nice evangelical churches and church leaders who wanted simply to stick to the purity of their church life and to evangelism. This is not something just in the Old Testament. Jesus himself in his teaching about what we owe to God and what we owe to Caesar has shown us that we have responsibilities on both sides (Matthew 22:21). Of course the priority is what we owe God but we cannot neglect what we owe the society in which we find ourselves. And sometimes we forget that. In the rest of the New Testament we find in St.

Paul in Romans 13 the doctrine of the godly ruler, and also in 1 Peter 2 – and there are many things to say about that. But for our purposes the point is that the godly ruler is supposed to approve of what we do when we do it for the good of society and to punish if people are working for its ill. 1 Timothy 2 also mentions this view of engagement with those who rule over us: to pray for them, but to also be active in society. And, in fact, this is what we find the early Christians doing.

Early Christians and Social Involvement
There is a discipline nowadays called the Sociology of the New Testament. I studied Sociology at one time so I'm always interested in these things. And one of the things that these sociologists of the New Testament and of the early church have discovered is that the early church grew because it was always serving the poor. It was always to be found in the disreputable parts of the cities and towns of the ancient world. It was arranging for the burial of paupers, it was raising funds to free slaves. Never believe people who say that the church was comfortable with slavery until Wilberforce came along. The church was never comfortable with it. It was always regarded as a social evil which, if possible, had to be ameliorated or eliminated; and buying the freedom of slaves was one of the good works that early Christians engaged in. Rescuing women who had fallen into prostitution was another. And for all these reasons of social involvement the church grew, as 1 Corinthians says, particularly among those who were poor and disadvantaged. It is not that social distinctions disappeared in society but that, for the early Christians, they ceased to matter.

Reformation and Radical Reformers
And this story has continued. Just to give one or two examples of it; at the time of Augustine all the Church could do was to plead for justice and mercy. We find St Augustine doing that in relation to the rulers of his day.[5] When the Reformation came there were two particular views about how Christian faith should

relate to the nation. One was the establishing of churches like the Church of England so that the Christian voice was at the heart of national life and the Church had a say in determining what *was* justice rather than just pleading for it. But the radical Reformation rejected that view and held that the task of the church should be to bear a prophetic witness to the nation rather than to be part of the structures of the state. Those from the radical Reformation who found themselves in the new world of the United States made sure that in the emerging polity of the new nation no church was established. But this did not by any manner or means imply that the Judeo-Christian tradition and ways of making decisions on the basis of that tradition, were to be neglected by those who are the founders of the United States. Again and again, in the Constitution, in the fundamental documents of the US, they appeal to this tradition.[6] What I'm saying is that, whatever Christian tradition you come from, you are not excused involvement.

Evangelicals and Activism

The evangelical revival came about because people were reading their Bibles again – as people should do – and it was this that led them, once again, to social involvement. I mean, why did people like Wilberforce develop a concern for the freeing of slaves, the ending of the slave trade and the abolition of slavery itself? Because they knew that you could not preach the Gospel of freedom that demanded a free response and enslave people at the same time. Why did they develop a concern for those men, women and children who were working all hours of the day and night in the mines and the factories of Britain early in the 19th Century? They knew that people could not be treated like this. Children working down mines for 16 hours a day without relief; people could not be treated like this – why? Because these people were also made in God's image. It comes back to the Creation story. So we need, on the basis of this rich heritage, to be involved in the civil and political life of our country in appropriate ways.[7] In some ways, these evangelicals were meliorists, they just wanted to make things better for the worst off, but their activism also ended up producing enduring social policies which became the basis of vital social institutions which survive to this day.

Obeying God rather than Men

We are told to obey those who are in authority. And this remains true for us except, according to the Bible, when those who are in authority over us command us to do what God forbids, and forbid us to do what God commands. So then we have to say like the apostles, "We must obey God rather than you" (Acts 5:29). Now I say this not just to make a point but because these are the areas where we will find more and more that we have to make a decision in Christian integrity. Are they asking us to do something that God has forbidden? We can't do it. I once signed a witness statement for a woman doctor who was on an adoption panel. All she asked was, when the panel was considering same-sex adoptions, that she should be excused from the panel since she believed that children are best brought up by a mother and a father. That request was rejected. She was told, "You will sit on the panel whenever it is sitting or you don't sit on it at all." She took her case to court. I signed a witness statement basically saying that her position reflects the teaching of orthodox Christian faith throughout the generations. There are now numerous cases like hers and we shall undoubtedly see many more.[8] The question is whether the consciences of Christians will be accommodated when what the law now requires can be delivered in other ways.

Salt and Light

Salt does not just provide us with taste in our food – though it does that. It is not only a preservative, but it is also an essential nutrient. I am constantly battling on this with my wife who keeps saying I have too much salt, and my view is that she has too little! We will see who is correct. But that is the function of salt. However, salt does this work invisibly. You don't see the salt in the food. It is working away invisibly preserving, providing taste, providing nutrition. The Church of England, for example, and maybe some other churches also, have been used to working with society in these ways, like salt. They have been 'hatching, matching, and dispatching' generations of people – very valuably. We were staying once with the Archbishop of Sydney and the next day he was taking the funeral of a policeman who had been tragically killed; a tragic occasion but also full of opportunity for the Gospel. This is working like salt, with the grain; going with the grain of society.

However, we may be approaching a situation where it is more and more difficult to work in this way with integrity. So the metaphor may need to change from salt to light. Light is the opposite of salt. Just as salt is invisible, light by definition is visible. Jesus said you don't light a candle and hide it under a bowl. You put it in a room where everyone can see it (Matthew 5:15). As the encroaching darkness grows, particularly in the West, so churches will have to learn how to be light - how to be visible and defined spiritual and moral communities that attract people from out of the darkness into the light. That is how it was in the early church; from the surrounding pagan darkness people were attracted to the light of the Gospel. So it will be again in our own context and we have to prepare for it.[9]

Notes

[1] *Pace* the individualism, in different ways, of both Rousseau and Hobbes. On the relationship between individual rights and society see Mark Hill (ed), *Religious Liberty and Human Rights*, Cardiff, University of Wales, 2002.

[2] See further John Goldingay, *Theological Diversity and the Authority of the Old Testament*, Grand Rapids, Eerdmans, 1987, pp59ff, and Kenneth Kitchen, *Ancient Orient and Old Testament*, Downers Grove, IVP, 1966, pp69f.

[3] On this see The Venerable Bede, *The Ecclesiastical History of the English People*, Oxford, OUP, 2008, and Catherine Glass and David Abbott, *Share the Inheritance*, Shawford, Inheritance Press, 2010.

[4] In the Annual Report of *Family Voice, Australia*, 2009, pp2ff.

[5] John Stambaugh and David Balch, *The Social World of the First Christians*, London, SPCK, 1986; E. A. Judge, *Cultural Conformity and Innovation in Paul*, Tyndale Bulletin 35, 1984; Francis Murphy CSSR, *The Christian Way of Life: Message of the Fathers of the Church vol.18*, Wilmington, Delaware, Michael Glazier, 1986; and Peter Phan, *Social Thought: Message of the Fathers of the Church vol.20*, Wilmington, Delaware, Michael Glazier, 1984.

[6] On this see Owen Chadwick, *The Reformation*, London, Penguin, 1990; and Herbert London, *America's Secular Challenge: the Rise of a New National Religion*, New York, Encounter, 2008.

[7] On the influence of the Clapham Sect see David Bebbington, *Evangelicalism in Modern Britain: A history from the 1730s to the 1980s*, London, Unwin Hyman, 1989, pp71ff; and Zerbanoo Gifford, *Thomas Clarkson and the Campaign against Slavery*, London, Anti-Slavery International, 1996.

[8] Richard Scott, *Christians in the Firing Line*, London, Wilberforce Publications, 2013.

[9] On all of this chapter see Lesslie Newbigin, *The Gospel in a Pluralist Society*, London, SPCK, 1989, pp222ff; Alasdair MacIntyre, *After Virtue: A Study in Moral Theory*, London, Duckworth, 2000, pp256ff.

5

CALLING ALL CHRISTIANS:
SHOULD WE BE PREPARED FOR EXILE?

In 1996 I chaired an ecumenical commission which produced a report called *The Search for Faith*. The difference between this report and many others like it was that it immediately became a cause célèbre in the media. The reason was its treatment of contemporary spirituality which it described as 'pick 'n mix' and as reflecting attitudes in culture not only to faith but to relationships, values and much else besides.[1]

The report also examined the persistence of belief, and the need to believe, even if the need to belong is no longer felt with such intensity or felt at all. This is shown again and again in the large number of people who describe themselves as Christian when modest percentages of the general population go to church on a given Sunday.

It gave considerable attention to what I have recently called 'nothing-but-ery', or a reductionist view of the universe and of the human condition – allegedly, but illegitimately, based on science. This is sometimes accompanied by an aggressive form of secularism which seeks to exclude religious discourse from the public sphere altogether, while continuing to espouse such values as the inherent dignity of human beings, or equality and freedom that, as I mentioned earlier, have ultimately been derived from a religious and, more specifically, a Judaeo-

Christian worldview. Such secularism favours individualism over community but also has a tendency to capitulate to culture. Not surprisingly, it is in thrall to scientific developments and can take a libertarian approach to how these are applied in the treatment of the embryo, the care of the person towards the end of life, or maintaining the integrity of the family in the face of assisted fertility technologies. In much of this, there is an implicit utilitarianism at work, with neglect of other considerations that may arise from a spiritual or categorical view of morality.

My participation in BBC1's *Soul of Britain* programmes in 2000 revealed not only the emergence of "nothing-but-ery" but also the continuing popularity of New Age, karmic and astrological beliefs. The Church's task cannot then be limited to responding to secularism, whether scientific or political, but must also take account of considerable credulity and even superstition in the country at large. On the one hand we have to uphold the God-given rationality of the universe. On the other, we must draw attention to its spiritual, even mystical, dimension.

How is the Church to respond to such a complex cultural situation and what is the Gospel or good news for the 21st century?

Christian attitudes to culture have varied over the ages depending on receptivity to the faith or hostility and resistance to it. Thus, Pope Gregory writing to Abbot Mellitus tells him to advise the missionary to the Anglo-Saxons, Augustine of Canterbury, not to destroy pagan shrines but to purify them and use them for Christian worship. Such a practice also seems to have been a feature of the evangelisation of the Netherlands by Willibrord and others. On the other hand, the English "apostle to the Germans", Boniface of Crediton, destroyed pagan temples and his felling of the Great Oak of Thor at Geismar sealed the success of his mission. When the pagans saw that he came to no harm in doing these things, they realised the falsity of paganism and the truth of the faith that Boniface was preaching.[2]

Both Pope Benedict XVI and evangelical missionaries like Charles Kraft have drawn attention to the ways in which the

Gospel addresses the deepest aspirations of cultures and, in fulfilling these, enables each culture to find its true centre. Kraft describes biblical revelation as "receptor-friendly". The (now) Roman Catholic West African scholar, Lamin Sanneh, refers to the "translatability" of the Gospel, i.e. its capacity for being rendered into the language, idiom and thought-forms of particular cultures. None of these distinguished scholars denies that the Gospel also challenges and transforms culture, but this can be gradual and from within. Such an approach reminds us of Richard Niebuhr's classic "the Christ of culture" category, where the message of Christ is not only the means for underpinning the social order, but also provides the resources for a critique of it and points society towards its destiny.[3]

An approach to culture of this kind needs to be balanced, however, by the Christ who can be "against culture" (another of Niebuhr's categories) and the Christ who is the "transformer of culture". The history of Britain is replete with those who, because of their faith, have stood up to the tyranny of monarchs, promoted basic freedoms, even at the risk of their own lives or liberty, struggled against slavery and on behalf of the poor. In our own day, we can think of Christian leadership against apartheid in South Africa, Anglican Archbishop David Gitari's courageous resistance at the time of dictatorship in Kenya, and Bishop Emmanuel Gbonigi's stand against General Sani Abacha in Nigeria who, it is said, admired the bishop for his integrity and courage. Just as these leaders had learnt much from the story of Christianity in Britain, so we can learn from it today as we seek not only to find receptivity to the Church's message in our culture but also, from time to time, resist in the name of Christ what is false, unjust or hateful.

A look at the Church worldwide also shows us how Christ can be the transformer of cultures. Again and again, we find despised, rejected and poverty-stricken groups of people who have been transformed by the Christian message of equal dignity. A change in their personal and social habits, love for the family and the neighbour, the pursuit of the good and of honesty in the workplace have been shown to lead not only to personal transformation but to social change.

In such a situation, where the Church has both to affirm what is godly in a culture but also to challenge what is mistaken or wilfully wrong, how are we to recognise the Church's mission and ministry?

We are faced with an overwhelming loss of personal and social integration: it has long been recognised that people are alienated from one another. The more individualistic society becomes, the more distanced we are from our neighbours. We are alienated from the natural environment around us because we see it only as something to be exploited to fulfil our own needs and not, as the Bible does, as having a destiny of its own. There is even an inner cleavage in ourselves such that our moral, spiritual, emotional and intellectual aspects are not working in harmony but, sometimes, against one another. Most fundamentally, we are alienated from the very ground of our being, the source of our existence and the One who gives us meaning and direction.

Alienation brings anxiety about life itself and the perceived threat to it. There is also, however, a sense of guilt, of not being what we have been called to be, of acting against our nature but being unable to atone for it. Such anxiety often leads to addiction. We seek to suppress it, to turn away from it and to deny it in enforced jollity and escapism. Addiction, whether to alcohol or drugs or to destructive behaviour or relationships, can be a way of forgetting, for a time, our real problems.

The Church's work has to address this personal and social situation which so many face. It cannot do this by simply repackaging the nostrums of social science or by imitating the methods of secular therapies. While the Church must be ever attentive to whatever is claimed as knowledge, it must also bring the Gospel of Jesus Christ to bear on the opportunities and problems of contemporary culture.

One of our great needs is to get out of the rut in which we are stuck and to start again. Repentance is a decidedly unfashionable term these days, but it is central to the Church's call to people everywhere. To know that we are forgiven deals with one of the basic reasons for the anxiety (or angst) experienced by so many. We are forgiven because Jesus Christ has, once again, opened the way for friendship with God. Instead of seeing the universe as indifferent or even as hostile to us, we can now see it as suffused and patterned by love. Such love is not only about the fulfilment of my desires or to do with my personal history, but with seeking the good, indeed, the best for the other, whether neighbour or stranger, friend or enemy. It is this experience of forgiveness and friendship which leads to a greater integration of our own personalities, whatever our quirks, experiences or even traumas.

Clearly, the Church's role has both a personal and social dimension to it. One of the great mantras of the modern Church has been "every member ministry", that is, a sense that God is calling each member of the Church to a particular ministry. The priesthood of all believers, as taught in the New Testament, is turned into the priesthood of each believer. This may be based on a misunderstanding of what the New Testament actually says but, whether or not every member has a ministry, every member certainly has to be a disciple of Jesus. In the business of making disciples, the Church will find that people have gifts which can equip them for particular kinds of service (or ministry) in the Church and in the world. How the local and national church discerns what the vocation of different members might be, how it prepares, commissions and supports them, will determine the Church's effectiveness in local communities and in the nation. Such effectiveness cannot be "bought" by becoming trendy or simply reflecting contemporary values, as politicians want the Church to do, but by making sure that all of the gifts given to Christians are being exercised to make the Gospel helpful, intelligible and liveable in our age, our locality, our nation, our world.

For centuries the Church has been committed to a presence in local communities: rural or urban, prosperous or deprived, mixed or monochrome. This has meant that the Church has been present when other services have withdrawn or only come in from outside to complete given tasks in a particular village, town or ward. The Church's presence must, however, be effective and this means a well thought out and well deployed ministry.

A basic assumption will be that the Gospel provides everything that a local church needs for its ministry and mission. The task of the wider church, and especially the stipendiary clergy, is to identify and enable those who are called to fulfil specific ministries in the local church, whether that is in serving the community, building up the faithful, teaching children or being prophetic about issues of justice and the proper use of resources.[4]

In the recognition of gifts for ministry, how God is calling women and men to serve him in the Church is a specific consideration. While men and women are equal because both have been made in God's image and given a common task, they are also different and fulfil their vocation in distinctive ways. Just as families and communities need a proper recognition of the distinctiveness as well as the complementarity of genders for balanced flourishing, so also the Church needs this for ministries which are balanced and complementary. The modernist and proto-feminist "one-size-fits-all" approach does not take difference into account and thus presses women into male patterns of work and recreation. The Church may be in danger of repeating this mistake just when the world is abandoning it.

Although there have been women deacons in the Eastern churches and, to a lesser extent, in the West, women have not been ordained priest or bishop in either the East or West, except in some schismatic communities. This should not be taken to mean, however, that women have not had hugely significant ministries in the Church. This is what the Orthodox Women's Consultation in Istanbul in 1997 had to say about the ministries of women in both the Eastern Orthodox and the Ancient Oriental churches:

Throughout the history of the Church, we have the testimony of countless women saints who responded to Christ in many ways, such as apostles, evangelists, confessors, martyrs, ascetics and nuns, teachers, mothers, spiritual and medical healers and deaconesses. We Orthodox women of today, inspired through the prayers and examples of these women saints, now endeavour to continue in their footsteps.[5]

From an evangelical point of view, we could add missionaries, counsellors, educationists and family-workers.

The historic churches, such as the Roman Catholic, the Orthodox and the Ancient Oriental, do not admit women to the order of priest or of bishop and biblical evangelicals do not generally appoint them to public roles which involve leadership of a congregation or an organisation. Together, these churches represent, of course, an overwhelming number of Christians throughout the world. I am not an "impossibilist" in the matter of women's ordination but the question of universal consent is important. The Church of England, or even the Anglican Communion, cannot claim to share the ministry of the ancient churches and then seek to change it unilaterally. There has to be at least permissive consent, if not uniformity of practice. Until then, any such ordinations will have to be seen as subject to the process of reception (which includes the possibility of these not being received). Naturally, such a situation raises questions in the minds of the faithful about things like sacramental assurance: the need to be sure that they are, indeed, receiving God's grace in the sacraments through duly accredited ministries.[6]

One thing is not negotiable: God is calling both women and men to ministry in the Church and mission in the world. Whatever decision the Universal Church comes to in due course, this should not be in doubt. Such a position does not necessarily mean pushing women into male patterns of ministry, whether these patterns have emerged because of God's will or social standards or both. Rather, we should be praying for and working towards patterns of ministry which take the God-givenness of gender seriously. Such patterns can be those of orders of pastoral workers, teachers, evangelists etc, or they can be particular offices in the Church that bring the specific gift of women to bear on ministry and mission.

What we should have then is a situation of women and men ministering together but each in their own way, showing common and distinctive gifts for the good of the Church and the spread of the Gospel.

The partnership of men and women in the Church is not the only partnership the Church needs. When I was a diocesan bishop, we held a consultation with our partners, and representatives of more than 40 local and national organisations turned up. These included educational agencies, social workers, youth organisations, statutory bodies and others. For the Church of England, with its heavy responsibility for a significant portion of our national heritage, in terms of historic buildings and the like, a new and honest concordat with the state is also very important. Congregations alone, some of them rural and small, cannot be burdened with the upkeep of what belongs to the nation as a whole. If these buildings are to survive for the purposes for which they were built, rather than as museums, they will have to be adapted and extended to meet present-day needs. This requires resources which the Church, local or national, cannot provide by itself.

As far as "establishment" is concerned, if this means a desire by the people of this country to hear the Church's voice in the councils of state, there can be little objection to it, but this cannot be at the expense of compromising the essential message which the Church has been called to proclaim. This means that the Church should have control over what it believes and teaches, its worship and, however wide the consultation, the appointment of its leaders. If such is not the case, there is always the danger of capitulating to the culture and to power structures, whether through seduction or coercion. In turn, the Church has an obligation to remind the nation of the Judaeo-Christian basis of its life as set out, for example, in the Coronation Service and the Coronation Oath.

Even if there is disestablishment, formal or de facto, two matters will still need to be borne in mind: the Church of England could remain the national church of the land to which people turn in national celebration or mourning and for the "hatching, matching and dispatching" rituals which any culture needs. Second, even if there is no established church, the moral and spiritual resources of the Judaeo-Christian tradition will still be needed in debate on policy and legislation over a whole range of issues such as the status of the embryo, the ethics of cloning, abortion, euthanasia and assisted dying, marriage and family, justification (or not) of armed conflict, the treatment of refugees, and many others. It would be very unwise to lose such a rich heritage which has provided our worldview just because of the disappearance of an established church and when there is no other viable worldview in sight.

It may be that establishment is gradually being eroded by atrophy and attrition. The Church of England will have to decide whether to struggle to maintain it or to lose it gracefully, thus lightening its load for the sake of a clearer witness to the nation. A secularist and secularising paradigm is being set in place in terms of the assumptions of policy, legislation, charity laws and the like. In such conditions, all the churches need to prepare for exile to begin to see themselves as gathered moral and spiritual communities which attract those in the surrounding darkness by their light and become centres for a Christian vision of society.

A missionary church will be light in its structures. At the very least, it will have the capacity to gather people. Such a gathering must, first of all, be for the purposes of prayer and the giving of thanks (*eucharistia*). There should be the opportunity then to consult and to decide together. According to the pattern set by the very first Council of the Church at Jerusalem, as recorded in the Acts of the Apostles, bishops, clergy and the faithful will all have a presence and a say but in the decision-making they will have distinctive roles and duties. This is, in fact, the true meaning of "synod" or walking together in the same way. It is very far from mimicking parliamentary structures and procedures, not to speak of the considerable bureaucracy this requires.

No one is an island and this is all the more so in the Church. We need one another so we can learn from one another, support one another, pray for one another and, when necessary, complement and even correct one another. What is true of Christians in the local church is also true of relationships between churches throughout the world. Every local church has the primary responsibility for mission in its area but it must carry this out mindful of its relationship with all the other local churches. It cannot relate to the state or to culture in such a way that its sister churches fail to recognise the Church of Jesus Christ in it.

At the local level those with pastoral and teaching responsibility must sometimes declare the faith of the Church. This is one of the most important roles of a bishop in the diocese. Universally also, there will be occasions when, to settle a disputed matter or to situate the Church's position in some crucial area, the faith of the Church has to be set out clearly. Those with such responsibility must only declare what the Church has always believed, even if it is being applied to contemporary issues. They must do it in manifest continuity with Scripture and apostolic teaching and, as far as possible, they must do it along with others who have similar responsibilities.

The Church's mission in society has two poles to it: that of embassy, of going out into the world, and of hospitality, of welcoming people to the Church's proclamation, worship and service.[7] Embassy can, of course, be a literal going out, as was the case with numerous young people who went out from this country in the 19th century to open up the interior of West Africa to the Gospel, knowing that for many of them it would mean death from disease to which they had no resistance. Less dramatically, but also importantly, the ministry from Rochester Cathedral during the seemingly endless Dickens festivals is also an instance of embassy: whether through the singing of hymns, invitations to pray in the cathedral (which produce a staggering response in terms of numbers) or counselling those who find themselves in need, the Christian community is going out to those around it. Embassy need not just be a physical going to another part of the world or even into the local high street. For many Christians it is simply going to work and bearing witness

76

to their faith there. As this becomes more difficult, we need to be advocates of respect for conscience and for reasonable accommodation of belief and the manifestation of belief at the workplace. The involvement of Christians and churches in public life or in the media (including new media), however difficult this is found to be, is another area where embassy is a necessity.

Welcoming people is as important as going out. Again and again, I am embarrassed at how the stranger, the person with special needs or the loner is simply left out at church. We must make sure that everyone is welcomed, made to feel at home and helped. Welcoming does not, of course, mean that we affirm or agree with everything people do or believe. The very distinctiveness of the Gospel that warms and heals cannot be compromised by an inclusion that does not challenge or change. At the same time, a welcome must include engaging with people's beliefs and values and seeking to find connections between them and the faith proclaimed by the Church.

The false will then be challenged and rejected but what is true will be recognised and fulfilled. It has ever been so and must continue to be so.

For the Church to be effective in embassy and hospitality, it must be visible in the society in which it finds itself. For some, like Philip Larkin, iconic buildings are enough, as they breathe an atmosphere of transcendence. For others, it is the people of a community gathering for worship in a place that has been used, perhaps for centuries, by their forebears. We must not neglect such traditional understandings of visibility, but there has to be more.

One feature of the Church most appreciated by ordinary people is the sight of clergy "on the beat": walking the streets, visiting homes and shops and chaplains at the workplace. Processions on important days like Good Friday, Palm Sunday and Easter, worship outdoors, especially at holiday times, evangelistic and prayer rallies and accessibility to worship in ancient buildings all contribute to that sense of visibility among the population. The papal visit to Britain in September 2010, and Billy Graham type missions, can reveal how Christianity can contribute to a deepening of people's spiritual lives and enable them to address everyday moral questions.

Too often debate about the future of the Church and of the Christian faith has been adversarial and polarised: tradition is set against innovation, authority against democracy and community-mindedness against "congregationalism". Such polarisation is not always helpful and needlessly forces people into exclusive and excluding models of the Church's life. We should be promoting a "both-and" rather than an "either-or" view of the Church so that tradition and renewal, order and spontaneity, leadership and consent, mission and maintenance can be creatively held together.

An action plan for today's Church will therefore include an understanding of the culture and context in which the Church is placed and how the Gospel can address its strengths and weaknesses. There will be an emphasis on partnership among churches but also with the state, local authorities, statutory and voluntary agencies. It should be clear, however, that the Church's integrity cannot be sacrificed to short-term advantage, and government especially will have to recognise the nature of the Church and its obligations in its partnership with Christian communities of different kinds. The churches should not only be concerned with decline and with needy areas, important as those are, but actively seek and support those at the cutting-edge of opportunity—young families, students and ethnic and other kinds of groups.

Local Christian communities should largely be responsible for mission and ministry in their neck of the woods with support from stipendiary clergy and specialists in education, youth work, worship, music and, particularly, the identification and preparation of leaders. This should lead to a streamlining of bureaucracy at every level, as should reinventing how churches gather for making decisions that affect them all.

At the same time, local and national churches should be aware of the world-wide dimension of the Christian faith. Our partnership with brothers and sisters overseas should be mutually enriching but it may also involve waiting for one another and, from time to time, being willing to be corrected and extended in our particular reading of the Christian tradition.

We should not be intimidated by the challenge of our times but see it as an opportunity for a vigorous engagement with the needs and questions of the day, confident that the good news of Jesus Christ remains just that—even, perhaps especially, for our own times.

Notes

[1] Mission Theological Advisory Group, *The Search for Faith and the Witness of the Church*, London, CHP, 1996.

[2] Anton Wessels, *Europe: Was it ever really Christian?*, London, SCM, 1994, pp11f and Bede, *The Ecclesiastical History of the English People*, Oxford, OUP, 2008, pp56f.

[3] See further my *The Unique and Universal Christ*, Milton Keynes, Paternoster, 2008, pp60ff.

[4] See my *Shapes of the Church to Come*, Eastbourne, Kingswat, 2001, pp41ff.

[5] See *Turn to God: Rejoice in Hope (Orthodox Reflections on the way to Harare)*, Thomas FitzGerald and Peter Bouteneff (eds), Geneva, WCC, 1998, p83.

[6] See further the *Rochester Report: Women Bishops in the Church of England?*, London, CHP, pp136ff.

[7] See my *Citizens and Exiles: Christian Faith in a Plural World*, London, SPCK, 1998, pp115ff.

6

THE CONSTITUTIONAL AND SACRAMENTAL
SIGNIFICANCE OF THE CORONATION

The Queen remains in robust health but, inevitably, as she gets older there is speculation about the form and content of the next Coronation service, when it is needed.

We should not forget that the service is, perhaps, the oldest ritual in the country. Its history goes back to before the Norman Conquest and it has influenced significantly the development of similar rites in other parts of Europe. During these centuries, it has changed very little; it has become a little more elaborate, been translated into English, had the Eucharistic material conformed to the Book of Common Prayer and in 1689 the Oath to maintain the 'reformed religion established by law' was inserted by Parliament. Any other changes have been minor and incidental. The overwhelming impression is that of a fundamentally Christian act of worship during which the new monarch is crowned and enthroned. This is preceded, however, by the giving of a Bible with the words: "We present you with this Book, the most valuable thing that this world affords. Here is Wisdom; this is the royal law. These are the lively Oracles of God".

The new monarch has already promised in the Oath to "maintain the Laws of God and the true profession of the Gospel". These are not just words. We know that in the course of time, the Bible has profoundly influenced the thoughts and actions of kings and queens. The emergence, under Alfred, of a Common Law tradition consistent with the Judaeo-Christian teachings of the Bible, St. Dunstan's fashioning of a Coronation oath and Henry's Charter of Liberties (so influential for Magna Carta) are all examples of the role the Bible has played in the development of the monarchy and of other political institutions in this country.[1]

The promise to uphold the Laws of God and to govern people according to law are basic to the idea of a constitutional monarchy, which is itself derived from biblical ideas found, for instance, in Deuteronomy 17:14–20 (cf 1 Samuel 12:14f). The Bible recognises both a distinction between Temple and Palace, Priest and King, and their inter-relatedness. This is the background to Jesus' comment to give to Caesar what is Caesar's, and to God what is God's. It cannot be an accident that this is the part of the Gospel set for the Coronation Service (Matt 22:15–22).

The whole service has a sacramental feel to it. It is, of course, set in the context of celebrating the Eucharist but one of its many remarkable features is the anointing of the monarch. The King or Queen is anointed with holy oil on the palms, the breast and the head. This is said to be in continuity with the anointing of kings, priests, and prophets in Israel. In the Bible, anointing is what *God* does through his servants and it is for the fulfilment of certain tasks, according to God's will. It is impossible to say what effect such a solemn act has on the consciousness of the one anointed but it cannot be insignificant.

Every act in the service, every symbol of monarchy is immediately and explicitly tied to the Christian faith. The ring of kingly dignity is described as the seal of 'Catholic Faith' so that the monarch will continue to defend Christ's religion (note, not every religion or some vague concept of 'faith', though freedom of belief can well be seen as part, even a necessary part, of Christian faith).

The Orb is set under the Cross as a reminder that the whole world is subject to the power and empire of Christ our Redeemer.

The sword is presented and the prayer accompanying this describes the monarch as a minister of God for the punishment of evildoers and for the protection and encouragement of the virtuous. This is taken directly from St. Paul's description of the godly ruler in Romans 13 and 1 Peter 2:13–17 (the epistle set for the Coronation).

It is worth noting that at both the anointing and at the communion the monarch divests himself or herself of all the panoply of power in a gesture of humility before God. This reminds us that the virtue of humility is a peculiarly Christian virtue which we learn from Christ himself who, though he was in the form of God, emptied himself and took the form of a servant for our sake (Phil 2:6–8).

The monarch is an example of the public virtues of service, sacrifice and selflessness which spring from such humility. Whilst constitutional monarchy precludes an overtly political role for a king or queen, the coronation service clearly gives the monarch a role of moral and spiritual leadership. At the communion, the monarch brings the offering of bread and wine, makes the confession and is absolved before receiving in both kinds. This is the climax of a service that has been sacramental throughout and also reveals the character of Christian monarchy.

When the new king or queen pledges to uphold the Christian faith, this is a most solemn acknowledgement of the basis for the nation's institutions, laws and values. It is right that the atmosphere for making such a declaration should be as ecumenical as possible. I cannot see, however, how such a service could be multi-faith. Its very sacramental nature would seem to exclude such a possibility but it is also significant that distinctive Christian beliefs are stated and advanced in every part of the service. For instance, one of the leading features of the service is to declare the monarch's dependence on divine providence. Naturally, those who belong to non-theistic religions, such as certain kinds of Buddhism, will not be able to join in such a declaration. Other religious traditions may not see a distinction between what is God's and what is Caesar's as is set out in the Coronation Gospel.

There are some, of course, who advocate a whole-scale

revision of the event so that it becomes wholly multi-faith or even secular. This would have very serious implications for the constitutional arrangements of the nation and would run the risk of incoherence, in the service itself and, more generally, in national life. The basis, justification and legitimacy of the monarchy is set firmly within the Judaeo-Christian tradition and to tamper with this could lead to an unravelling of the monarchy's *raison d'etre*. I do not believe, however, that such a radical step will be taken in the foreseeable future. We should proceed then on the assumption that the traditional rite will be used and that this will involve the nation, as well as the monarch, in reaffirming the Christian basis of national life from which our leading values derive. One of these values is freedom for those who have other ways of viewing the world and human destiny. Hospitality and an invitation to them to contribute to the developing life of the nation also spring from the non-coerciveness of the Christian faith (even if the churches have not always been true to the Gospel in this matter).

The Coronation should, therefore, at once be a clear declaration of the Christian basis of society *and* a welcoming of those of other faiths and, indeed, of none. What might this mean in practice? People of other faiths should certainly be invited and their leaders given an honoured place, if they are willing to attend. After the service, in Westminster Hall, or some suitable location near the Abbey, they, and others, should be able to bring greetings and pledges of allegiance. Nothing in the service itself should occur, however, which is indicative of any departure from the doctrine and practice of the Church.

The Coronation is not merely a civic or national event in which the Church is simply being asked to be 'chaplain to the nation'. It is a deeply Christian ceremony in its own right and has the central mystery of the Christian faith at its heart. By communicating, the monarch demonstrates that he or she is a communicant of the Church of which he or she is to be Supreme Governor. By deferring to those who have responsibility for the ordering of the Church's life in being crowned and enthroned by them, the monarch is reminded that "we give not our Princes the ministering either of God's Word or of the Sacraments" (Article 37). In other words, the distinction but also the inter-relatedness between the work of God and that of Caesar is clearly set out as an object lesson to the nation at large.

Let us hope that we will not need another Coronation very soon but, when we do, let us use with reverence this rite which has been shaped by such piety and which has led to such fruit in our national life. Such a sign of rootedness will not offend people of other faiths. It will honour Christ and will evoke genuine respect among our friends of other faiths and even among many who do not profess a faith of any kind.

Note

[1] Catherine Glass and David Abbott, *Share the Inheritance,* Shawford, Hants, Inheritance Press, 2010.

7

WHY CAN'T THE VOICE OF CHRISTIANS BE HEARD?

For more than 1500 years Christianity has formed and undergirded the public law of this land. Now the Lord Chancellor and the Lord Chief Justice, by disciplining Richard Page JP for declining to place a child with a same-sex couple on the grounds that it was not in the interests of the child, have declared war on even residual notions of the faith having any place in our legal processes.[1]

Until the recent 'equality' legislation, the teaching of the Book of Common Prayer's Marriage Service was reflected in the law on marriage. Now even to allow such teaching to be taken into account, in reaching a legal decision, is said to be 'bigoted' and 'prejudiced'.

This is but the latest in a long line of cases having the effect of excluding Christians from public service and holding public office. Both the Universal Declaration of Human Rights and the European Convention guarantee not only freedom of belief and conscience but also the right to manifest such belief in public or in private.[2] In spite of subscribing to the UN Declaration and the European Convention, and contrary to our own Human Rights Act, the government and law officers, it seems, are intent on preventing Christians from manifesting their belief in the public sphere.

Indeed, the implications are wider than that, for what is said about Mr Page could apply equally to Jews, Muslims and others. The chief law officers of the Crown, and those who have complained to them, allege that Mr Page has improperly allowed his religious beliefs to influence his decision.

It is true that Mr Page cannot exclude what his faith teaches from his consideration of these matters but, as he says, his decision was not based solely on his religious beliefs, or, indeed, simply because of the sexual orientation of the couple involved. It was taken for objective reasons in the interests of the child and for the common good. The complaint against Mr Page tells us that there is research showing that children adopted by same-sex couples do better than children in traditional families.

So much for the rest of the world believing that children need both mothers and fathers for the best outcomes in life! It would be interesting to know the credentials of this research. How was the sample recruited? What was the period covered? Was the research randomised? Was there a control group, to whom were these children compared? We are given none of this information, only the word of a clerk about research conducted by an agency with an interest in the issue.

Against this, the wide-ranging University of Texas study by Mark Regnerus certainly found that children brought up by same-sex parents look 'markedly different' on numerous outcomes such as education, mental health, employment or use of drugs when compared to those from families with both a mother and a father present. In addition, evidence from Denmark, the United States and the CIVITAS think-tank here has shown the need that children, particularly boys, have for a father.[3]

Fathers relate differently to the child than the mother, and children need both mothering and fathering for all-round development, the formation of healthy same- and other-sex relationships and for self-esteem. There may be tragic circumstances where a child does not have a present father or mother. Such children and the present parent must, of course, be supported in every way but this is very different from planning to have children who will never know a mother or a father.

There has been a long tradition in Britain of making room

for conscience. Even in times of war, this has been recognised. The 1967 Abortion Act and the 1990 Human Fertilisation and Embryology Act both respect the consciences of those who have scruples about the manipulation or destruction of foetuses (though recent judicial decisions seem to be limiting even such respect). Why should Mr Page's conscience not be respected and why should there not be reasonable accommodation of his beliefs?

The complaint against him alleges that he would not sign the final decision taken by the majority, when it was the 'convention' to do so. Why is there a convention that does not recognise conscientious dissent? The highest law officers of the land have not only issued a 'reprimand' to Mr Page but require him to receive 'remedial' training.

This smacks to me of the 're-education' camps so beloved of totalitarian Marxist states. Is this the way to promote liberty, or is freedom of speech and belief only for a liberal elite with politically correct views?

Notes

[1] Daily Mail, 18 January 2015.

[2] Article 18 of the UN's *Universal Declaration of Human Rights* and Article 9 of the *European Convention for the Protection of Human Rights and Fundamental Freedoms*.

[3] Mark Regnerus, *How different are the adult children of parents who have same-sex relationships?*, Social Science Research 41, 2012, pp752-770; Morten Frisch, Anders Hviid, *Childhood Family Correlations of Heterosexual and Homosexual marriages: A National Cohort Study of Two Million Danes*, Dept. of Epidemiology Research, Danish Epidemiology Science Centre, Copenhagen, 2006; CIVITAS, *How Fathers fit into the Family,* Institute for the Study of Civil Society, London, 2001.

Part Three

FREEDOM AND RESPONSIBILITY

An immediate feature of our experience is awareness of being able to act, or to restrain action, of freedom to choose this or that course of action, and of rightness or wrongness of the action we have chosen. Much that is of significance in human lives and in our societies arises from such awareness: our work, how we manage our environment, the achievement of science and the accomplishment of the arts, our day-to-day and most intimate relationships are all seen to have meaning because of our capacity (however limited) of self-direction and our consciousness of responsibility because we have such capacity.

It is true that moral awareness is not enough: the prodigal son in Jesus' parable had not only to become aware of his plight (Lk 15:17) but had to repent of his rebellion when he encountered the freely offered and sacrificial love of his father (v.21). We may say also that even moral awareness is a work of grace in creatures who have allowed our sensibilities to be so degraded by our selfish appetites that we cease to be able to distinguish right from wrong.

Even vestigial awareness, however, leads us to affirm fundamental freedoms of movement, of owning property, of work, of relationships and, above all, of belief, of practising our beliefs, in public and private, and of arguing for them.

But, of course, freedom always has to be balanced with responsibility. Such responsibility must be about protecting others from harm which our activities may cause them but it cannot be just about individuals, and 'not causing harm' must extend to the most vulnerable and not only our 'peers,' however that is perceived. This leads not only to valuing and promoting a 'culture of life' in addressing the various moral dilemmas of contemporary life, but to a strengthening of vital social institutions such as the family (both immediate and extended), local community, the church and civil society.

In the chapters that follow, attention has been given to some of these aspects of freedom and responsibility.

8

FREEDOMS WE RISK LOSING

Let us begin with the Cylinder of Cyrus in the British Museum. It is the Proclamation of Freedom by Cyrus the Great (Kourosh-i-Kabir as he is called by the Iranian people today) when the Persian Empire reached its zenith. The emperor is mentioned in the Bible as one of God's anointed who was to bring liberation to the people of Israel who were at that time in bondage (Isaiah 45:1–7).[1]

The Cylinder of Cyrus was loaned to the National Museum in Tehran for a year or so (so that it was back home, if you like). At the time, I was engaged in a kind of dialogue with the Iranian authorities and I thought that I would begin my part of the dialogue by saying something about the Cylinder. I said how wonderful it was – this tradition of freedom and tolerance in Iran that goes back to Cyrus the Great. After I had finished, the man who was chairing the meeting on the other side looked at me and said, "Bishop, we are not interested in the past. We are only interested in the future." Well, can it be right for a nation to forget its heritage? Britain is busily forgetting its heritage and needs to be reminded, but what about Iran and Cyrus?

As I go around the world, in even the most unpromising places, I find a heritage of freedom and toleration. A couple of centuries after Cyrus, we have the Indian king Ashoka, who, after a very bloody reign, became a Buddhist and then proclaimed freedom for people in his empire. He erected a number of pillars proclaiming peace and freedom which we can still see. Today many people who are Buddhists profess peace and reconciliation for themselves, but there are many countries where Buddhism is the official religion and where there is a great deal of conflict — Sri Lanka, for example, or Burma, where both Christians and Muslims find themselves oppressed communities. If people are going to learn from Cyrus, why not from Ashoka?[2]

Then there is Constantine the Great's Edict of Milan (which wasn't an edict and wasn't from Milan, but let that go for the time being). The interesting thing about the Edict of Milan, as far as Christians are concerned, is that we often think it was about freedom for Christians, at last, who had been persecuted by the Roman Empire for so many years. It was certainly that, but it was also a proclamation of freedom of belief for everyone. Constantine wasn't just saying Christians are free now, he was saying everyone is free to practise their beliefs, and I think in that sense the Edict of Milan is very significant.[3]

Coming back to Persia, the true parallel to Milan is the Emperor Yazdigard's Edict, which brought about freedom and toleration for Christians, and indeed for other communities in the Persian Empire. This notion of millets (tolerated communities) became important for their later status in the world of Islam.[4]

Then there is what is known as the Constitution of Medina. When the Prophet of Islam arrived in Medina there were strong communities of Jews and Christians there and he promulgated the Constitution of Medina (*Sahifat Al-Medina*), in which he recognised the equality of Jews, Christians and others with the Muslims in the new city state. The Constitution of Medina marks the first Islamic state and when people say to me, as indeed they do quite often in my travels, that they want an Islamic state in this or that place, I say to them, will it be like the first Islamic state? And if not, why not?[5]

Of course, there is our own history in this country. King Alfred the Great brought together from diverse sources a common law, but he made very sure that it was in agreement with the teaching of the Bible, although he also drew on Anglo-Saxon and Roman Law and the customs of the Celts. The great Charter of Liberty that Henry I was compelled to accept (that was a condition for his being crowned King by Archbishop Anselm) is the background to Magna Carta and once again the recognition of freedom for ordinary people. The first purpose of the Magna Carta at that time was a limitation of the powers of the King. That is also a biblical idea. The constitutional monarchy goes back to Deuteronomy 17 and to what the Prophet Samuel said to Saul and to David. So Magna Carta was certainly about that, but it also had the effect of promoting freedom more generally.[6]

The question that I ask myself is: if there are all these traditions of freedom and tolerance in so many different cultures, why are we losing these freedoms today in the 21st century when you might have thought there was more fertile ground for their flourishing? If I asked you when the modern age began, what would you say? Was it the Industrial Revolution, the Renaissance, or the Enlightenment? These are all very good answers and I am not saying one of them is right or wrong, but I think there is a sense in which the modern age for our purposes begins in the 13th century.

What happened in the 13th century was that the Western world received back the writings of Aristotle from the Islamic world where they had been translated, studied and commented upon. That much is common knowledge — you hear it in politically correct classes. What is not as often heard is how the Islamic world got it. The answer is that the Islamic world got not just Aristotle but Greek knowledge in general, of science, philosophy and so on from the work of mainly Christian clergy who translated either directly from the Greek into Arabic or from Syriac. This knowledge was transmitted to the West either through Jewish traders or through the Arabic-speaking Christian communities in the West, in particular the Iberian peninsula. In the past the emphasis had been on a divinely-ordered society, governed by a mixture of divine, natural and positive law. The emphasis now was on the providential nature of the world itself

– that it was governed by natural law – on the particular, and therefore on the human person having his or her own identity and place within this world that was ordered in this kind of way. To this, the Christian, out of the teaching of the Bible, added that human beings had been made in God's image, and this was something quite new — we don't find it in Aristotle. Aristotle believed in what you might call natural subjection, that there are some people who are born to be free and others who are born to be slaves. He said notoriously or famously, depending on your point of view, that people living in the northern part of the world could be enslaved because they had courage without intelligence, and people in the southern part could be enslaved because they had intelligence without courage. The Greeks, of course, had both. So the idea of inalienable human dignity is not to be found in Aristotle and is of Judaeo-Christian provenance.[7]

But this new importance of the person resulted in a greater recognition of freedom and of conscience. From it emerged the idea that such persons had to consent to how they were governed, and so a new kind of democracy, different from the harshly selective model of the Greeks, could gradually develop. From it also arose the idea of natural rights which belonged to us inalienably and could not be taken away. This assumed especial importance in the New World as some Christians tried to defend the fundamental freedoms of the indigenous people. The Enlightenment received these ideas and embellished them and they serve as the background to contemporary documents such as the Universal Declaration of Human Rights. It is interesting to note that in equivalent Islamic declarations, Article 18 (which guarantees freedom of thought, conscience and belief) is entirely absent.[8]

Most countries are signatories to the UN Declaration, so why are we facing the situation that we are and what are the threats to this hard-won tradition of freedom and tolerance that we have?

It seems to me that there are several such threats. The first is old-fashioned tyranny; that's not gone out of business. Eritrea is a very good example. The most terrible persecution of Christians started with the evangelical Christians in Eritrea but has now also spread to Orthodox and Roman Catholic Christians: people being imprisoned in containers, left out in the heat of the day and the cold of the night: torture, beatings, all sorts of things, and the reason, as far as I can tell, is just personal tyranny and the fact that the rulers of Eritrea seem paranoid about these different Christian churches and people. The Orthodox Patriarch has disappeared and no one knows where he is, but this is an example simply of paranoid dictatorship, nothing else.[9]

Another threat is totalitarian ideology, for example, in the form of one kind of Marxism or another. The situation in China is much improved, partly because of the sheer numbers. In 1949 there were perhaps five or six million Christians (Catholics and Protestants) in China; there are now perhaps a hundred million, maybe more, so the numbers are such that they cannot be ignored and their situation, at least in the big cities, has improved in terms of freedom of worship and of witness. But it remains serious in other respects, particularly with the unregistered churches, the so-called house churches, although many of them are so big that you cannot really call them house churches. The situation of those Catholics who still profess a loyalty to the Pope remains serious. Some Catholic bishops are still either in prison or under house arrest and many clergy of that part of the Catholic Church have been in prison, have been tortured or been in labour camps, as have the leaders of house churches. So there is a long way still to go as far as freedom is concerned for the people of China. The other example of these remnants of Marxism is Vietnam, where the evangelical churches have grown exponentially. While Roman Catholic Christianity has been present in Vietnam for a long time and has also suffered grievously at the hands of the rulers, the evangelicals are now finding that the heat is on them and people are being prevented from worshipping, their churches are being destroyed, they are being deported from their villages to other villages and sometimes being detained and fined simply for being Christians. Again and again villagers are told, "In this district you cannot be a Christian." Laos is another example of continuing terrible persecution for evangelical Christians, partly as a remnant of Marxist ideology.[10]

There are other examples of persecution. As I mentioned earlier, regrettably, in spite of the example of Ashoka, there is the persecution of Christians and Muslims in Burma, sometimes (I am sorry to say) led by Buddhist monks. This is also the case in Sri Lanka, both with regard to Christians and also in terms of the Tamil ethnic minority. The West has a rather idealised picture of Buddhism, but that is not so in Burma or Sri Lanka and some other countries. In India there has been persecution of Christians, again because of the ideology of Hindutva, that is to say, the belief that the only real citizens of India must be Hindus, that others — such as Christians and Muslims — cannot really be citizens of India unless they become Hindu in some way or other.

All of this is real and has to be noticed but, as Rehman Chishti MP has said, 80 per cent of the persecution of Christians that is taking place today is taking place in the Islamic world. This is a fact that cannot be denied, and the question is, why? We are faced in the Islamic world and indeed beyond that, with something that is not just the faith of pious Muslims – Christians should respect the faith of other people even if they disagree with them, and they should certainly love the other person even if they disagree with that person — but this is not about personal faith or even the faith of a community; this is about a comprehensive political, social and economic ideology. That is what Islamism is. Now there are moderate Muslim voices. Many of them are my friends; I admire them. Sometimes they are very courageous, like the former Grand Mufti of Egypt, but in most places their voice is not prevailing, so we have situations of increasing hardship for Christians and others in the Muslim world.

Some Muslim organisations now say that they have renounced violence. We welcome that. The Muslim Brotherhood in Egypt claims that it has renounced violence. That's excellent but we still have to ask who has been responsible for the recent violence against Christians and others. The Tablighi Jamaat say they have never been violent; I think that is true. The Jamaat has one of its headquarters in Raiwind, of which I was Bishop, so I do know a little about this, but the question is: if people belong to an ideological movement like the Tablighi Jamaat, or like the Ikhwan, can they then go on to something that is violent and extremist? If so, what is self-professedly non-violent Islamism doing about it?

The Western press has had a love affair with the Arab Spring. The name itself was coined here, but the Arab Spring is not all that it seems. The real test of democracy is not taking power through the ballot box but the willingness to give up power through the ballot box, and there, as far as many Islamist movements are concerned, the jury is still out. Bishop Kenneth Cragg, who died very recently just short of 100 and writing up to the very end — a distinguished teacher of mine and a very sympathetic Christian student of Islam — was asked once, "Well, in the end, Bishop, what is the difference between Islam and Christianity?" He said something that is relevant today: "It's the difference in the attitude to power." Christianity teaches that it is by giving up power that you change the world. Islam teaches that it is by taking power that you change the world.

Democracy may be the darling of some in the media here, but it is not enough. In the Middle East certainly and in many other parts of the world, democracy is not enough because democracy can become a tyranny of the majority. It's no less tyranny because it's of the majority. In fact, in the referendum in Egypt it wasn't the majority that voted for the referendum, it was actually a very small minority. Nevertheless, we couldn't just say that because so many people had voted for something, it was legitimate now for a country like Egypt to have a constitution that finds its source only in Sharia. It's not enough. We also need a Bill of Rights. Why was a Bill of Rights needed here in 1689? Or after Independence in the US? Why did we need at a global level the Universal Declaration of Human Rights, and so on? I think in many countries in the world today we need a Bill of Rights, particularly where we are faced with a strong Islamist movement that demands the imposition or enforcement of Sharia in the way in which they interpret it.

In Egypt, to take an example, a Bill of Rights was needed first of all to affirm the equality of all before the law. Because under Sharia it is not at all clear that the equality of all can be taken for granted, because Sharia is structured in such a way that, for example, Muslims and non-Muslims are not equal. By definition, women and men are not equal. So we need to ensure the equality of all before the law and one law for all. I was a great admirer of the late Pope Shenouda, Patriarch of the Coptic Church (who has recently died) for his courage in difficult circumstances throughout his period as Patriarch in Egypt. But towards the end, when it seemed that Islamists would actually come to power, he said something that made me quite anxious. He said, "Let them have their Sharia as long as we can have our own law." That is exactly the definition of the *dhimmi* (the system by which certain non-Muslims were allowed to live in the Islamic domains), with Christians being relegated to a second-class status, with certain disabilities, by definition, and exclusion from participation in public life. So, in a Bill of Rights one law for all is very important. We may take the idea of common citizenship for granted but those who have lived under the *dhimma* certainly do not. That also is important. For hundreds of years, Christian and Jewish subjects in the Islamic empires suffered from very serious disabilities. They included lack of freedom of worship, of building churches or synagogues, of having to pay special taxes, of systemic discrimination and sporadic violence. All of these became characteristic of the *dhimma*. It is encouraging that the new Egyptian Constitution and the present leadership are emphasising fundamental freedoms and common citizenship. Many others can learn from this example and more should be done.

When I began my work with the persecuted church over six years ago, I had imagined most of it would be overseas. It has not turned out exactly to be so. I have been drawn, more and more, into what is happening in Britain. In the House of Lords there is a room called the Hume Room, where you can go and get public school-type lunches quite cheaply. The only condition is that you sit at the very next vacant chair at the dining table, so you find yourself sitting next to all sorts of people you wouldn't otherwise meet. I found myself sitting next to the gentleman I mentioned earlier who expressed great regret for his part in the Sunday Trading Bill campaign. It had, he now believed, destroyed a common day for the family, and it meant the poorer sections of society would be the ones who would be forced to work because the wealthier people could always take the day off, if they wished to do so. I found his outburst quite revealing and I wish there were more *mea culpas* of this kind. But in spite of an intervention by myself, a court has ruled recently that Christians have no right to ask for time off for worship and fellowship with other Christians on Sunday. And in fact my intervention was used in a sense that I had not intended at all — to establish this case that they were making. The result will be that poorer people will be forced to work on Sundays. Poorer Christians, younger Christians, will be forced to do this and not be able to go to church. We have actual cases that have already occurred.

Then there is the legislation against hate speech. It is true that the legislation was at the last minute improved, in the House of Lords as it happens, to recognise to some extent legitimate activities of preaching, evangelism, criticism and so forth. Nevertheless, it has already been used to prevent people preaching, evangelising or simply exercising their right of free speech in public, such as policemen saying to a Christian evangelist in a large British city: "You can't preach here. This is a Muslim area." In several other cases, where people have simply been quoting the Bible or even where a quotation from the Bible has appeared on a screen, this has led to their arrest and the threat of prosecution. There are people who have had personal experience of having said something on the radio and then, by the time they got home, the police were waiting for them.

Then there are those Christians and Christian bodies who feel that equality legislation is such that they cannot in conscience agree with some of the things that those who have legislated for equality in this way are asking of them. The closure of the Catholic adoption agencies is an example. They had been doing valuable work for 150 years, placing difficult children in adoptive homes. They were not allowed even this exemption, which is all that they were asking for, that they be allowed to continue working as before, placing children with stable married couples. They weren't asking for anything new, and they were not allowed to do that.

There are now more than a hundred cases where, for reasons of conscience, people have lost their jobs or their place in public life, on panels of experts, on the magistrates' bench, or their registration with professional bodies. It seems to me that this is a growing phenomenon. This is not going to decrease; it will increase in terms of people who will be affected. And what are we going to do about it? It is no use comparing it with the severe persecution which Christians and others experience in some countries. However, if you lose your job or your place in the community, that must feel like persecution to those who are affected. Indeed, in my experience, discrimination and exclusion from public life is often the beginning of other kinds of persecution.[11]

It seems to me that legislation, and indeed policy or procedures, have ignored certain things that we need to be reminded of. The first is conscience: that is why I mentioned conscience as something that had been rediscovered because of Christian teaching in the 13th century. But we are now in danger of forgetting its importance. Indeed, British lawmaking has often recognised the place of conscience: conscientious objection during times of war is recognised; people, even in the Second World War, were exempted from combat and given other jobs to do. Even the 1967 Abortion Act, which in many other respects I deplore, recognised conscience in exempting people because of their beliefs from taking part in procedures that may lead to the termination of a pregnancy. But now in this most recent spate of equality legislation, conscience has not been recognised. Why is that? Why have we reached a stage where conscience is no longer important? It's not just that it's been forgotten or neglected because when it has been pleaded, when people have said, "I can't do this because of conscience," the courts have not recognised it. In every instance, freedom of expression and of association has been trumped by certain notions of equality.

I realise that you can't take conscience of every kind, in every way, in every case, into account. But we are talking about the consciences of those who stand in well-formed spiritual and moral traditions. I'm talking about the Christian churches. Jewish people may want to talk about their traditions and Muslims theirs, and so on, so we are not just talking about an eccentric exercise of conscience but a well-formed one.

What has been ignored is the idea of reasonable accommodation. This is not particularly a British idea but an American one. It has come out of the First Amendment to the American Constitution on Freedom of Belief, and also the Civil Rights Act of the 20th century. There is a huge amount of case law in the United States which recognises religious belief, the expression of religious belief and the need for people to manifest their belief at their place of work. In some cases there has been accommodation of even unreasonable belief, or at least that's how it seems to me. But in Britain we have a peculiarly Benthamite "the law is the law is the law" mentality. The difficulty with legal positivism is how to change bad law. In every age and every clime there have been laws that have been bad and people have struggled and campaigned to have them changed. What is wrong with that — even to recognise the possibility of mistakes? With this most recent legislation, however, I have been told at the highest levels that because the legislation has been passed, nothing further can be done about it.[12]

Well, I think something can be done. Conscience can be recognised, reasonable accommodation at the workplace and in public life can be made, provided it does not jeopardise the business in which the employer is engaged or the business of public life. This can be applied to particular cases. Take the case of the registrar who asked to be excused from having to conduct civil partnership ceremonies: plenty of other registrars were willing to preside at such ceremonies. There was no threat of any jeopardy for what the law was now asking, and it may be that a registrar who was not willing to preside at such ceremonies could be given extra duties or other duties, but reasonable accommodation was not made. Similarly with the counsellor who, as I understand it, was willing to offer non-directive counselling to homosexual couples, but was not willing to offer them sex therapy. He was willing to go as far as it was possible for him to go with integrity. For those who wanted such sex therapy, there would be other counsellors in the organisation who could offer such therapy, and reasonable accommodation could therefore be made, but it wasn't.

So I think conscience and reasonable accommodation are the ways forward here. The European Court judgments in four cases that were before it point out that every government must balance competing rights. The question is, in this country, whether competing rights have properly been balanced. If the government wants to give the homosexual community certain rights and privileges, there is a democratic process to do it. The question now is whether the rights of believers, of those who for ethical, religious, spiritual and moral reasons want to exercise their right of conscience, have been recognised enough. And the European Court leaves that question open. I am sure it is a question that is not finally closed and will have to be reopened.

We find a situation where the Church is growing rapidly in many parts of the world and sometimes in places where there is great hardship. We praise God for that and we praise also those Christians, our brothers and sisters, who are living their faith in those difficult situations. But at the same time we need to think about ways in which their lives, sometimes their way of life, can be safeguarded, and not just to endorse uncritically popular movements that appear to us to be attractive.

Here in Britain the danger is of forgetting the Judaeo-Christian tradition which is the basis for this country's common life and has been for more than a thousand years. As you may have noticed, earlier in this book I've written a chapter on the sacramentality of the Coronation service. Obviously I had to read the service to write the chapter, and it is shot through with Christian symbolism and Christian teaching. As I mentioned before, at the very beginning, the sovereign to be crowned and enthroned says that he or she will uphold the laws of God and the true profession of the Gospel. And so it carries on throughout: the Anointing, the receiving of Holy Communion, the giving of the ring to uphold the Catholic faith in the form of the reformed religion established by law.[13] This is the basis for national life. It seems to me that sometimes the nation is saying: "We don't really want to be reminded of this." That may be so, but if they don't really want to be reminded of it, what is the alternative?

Secularity has undermined so much of what has been held in common by the people of this nation, but it has not provided an alternative world view. When we need to decide moral questions about the dignity of human life at its earliest or latest stages, when we want to talk about the family, when we want to talk about equal opportunities, we need some kind of moral and spiritual basis to do so. If it's not going to be the Judaeo-Christian tradition, what will it be?

Notes

[1] On this, see further Claus Westermann, *Isaiah 40-66,* London SCM, 1969, pp152ff.

[2] Elizabeth J. Harris, *What Buddhists Believe,* Oxford, One World, 1998, p34.

[3] Henry Chadwick, *The Early Church,* London, Penguin, 1967, p122.

[4] On this see William Young, *Patriarch, Shah and Caliph,* Rawalpindi, 1974, pp27ff.

[5] For the text, see Ibn Ishaq, *Sirat Rasul Allah,* trans. A. Guillaume, *The Life of Muhammad,* Oxford, OUP, 1955, pp231f.

[6] Catherine Glass and David Abbott, *Share the Inheritance,* Shawford, Hants, Inheritance Press, 2010, pp22ff and *Magna Carta Unravelled,* London, Wilberforce Publication, 2015.

[7] On all of this, see Nazir-Ali, *Conviction and Conflict: Islam, Christianity and*

World Order, London, 2006, pp69ff; Maurice Cowling, *Religion and Public Doctrine in Modern England*, Vol I, Cambridge, CUP, 2003, pp408ff; Roger Ruston, *Theologians, Humanists and Natural Rights* in Mark Hill (ed) *Religious Liberty and Human Rights*, Cardiff, University of Wales Press, 2002, pp14ff.

[8] Colin Chapman, I*slam and the West*, Carlisle, Paternoster, 1998, pp113ff.

[9] For a personal account of this persecution see Helen Berhane, *Song of the Nightingale*, Milton Keynes, Authentic, 2009.

[10] Rupert Shortt, *Christianophobia: A Faith under Attack*, London, Rider Press, 2012 and John L. Allen Jr, *The Global War on Christians,* New York, Image, 2013, are two books by well-known journalists on the persecution of Christians.

[11] Richard Scott, *Christians in the Firing Line*, London, Wilberforce Publications, 2013.

[12] Paul Coleman, *Issues relating to Reasonable Accommodation: with a particular focus on employment law.*

[13] Nazir-Ali, 'The Sacramental Significance of the Coronation', *Ecclesiastical Law Journal*, 2013.

9

WHAT SHOULD WE DO WITH THE VEIL?

In a free society the debate about the *niqāb* or the full-face veil (which covers the entire face including the eyes) cannot be about being "affronted" or "offended", nor can it be only about preferences, whether personal or social.

The presumption must be for people to dress as they choose, provided this does not cause disruption or disorder as we go about the normal business of life. There are two dangers to guard against: one is of young women (or even girls) being forced to wear the veil by their families or the religious community to which they belong. The other is the ultra-feminist war cry, already heard, that people must be forced to be equal even against their will!

The veiling of women, in the sense of wearing a headdress, was common in the ancient world. It also characterised Christian women, especially those engaged in some kind of public ministry (1 Cor 11:2–16) and, from the 3rd century, it was given to those who had dedicated their lives to Christ in consecrated singleness. In modern times, it has survived not only in the habit of nuns but as head-scarves or hats and, on solemn occasions, even the face can be covered, for instance, at weddings or funerals.

In the case of Islam it is, of course, for Muslims to decide what is proper to the requirements of their faith. To an observer, the Qur'ān prescribes 'modesty' of dress (for both men and women- 24:30, 31) and a covering of the body for women (24:31b and

33:59). There seems to be nothing about covering the *face*.

Any decision made by society must be based on objective criteria which have to do with maximising freedom and maintaining fairness, justice and good order for all. It seems to me that there are a number of such criteria which would restrict or prevent the full-face veil or the *niqab* being worn in public places or in the course of professional interaction.

Paramount is, of course, the need for security. There have been a number of cases worldwide where criminals or terrorists have escaped arrest wearing a *burqa*. More often, there is a need to identify people for security reasons, and not only at immigration booths. Those dealing with our security need to be able to tell, by people's behaviour in public places including facial expressions, whether they are any danger to others. Schools and colleges in particular will want to be very sure of the identity of those in their buildings so that they can protect children and young people from those who may wish to harm them. Again, this must go beyond the checking of identity at the entrance but will extend to the rest of the premises during the course of the day.

There is then the need for personal interaction. Doctors and dentists will, naturally, wish to interact with their patients and teachers, similarly, with their pupils. More generally, employers will be wary of employing those who cannot interact freely with their colleagues at the workplace. Such interaction may be also necessary for social services, community policing and a myriad of other activities. The recent ruling in court that a witness or an accused must remove the veil whilst giving evidence is not enough as jurors and the judge may also wish to observe behaviour when others are testifying or when counsel are arguing their case.

Finally, there is the question of safety. Wearing the veil will be hazardous in situations where machinery is involved, where the terrain is difficult or the weather dangerous. Naturally, it will be extremely difficult for anyone to operate a vehicle safely but simply crossing a busy road or negotiating the underground may also be full of difficulties.

With such objective criteria, it should be possible both to uphold freedom for what people do in their personal lives, but also to regulate what is of common interest. Where there is a need for the security of others, where social or personal interaction is required and for reasons of safety, it should be possible to prevent the use of the *niqab* or the full-face veil, whilst continuing to uphold the freedom of people to believe and to dress as they please.

10

HOW TO SAVE MARRIAGE
FROM HITTING THE ROCKS

There has been a good press for marriage lately. More people are marrying and more people are staying married. This is welcome news. I have recently been with a number of community groups that promote marriage in schools, colleges and generally in society. This has been an encouraging and hopeful experience for me. But whilst we welcome this great interest in marriage, both in promoting it and defending it, it is impossible to do so unless we understand what marriage is and what the family is, and I want first of all to draw attention to that.

Not so many years ago, the Cambridge Group for the History of Population and Social Structure did a long-term and cross cultural study on the nature of the family throughout the course of history and in many different countries – Western and non-Western, Western Europe and Eastern Europe and so forth. They discovered that in nearly all these situations the father, the mother and the children are at the heart of family structure; even in cultures that have traditions of extended families – and I am well familiar with those – the father-mother-children cluster, if you like, is at the heart of these arrangements. This I suppose is the proper use of the term 'nuclear'. A nucleus is the centre, it's the heart, the core, the centre of a cell or an atom, or whatever it may be. It is not what it is taken to mean these days: isolated from everything else.[1] Now, this study in Cambridge was backed up by another study by another centre also in Cambridge, which showed how important it is for children to have both parents for their upbringing and that even in situations of conflict (provided they are not terrible) children prefer their parents to stay together.[2] I'm sorry that attempts have been made to negate the earlier work of these centres, but that is another story.[3]

These centres really were building on the discipline known as the *sociology of the family* which began in the 1940s and which spoke of the family in this sense, in the sense I have just described, as 'natural' or 'normative'.

Now, this natural or normative family, expressed as it is in different contexts, as I have said, is ubiquitous, found in many different cultures and over the course of history.

From the point of view of the Christian faith and of the Christian Church, the Church does not claim, of course, to have invented the idea of the family. What it has done, at its best, is to identify those things in cultures and places that were there already which needed to be affirmed and to be strengthened, sometimes to be corrected and on occasion, to be refuted. So, the Church builds on the Hebraic tradition of the family, as taught in the Old Testament and as practised in Judaism, but it also acknowledged some features of the Roman idea of marriage and the family and built on them. The Greeks were more difficult because on the one hand you have the statism of Plato, where parents give up their children to nursery governors – nothing new under the sun – so they can take part in public life. Aristotle, on the other hand, was overly biological in his understanding of marriage and the family.

The Christian Church based its approach on marriage and the family, as it found it to be in different places, on the one flesh union of man and woman, not only created together and given a common mission – what is known as the cultural mandate in the world – but created and ordered towards one another. So, not created in isolation but created *toward* one another. For the sake, of course, of the birth and nurture of children, but also for the sake of their own fulfilment and their own security. This is very important to understand. Because the Church understood marriage as being between *persons,* it took consent seriously and it emphasised *mutuality* because that is characteristic of the Bible's teaching on family and society.[4]

Throughout the course of Christian history there have been many expressions of this understanding of marriage and the family but I want to take just one. It is a name difficult to avoid in this situation and that is of Saint Augustine, the great Bishop of Hippo in North Africa. Augustine saw marriage first of all as the coming together of man and woman for the sake of children but also for the sake of the security of the partners. So this is what you might call the contractual view of marriage. It needed to be understood in a lifelong sense because, apart from anything else, the human child takes a long time to grow up.

But Augustine didn't stop there, he went on to speak of the commitment that is necessary – contract is not enough – to each other as persons so that we are not using one another simply as a means to our own selfish ends, whatever they may be, but the commitment has to be to the other as a person.

And then, arising from all of this, Augustine also spoke of the sacramental bond which means that you are now not talking about two but one; the unity that is created by the complementarity of man and woman. The unity is a unity that arises out of similarity and difference. There has to be another in the marriage so that we can come together in this particular way for the sake of the common good, for the sake of children and for their own fulfilment.[5]

Augustine has remained important in nearly all the thinking about marriage, certainly in the Christian Church but indeed well beyond that, I think we can say – for example, to the Enlightenment. You have to justify everything by the Enlightenment these days, so let's take three typical thinkers of the Enlightenment. John Locke emphasised the importance of the contractual side of marriage and particularly the contract that is undertaken for the sake of the birth and the nurture of children. And so the implication is – I don't think Locke ever brings this out explicitly – that the contract might not last beyond the growing up of the children. That's the weakness in the Lockean position, whereas we would have to say, would we not, relying on Augustine, that the contract is not just for the sake of the children but also for the security of the partners? What happens when you have brought up the children and then you are abandoned? This is not a story that is unfamiliar to us these days.

The other great giant in the Enlightenment period, Immanuel Kant, on the other hand (you won't be surprised to know) emphasised the unbreakable promise, the commitment aspect. Remember Augustine's emphasis on commitment. Kant developed that into what he called the unbreakable promise; that when you undertake a vow it is then your duty to keep that vow and there is no duty for him higher than the keeping of a promise.

Contract and commitment in this sense of duty, of unbreakable promise, are important things but it was Hegel, another great Enlightenment figure, who talked about the mystical union. Here we are coming very near the Augustinian idea of the sacramental bond. And so for Hegel the differences that there are between the two persons are overcome so that there is a real unity of thought, of direction, of destiny in the marriage and from the marriage. Whilst in the Christian tradition, marriage between the baptised is thought of as sacramental because it is a sign of unity between Christ and his Church, Hegel extends this to marriage in the natural sense (this is reflected to some extent in the Anglican emphasis on marriage as a creation ordinance).[6]

If Augustine laid the groundwork and the Enlightenment figures developed it, the sad fact is that there are threats to all of these ways of understanding marriage today. Even if you think of it as mere contract, what has happened to that? Since the arrival of 'no fault divorce' without consent, is marriage even a contract any longer, if you can get out of it, more easily than you can get out of your mortgage, for example? What kind of contract is marriage now? So there has been a huge threat, and a destructive impact, caused by the so-called reform of divorce laws on marriage in this connection.

What about commitment? Well, there is little social

disapproval now. If long-standing spouses leave one another for whatever reason, there is no social disapproval for breaking this unbreakable promise and clergy perhaps have more experience of this than some other people. How tragic that again and again the pastor in his study is to be confronted by the breaking of what is supposed to be unbreakable and, so often now, unilaterally.

What about the mystical union, the sacramental bond? Well, we are living in an age when people have been commending what they call 'free or pure relationships', which last only as long as the partners want them to last and they can be ended if one partner does not want the relationship to last any longer.[7]

So these threats have been felt on all those aspects of marriage that have been regarded from Augustine's time as important, indeed, essential.

What then do we need to do? It is very urgent for us to struggle for the restoration of a public doctrine of marriage in this country. Both divorce reform and other kinds of legislation have not just damaged but almost destroyed, I think, any public understanding of marriage. What is marriage in this country? For many years, centuries perhaps, the public doctrine of marriage was that of the Book of Common Prayer as it is set out in the preamble to the marriage service and one by one, as I have just pointed out, all of the aspects of marriage in the preamble have been placed under severe threat at the very least, if not more than that.

Why do we need a public doctrine of marriage? The Roman Catholic bishops in their recent letter on the subject have given some of the answers which bear repetition. These are because (a) marriage is good for society: marriage is one of the basic building blocks of society and as far as I know, there has never been a society which has not had marriage and the family as a basic unit of it; (b) it is good for children: the best outcomes for children are to be found within marriage, whether that is how they do at school, or in terms of delinquency, the likelihood or not of children getting into crime or other kinds of anti-social behaviour; and (c) marriage is good for the partners themselves: all the studies show that people who are married live longer, are healthier, perhaps even happier (that would be something, wouldn't it?) So there is that aspect to marriage, the fact that it is good for society, good for children and, of course, good for the partners themselves.[8]

Having said that, human beings have many different kinds of relationships. We are social beings and, of course, we have relationships with parents, with siblings, with relatives and with friends, and it is important for us to recognise the significance and richness of relationships, that there should be in people's lives. I'm so sorry that so many of these relationships, because of the patterns of modern life, are nipped in the bud and not allowed to flourish. It may be right for us as a society, and indeed for the government, to recognise and to support some of these relationships. It may be right for people in a particular kind of relationship, whatever that may be, to take legal steps for that relationship to be one that is just and fair to each person in that relationship. I'm certainly not against that. In the House of Lords, when the Civil Partnerships Bill was going through, some of us sought to widen its remit to include people who were sharing domestic arrangements on a long-term basis for a number of reasons. In fact, the amendment was passed in the House of Lords and was only set aside in the other place.

The point is that whilst we want to recognise and support a whole number of different relationships that people have, these cannot be confused with marriage. The flourishing of relationships is one thing. Marriage is a particular kind of relationship ordered to a particular end for certain purposes and it is a category confusion, if you like, to say: "We want to improve relationships between people whatever they might be, so therefore we should get them married". This would be absurd in many circumstances. You can see the absurdity of it; the integrity of each relationship has to be recognised on its own terms and not in terms of something else. We really must draw back from this category confusion. This is not the place to comment on gay relationships. The Church's teaching is clear about this but, if those in such relationships feel that they need legal protection, they should be able to have it without confusing such an arrangement with marriage.

If there is to be a public doctrine of marriage, what would be its practical implications? The importance of marriage preparation is often mentioned. Again, clergy have some experience of this. Most clergy engage in marriage preparation for couples they are going to marry – badly or well. I can't hand-on-heart say that it is always done very well but at least they have a shot at it and we need to help them to have a better shot at it. There are now many resources available for this.

But what about civil marriage? The press delights in telling us that more and more people are now not getting married or, if they are getting married, they are not getting married in church, they are getting married in register offices or in one of these wonderful 'New Agey' places that there are all around. What preparation is there for such people? I was at such a marriage recently. The groom, to keep up his nerve, had had quite a number of drinks and he was having another one, so I said to him: "Do you really need to have this drink?" and he said: "Oh yes, I do because in a few minutes (this was just an hour or so before the ceremony) I'm having my preparation with the officiant at the ceremony". Well, how much? What sort? What would be the influence of such preparation on a person who had already had more than his fair share of alcohol? This is simply unacceptable. This is heading for disaster and, if Parliament can do nothing else, it should encourage all-round marriage preparation for people, whether that's in the context of church, or in the ceremony of another faith, whether it's a *nikāh*, whatever it may be, or if it's on civil premises.

What should be the content of this preparation? This is very important. Of course, people will present this preparation in different ways. There will be DVDs, manuals and all sorts of things like that. We welcome that. But the content we can debate about. At the very least the preparation should be such as enables the integration of various kinds of motivation that lead people to marriage, particularly for men. You may want to challenge this but let me say it: particularly for men it is important that the sexual instinct is integrated with their capacity for affection (men do have a capacity for affection, appearances not withstanding) and also with the commitment to nurture. If these three very elemental aspects of human nature get out of kilter, then the marriage is at risk from the very beginning. So, in fact, I'm not saying anything new; Augustine had already seen this. The integration of the sexual instinct with the capacity for affection and the commitment to nurture must be a part of marriage preparation, however it is done, at least for men. I look forward to hearing what women have to say about themselves.

The preparation must take people through what we call 'stages of intimacy' or perhaps better 'aspects of intimacy'. You have courtship and then you have the honeymoon period. That's great but then you have conflict brought about by competition. Married people are just like other human beings; they occupy the same space and they want to get their bit of the space and their bit of the resources and so on. Married people need to know that this will happen, that after courtship and perhaps even during the honeymoon there will be competition for scarce resources even within the marriage (after all, it is the basic unit of society), that there will be conflict, and how to deal with competition and conflict, rather than for that to put the marriage on the rocks. And then to know that this also leads, or can lead, to cooperation and in the end not only to cooperation but to that unity of mind and being that Augustine called the sacramental bond, and Hegel the mystical union.

I hope that with the help of psychologists and those, like clergy, who have so much experience in these matters, that good preparation can be made available not only for people who get married in Church but most importantly for those entering into civil marriage.

I'm so glad that there is more and more consciousness now of the importance of parenting. The word, however, is a misnomer to some extent. There is really no such thing as parenting; there is mothering and fathering because how mothers parent their children is different from how fathers parent their children. The difference is obvious to anyone who has brought up any children. All the research is telling us that fathers relate to their children differently from how mothers relate to their children. Fathers even play with their children differently and it is very important from a developmental point of view that both parents are able adequately to relate to their children. So I commend the campaigns that there have been to make sure that fathers are present for their children – these campaigns (extremism not withstanding) are very important as they have to do with a child's sense of identity, with developing good all-round relationships and with proper nurture. I salute single parents who bring up their children and bring them up as well as they can. Nevertheless, I think they would be the first to say that it takes two to bring up a child. They know best of all, in fact. Home-Start and many other agencies are involved in showing people how to be mothers and fathers; whatever else happens, please don't withdraw support from them.

Having looked at marriage preparation and parenting, I want to say something about pre-nuptials. In the press pre-nuptials simply mean agreements about money. That's very sad and it's not what I want to talk about. Given that we live now in a situation of no-fault divorce without consent, how can people be encouraged to take marriage more seriously? In the United States, in a number of the states there are experiments to allow couples to undertake what they call 'Covenant Marriage' where, at the beginning of a marriage, the couple agree about what will happen if there are difficulties. This can include the necessity to undertake counselling, for example, but also specifying the conditions under which there may be divorce. To move, therefore, from a situation where there is no-fault divorce without consent to couples agreeing between themselves what would be the sufficient reasons for a divorce: desertion, adultery, cruelty, whatever it may be. We ought to think of this more seriously and see how we can encourage people to take marriage as a step that is solemn, that is serious, and that should be more difficult to bring to an end than it sometimes is in our culture – in our country and in many others.[9]

Turning to the post-nuptial part, the direction of the divorce reform, as it is called in this country, from 1969 onwards has all been one way, which has been constant liberalisation. I can understand some of the reasons for it but the issue is now about justice and reliability. For judges not to be able to even take into account an injustice or a wrong that has been done, does not speak well for our commitment to justice in the land. Current divorce law does not recognise how responsible each partner has been in the marriage, and something should be done about this. People involved in marriage support have consistently said this: that they are amazed at the irresponsibility of people in the divorce courts. There is, therefore, an issue of justice that needs to be addressed when, tragically, a marriage does come to an end.

Finally, there is the question of preference for marriage. If there is a public doctrine of marriage – this is one of the reasons why a public doctrine of marriage is necessary – then there will be some preference for marriage and for the family, for example, in the tax system. I was glad when the Conservative Party before the 2010 election made a pledge that there would be such a preference. After some delay, the pledge was eventually honoured, but not before redefining marriage in terms of 'coupledom' rather than children, and then only making a marginal provision.[10] It is very important, if people are to mean what they say – whether the Conservative Party or the Prime Minister, whoever it may be – that marriage is important for society and important for the family, that it is then recognised in some way. One obvious way to do it is through the tax system. However it is provided, whether through some kind of restoration of the married couples' allowance or the transfer of tax allowances between one partner and the other, or the support of marriage and families where there are children (the last being the pattern that is to be found on the continent – in France and in Italy), the purpose should be to strengthen the family. It must be done for the sake of marriage, for the sake of the family and for the sake of demography.

We are in a situation now which is quite serious insofar as the replacement of the population is concerned. The reason we don't see it more clearly is first, immigration and secondly, people living longer. But the whole of Western Europe is facing a critical issue of demography and there should be no shame in encouraging people to have children and supporting them through the state and the tax system, so that we can look after the elderly when they can no longer work.

Our present need therefore, is not to redefine marriage but to understand the nature of it and the threats to it. It is also to promote marriage and defend it – for the sake of society, for the sake of the children and for the sake of the spouses themselves. If only the consultation had been about these essentials rather than the narrow one about same-sex marriage in which the result was predetermined.

Notes

[1] See Peter Richards, 'The Family Way', in the *Cambridge Alumni Magazine*, No. 29, Lent 2000, pp19ff.

[2] Ibid, Pauline Hunt, 'Family Values', pp22ff. See also Brenda Almond, *Fragmenting Families*, Oxford, Clarendon Press, 2006, pp135f.

[3] See the same magazine, No 50, Lent 2007, pp18ff.

[4] On mutuality or reciprocity see Charlie Moule, *The Epistles to the Colossians and to Philemon*, Cambridge, CUP, pp126f.

[5] See further Michael Banner, *Christian Ethics and Contemporary Moral Problems*, Cambridge, CUP, 1999, pp21f.

[6] See Brenda Almond, op. cit., pp47ff.

[7] For a critique see Patricia Morgan, *Children as trophies?*, Newcastle, Christian Institute, pp27f.

[8] See further Most Revd Vincent Nichols and Most Revd Peter Smith, *A Letter on Marriage*, Catholic Bishops Conference, England and Wales, 2012.

[9] See Brenda Almond, op. cit., pp196ff.

[10] See *Transferable Tax Allowances for married couples and civil partnerships*, HM Revenue & Customs, London, March 2014.

11

BOYS, THE FAMILY AND THE NEED FOR A FATHER

In her highly regarded book, *The Fragmenting Family*, Professor Brenda Almond has shown the importance of the natural, or biological, family and its implications for human development. She claims that the debate about the traditional family is as much philosophical and sociological as it is religious. Whatever the value of people making choices, the importance of the genetic relationship cannot be neglected as it is bound up with the most fundamental aspects of human existence. Natural bonds are independent of preference and represent a continuity which cannot be 'deconstructed'. It is this continuity, from one generation to another, which the natural family represents. [1]

Almond's thesis seems entirely congruent with the views of Peter Laslett, the Cambridge historian of the family, who showed the widespread and long-lasting survival of the natural family in a variety of cultures and times. Even with extended families in non-Western cultures, the unit of father, mother and children is at the core of them. Although others males in the extended family may provide supportive roles in the nurture of the children, the father's role remains central. Cambridge University's Centre for Family Research was telling us at the turn of the Millennium how children suffer more from the effects of divorce than from a parent dying. It is claimed that the disappearance of a father, which so often happens after divorce, was significantly detrimental to the development of children.

How surprising then to find the same centre, albeit with different personnel, now claiming that there is no reason to think that a father's presence is essential to a child's well-being. How has such a huge change of perspective occurred in only a few years?[2] Alongside such claims, there is a strong lobby which seeks to minimise the effects of divorce on children. In the teeth of strong evidence to the contrary, it claims that divorce can be 'a healthy experience for children'. We must ask what it is that lies behind such hostility to the natural family. Is it social and personal self-justification for what Professor Almond has called 'families we choose' with the plethora of life-styles which this involves, or is it a search for 'pure relationships' which are not anchored in any social structures, conventions or laws?[3] Against all of this is the mounting evidence that children who grow up with both their parents are, on the whole, better off than children with lone parents or step parents, whether that is in terms of mental health, educational performance, crime or sexual behaviour. This is not, in any way, to devalue the sometimes heroic effects of loving single parents or step-parents. It is simply to note the importance of biologically-related families against the frantic and increasingly successful efforts to deconstruct them.[4]

How children relate to parents also differs in terms of the child's gender and that of the parent. A boy's identification with his mother begins to alter as he seeks to identify more with his father. Girls, similarly, need to be affirmed in their gender by their mothers and to develop a relationship with their fathers which will lead to them growing up at ease in their relations with other men. The gender of the parents is not a matter of indifference nor is the biological relationship of the child to each of the parents.[5]

The basis for such thinking is rooted in the Judaeo-Christian insight that women and men have both been created in God's image, that they have been given a common mission of stewardship in the created order which is particularly related to the founding and nurture of family and that they are called to fulfil this mission in ways that are distinctive for each of them. Equality in personhood, commonality in mission and complementarity in the approaches to common tasks have to be held together. The complementarity does not have so much to do with tasks each might perform in the domestic or social economy, but how each approaches a common task. This is especially true where the common task of nurturing children is concerned and, *a fortiori*, the task of bringing up boys.

More and more research is showing that boys develop differently and have distinct domestic, educational and social needs. At home they relate to their mothers quite differently from the way they relate to their fathers; each relationship meeting a number of emotional and developmental needs. We now know that skills like language acquisition, spatial sense and emotional intelligence develop at different rates and, sometimes, in different ways in girls and boys. A good educational approach, therefore, would be to take such difference seriously. A 'gender-neutral' approach would, paradoxically, advantage one gender or another depending on what is being studied.[6] Boys, in particular, need to be reconnected to learning through a number of strategies which include respect for differences in the rate of learning in certain areas, mentoring relationships with role models, respect for typically boyish characteristics such as a desire for adventure, physical energy and courage, endurance under pressure, and so on.

The Harvard psychoanalyst, James Herzog, has shown how desperately boys need closeness to their fathers for their own security and identity, as well as in developing appropriate patterns of masculinity. His book is revealingly called *Father Hunger*, and there is a burgeoning literature in this area. This literature tends to show that children brought up by both of their own parents are enriched in the care they experience. Their parents provide them with distinctive windows into the world. Mothers benefit from the support of fathers, and what the fathers contribute to household incomes remains hugely significant even in the context where both parents work outside the home. At play and work, fathers and mothers contribute in distinctive ways to a child's development and these have to do with differences in strengths and styles of parenting which make for a healthy mutuality and complementarity. Where boys are concerned, there is a connection between a good relationship with the father and a boy growing up with proper self-esteem, including being able to make good relationships with the people of the same or the opposite sex.[7] It is paradoxical and tragic then, that just as all the research is showing us the importance of fathers, we are writing them out of the law, legislating for the birth of children who will never know their natural fathers, not by accident of history but by design.

A number of researchers and practitioners have pointed out that good fathering, like all good parenting, and especially of boys, should be authoritative. That is to say, it should avoid the extremes of rigid authoritarianism, on the one hand, and permissive avoidance on the other. In terms of human development theory, children are progressing towards autonomy and, hopefully, towards autonomy-in-relationship or in mutuality. In the meantime, like everyone else, they need a framework for living; they need adequate, but not overbearing supervision and they need discipline that is loving but firm. The false belief that children are autonomous in the same way as adults is thought to be at the root of much adolescent alienation, not least among boys.[8] Even for adults, as feminist critiques of development theory have shown, autonomy needs continually to be balanced by connectedness, and for this a moral and spiritual framework is necessary.

As far as this last is concerned it should be a priority in education, and particularly in religious education, to show children how the values they are being taught are rooted in a moral and spiritual tradition. Instead of being presented, from an early age, with a smorgasbord of varied religious practices, drawn from the 'phenomenology of religion', children need first to be rooted in their own tradition so that they can have a vantage point from which to appreciate and assess everything else they are taught. Without this we will get only 'pick 'n' mix' spirituality which does not have the rigour either to be discriminating in accepting what is on offer, nor in being self-critical of one's own conduct or context when the need arises. In this culture, it is important to show boys how to express their spirituality and to be able to reflect on it.

In our consideration of the nurture and development of children, and especially of boys, we need to look not only at the physical, mental and spiritual development of children but also the importance of genetic relationships within the biological family and how children locate themselves within it, including broader relationships with siblings, grandparents and others. Where these are not available, for one reason or another, we should be looking urgently as to how we can compensate for their absence without jeopardising the normativity of the family. Active parenting, and particularly the role of fathers, needs to be acknowledged in the development of children and especially boys. The importance of mentoring and of appropriate role-modelling is also of huge significance in the wider socialisation of boys. Above all, as Judith Kleinfeld points out, boys deserve attention and respect. They need to be respected for who they are rather than always being compared to others. Their capabilities, aspirations and energies need to be directed towards their proper development rather than being allowed to be dissipated in activities born out of obstruction and frustration.[9]

If our society is to be whole and balanced, we need boys as much as girls to flourish. It is time to attend to boys before it is too late. Whilst respecting difference, we need to value and to channel the typically boyish markers (energy, endurance and a sense of adventure) on the playground, in clubs, schools and at church. We should focus specifically on the needs of boys in education and we need to give attention to strengthening the family, as well as to finding appropriate role models for boys. It is a tough agenda but if government, voluntary agencies, the churches and local authorities work together, it is not impossible to deliver.

Notes

[1] Brenda Almond, *The Fragmenting Family,* Oxford University Press, USA, 2006.

[2] Peter Richards, *The Family way* and Pauline Hunt, 'Family Values' in the *Cambridge Alumni Magazine*, No 29, Lent, 2000, pp19ff and Imagining Ourselves by Martin Thompson in the same Magazine's 50th issue, Lent, 2008, pp18f.

[3] See Sarah Womack, 'What Makes a Good Childhood' in *Britain Today*, 2003, Economic and Social Research Council, Swindon, pp31f.

[4] See further Patricia Morgan, *Children as Trophies?*, The Christian Institute, Newcastle, 2002, pp127ff.

[5] See, for instance, A Dean Byrd, 'Gender Complementarity and Child Rearing: Where Traditions and Science Agree', *Journal of Law and Family Studies*, University of Utah, Vol 6 No 2, 2005.

[6] Leonard Sax, *Why Gender Matters*, Random House, New York, 2006; Judith Kleinfeld, *Five Powerful Strategies for Connecting Boys to Schools*, White House Conference, 2006.

[7] J. M. Herzog, *Father Hunger: Explorations with Adults and Children*, Analytic Press, Hillsdale NJ, 2001. See also Ross Parke, *Fatherhood*, Harvard, Cambridge MA, 1996.

[8] See the Civitas paper, *How Fathers fit into the Family,* The Institute for the Study of Civil Society, London, 2001 and James Dobson, *Bringing up Boys,* Tyndale, Wheaton 2001, pp227ff.

[9] Kleinfeld, op. cit. pp. 6f.

12

DESIGNER BABIES ARE A DISASTER FOR SOCIETY

"Britain is to get its first NHS-funded national sperm bank to make it easier for lesbian couples and single women to have children."

This announcement raises some important questions about the future of our children and the role of men in our families and communities. The most important thing to say is that the needs of any child must be primary. It is the upbringing, welfare and education of the child that should be the prior consideration. It is not enough to 'want' a child, let alone one with particular characteristics.[1]

This bank will allow women to choose from profiles of donors, which will include educational attainment and 'attractiveness' criteria, raising the spectre of 'designer babies' born to the parents' specifications. What if the process of pregnancy and birth 'interferes' with the desired outcomes – will such babies then be rejected?

As previously mentioned, research shows that children are best brought up in families where both a mum and a dad are present. The role of fathers in the nurture of their children is unique and cannot be replaced by other so-called 'male role models' or, indeed, an extra 'mother'.

Research tells us that children relate to their fathers differently than to their mothers, and that this is important in developing a sense of their own identity. In particular, boys need closeness to their fathers for a sense of security and in developing their own identity, including appropriate patterns of masculine behaviour. The results of 'father-hunger' can be seen in educational achievement and on our streets, where it contributes to delinquency.[2]

None of this should detract from the heroism of single parents. They should be provided with every support by the State and by local communities. There is, however, a big difference between children growing up without fathers because of death or family breakdown, and actively planning to bring children into the world who will not know one of their biological parents, and where such a parent will never be part of the nurture of these children.

This also brings the question of anonymity to the fore. The change in the law so people could, at a certain age, find out who their biological father is, has certainly contributed to the 'shortage' of donors in response to which the sperm bank has been set up. If there is no anonymity, will potential donors come forward, or will the bank face these same 'shortages'? It seems that the latter will, increasingly, be the case.

What then? Will it rely on overseas donors? What implications will this have for anyone wanting to be in contact with their biological dad?

The removal from the Human Fertilisation and Embryology Act of the need of a child for a father may have been a triumph for radical feminists, but we should not be planning for bringing significant numbers of children into this world who will not know their fathers. This will be disastrous, not only for the children, but for a sense of self-worth in men and, therefore, for society generally.

We have had enough of children being the recipients of endless, fashionable, social experimentation. Let us give them the love they deserve rather than just gratifying our own desires.

Notes

[1] The Human Fertilisation and Embryology Act 1990 (as amended in 2008) specifies that, in any assisted reproduction procedure, account must be taken of the welfare of any child born as a result, and of any siblings such a child may have.

[2] J. M. Herzog, *Father Hunger: Explorations with Adults and Children*, Analytic Press, Hillsdale, NJ, 2001. Also, Ross Parke, *Fatherhood,* Harvard, Cambridge, MA, 1996.

13

THREE-PARENT BABIES:
AN ETHICAL BOUNDARY HAS BEEN CROSSED

Scientists, naturally, like to make advances in science and the fact of mitochondrial disease being passed on by parents to their children is clearly one which science should investigate. But are three-parent embryos or three-person IVF really the way forward?

The Government's own consultation reveals considerable public hostility to the procedure, as do opinion polls. Whilst 1 in 200 children are born each year with some level of mitochondrial disorder, only 1 in 10,000 are severely affected. This means that only a very few births would be involved if the proposed technology were to be introduced. Not that what is being proposed is a cure. The new techniques may prevent babies being born with mitochondrial disease but they will not cure those who have been born already. Moreover, babies will continue to be born with these conditions since parents will not always know of the risk until the first baby is born.

We need to remember that an ethical boundary is being crossed. The proposed technology will interfere with, and change, the germ line for ever. This is breaking an international consensus that genetic engineering should not be used to modify human eggs or sperm in such a way as to alter the characteristics of future children. It is sometimes claimed that mitochondria are only batteries in cells and carrying no significant hereditary characteristics but, if that is the case, how is it that they carry heritable disorders? As both the responses of scientists and of the churches have pointed out, we simply do not know the risks involved in this kind of interference in the germ line. The technology involved in the process has not been known for its success in therapeutic cloning or in the creation of 'cybrids', over which there was much hype in the past. How can we be sure of its success this time around?[1]

A large number of eggs will have to be 'harvested' from women willing to donate. This is, in itself, a hugely invasive procedure with considerable health risks for the women involved. How many embryos will be created and destroyed during research? One of the techniques involved could make future destruction of embryos likely.[2]

The psychological and social implications should also be considered. There are questions here about a person's identity and wishing to know all the genetic characteristics which make me who I am. Will children be able, in future, to ask for the identity of the 'second mother'? Will donors be able to know the identity of children they help bring to birth? Lord Winston has himself warned of the risks of 'meddling with nature'. We should take this warning seriously in this context.

Conservative MP Fiona Bruce's points are well-taken. Safety tests have yet to be carried out and reviewed. No other country has legalised this procedure for ethical reasons. The procedure would cause the germ line to be interfered with and changed and human embryos could be destroyed in the process. It is unclear whether the UK would be violating international agreements on germ-line interventions and there has been no informed debate on the issue. It is regrettable, that her motion in the House of Commons expressing her reservations and asking for further scientific and ethical work was rejected. We must beware of undue pressure, in the name of science, pre-empting proper ethical consideration of issues raised by scientific developments and possibilities.

Moral thinking must be allowed to keep pace with such developments. At present, apart from various 'ethics committees', there is no overall representative body to consider bioethical issues and to advise on them. Do we need to learn here from the President's Council on Bioethics in the USA as to how we provide an adequate moral lens through which to study scientific developments and their possible impact on society?

In the UK, successive governments have considered creating some mechanism to enable such reflection but, so far, have done nothing.

Notes

[1] See further John L. Ling, *Bioethical Issues,* Leominster, Day One Publications, 2014, pp112, 163.

[2] Peter Saunders, *3 Parents and a baby*, Christian Medical Fellowship, 2 February, 2015.

14

A CHRISTIAN VIEW OF THE DONATION AND TRANSPLANTATION OF ORGANS

From a Christian point of view acts of mercy are a part of the self-sacrifice which God requires of us (Mic 6:6–8). The paradigm of such self-giving is Jesus Christ himself and any self-giving on our part is an aspect of following in the way of Jesus. Willingness to donate an organ so that another can have life may well be seen, therefore, as part of our discipleship, motivated by compassion and a sense of social responsibility. Christians should, generally, be encouraged to help others in need and organ donation, even if it is post-mortem, can be a very concrete and sacrificial way of helping. I know a couple, personally, where the wife has given one of her kidneys so her husband might live. Her sacrificial action has greatly enriched and strengthened the marriage.[1]

For Christians, the question of consent is very important. This is obviously the case where a live donation is involved. This must respect the principle of *primum non nocere* (first of all do no harm) and it must be clear that no undue pressure has been brought to bear on the donor. The donation must be made freely out of a spirit of altruism and not for commercial or other gain. It is particularly important to monitor very carefully any such donation by children or adults with learning difficulties. Donation should also be subject to the prior consent of the donor while alive and to the consent of the next of kin after death. Published surveys show clearly that next of kin usually respect the wishes of the deceased in these matters, although, the surveys consistently underestimate the opposition to, or uncertainty about, 'presumed consent'. We welcome the Department of Health's decision that the donation of organs must be unconditional and non-discriminatory.

Respect for the dead is another important principle and one which makes the issue of prior consent crucial. This principle also involves some recognition of the continuity between the deceased person and the body. Such a body, at its burial or cremation, should be recognisably the body of the person who has died. The harvesting of organs should not be such as to violate this continuity or to cause unnecessary distress to the mourners.

It is extremely important to be clear about the point of death. If 'brain stem' death is generally accepted as such a point, we must be clear that this involves the irreversible loss of capacity for bodily integration, of cognition and of sentience. Moral theologians of different views have often warned about the dangers of pronouncing death too quickly, especially when the use of organs is on the agenda.[2]

In certain cases, individuals who are brain dead are kept 'alive' through mechanical and medical means so that their organs may not deteriorate before they are removed for transplantation. Questions have been raised as to whether 'elective ventilation' means that the point of death has been postponed. If so, is it moral, indeed legal, to harvest organs while, for example, a person's heart is still beating? The process also appears to involve a 'stripping' of the body's parts. Is this consistent with the principle of respect for the dead? It is true that major medical and surgical procedures are rarely without their gruesome aspects, but usually they are for the benefit of the person concerned. 'Elective ventilation' is for the benefit of others and, therefore, a different category.

The recipients of organs clearly benefit from the transplant-ation, if it is successful. Such a benefit is not without cost, however. To some extent, the integrity of the body has been violated when an alien organ is transplanted into it. Medical practitioners are well aware of the balance that has to be struck between the immuno-suppressive drugs the person must take to help the body accept the new organ, and the need for the immune system to continue its work against other invasions of the body. Having another person's organ in the body involves a drug regime and a lifestyle which certainly prolongs life, but also affects its quality.

The chronic shortage of organs has caused researchers to turn to alternative means of meeting the need. If these are pharmaceutical or mechanical, few ethical questions arise. There are, however, two areas of research which may be worth a mention. First of all, there is the question of xenotransplantation. That is to say, the producing and rearing of animals solely for the purpose of harvesting their organs for use in humans (I understand that the Roslin Institute in Edinburgh has produced, in addition to Dolly the sheep, five 'pollies', or pigs, which might be used in this way). Such procedures are encrusted with difficulties of all kinds, not least the rate at which the organs of animals, especially cloned animals, age.

There are physiological difficulties: for example, would the kidneys of a pig function in a human body? There are immunological difficulties. We have seen how a balance needs to be struck between the drugs needed for the body to accept an organ from another human and the need for the immune system to be able to resist disease. It would appear that the drugs needed for the body to accept an animal part might be such as to jeopardise effective functioning of the immune system. There are microbiological difficulties. The placing of animal tissue in the human body will break the barriers between species, and a weakened immune system may not be able to cope with any animal viruses which may be introduced into the body. Some of these viruses may be lethal to humans while being relatively benign in animals. The risk of xenotransplantation is not only to the individual (an individual may accept such risks if death is the only alternative). There may be risks to entire populations which may become susceptible to certain diseases. There are also ethical difficulties. Should we produce and rear animals solely for this purpose? Are animals merely a means to a human end? One answer might be that we do this already when we produce animals for eventual slaughter. But the word eventual may be important here. Such animals usually have some opportunity for a normal life and for socialisation. Animals produced for organs would be denied such opportunities. They would have to be reared in isolation.[3]

There is also the issue of therapeutic cloning, where the nucleus of an adult cell is transplanted into a fertilised egg whose own nucleus has been removed. The resulting embryo can then be harvested for stem cells from which, it is hoped, organs can be grown. These would be compatible with the tissue of the person from whom the cell had been taken in the first place. One of the difficulties with this possibility is the scarcity of eggs. The main ethical issue which arises, however, is the use of an embryo for purposes other than human reproduction. According to current legislation, such an embryo could not be used for reproduction and would have to be destroyed within 14 days. In fact, the most fruitful developments have not been in the therapeutic use of embryonic stem cells but in the use of stem cells already existing in the adult, or in inducing adult cells to behave like stem cells. It is indeed likely that some organs at least will be grown from such stem cells.[4]

It will have been seen from this discussion that organ donation is an 'intermediate technology' which may be acceptable to Christians while other, ethically acceptable, alternatives are being developed. Such alternatives should be such as to minimise harm and maximise respect for the dead. As we have seen, considerable harm may be involved in xenotransplantation and in therapeutic cloning. Carving up dead bodies does not maximise respect for the dead and transplantation poses some questions about the integrity of the recipient's systems. Is there a future which minimises harm and maximises respect for the dead? It has been suggested that the generation of tissue and organs from somatic (not germ line) cells may be possible. If the research goals for organ donation and transplantation, in addition to improving current procedures, could include research into methods which would minimise harm and maximise respect, this would be an advantage from the Christian point of view.

We have considered what is acceptable for Christians and where questions need to be asked. We have looked at altruism and self-sacrifice where donation is concerned but also at the need for consent. We have acknowledged that a 'lesser evil' may be involved in promoting a 'greater good' and we have asked for research which minimises harm and maximises respect. A Christian view would need to take all these factors into account.

Notes

[1] See my 'Acts of mercy are part of Christian Faith' in, *Organ Donation and Transplantation – the multi-faith perspective*, Bradford, 2000.

[2] On all this, see R. Y. Calne, 'Tissue Transplant' in a *Dictionary for Medical Ethics,* London, DLT, 1977, pp323ff.

[3] For one perspective see E. David Cook, 'Xenotransplantation', in John F Kilner *et al* (eds), *Cutting-Edge Bioethics*, Grand Rapids, Eerdmans, 2002, pp18ff.

[4] John R. Ling, *Bioethical Issues*, Leominster, DayOne, 2014, pp121ff.

15

LET US HELP PEOPLE TO LIVE RATHER THAN TO DIE

It is absolutely right for us to feel compassion for those who have a terminal or an incurable illness and for their near and dear ones who wish to relieve them of this burden, even if this means the death of the one who is ill. Hard cases, however, make bad law. We should be very wary of changing the legal tradition of the Western world based as it is on the Judaeo-Christian view of the human person, because of extreme situations which have been given massive media publicity and because there may be a few people in a coma from which a return to conscious life seems impossible.

It is natural for a person to feel helpless and hopeless when a terminal or incurable condition is first diagnosed but, given the right support by family, friends and the medical community, it is quite possible to come through this phase and to enjoy some quality of life and even its enrichment. As Dame Cicely Saunders, the founder of the Hospice movement, has said, "Our last days are not necessarily lost days". Not only can they be used to recapture the past and to strengthen relationships but they can also be the opportunity for contemplation and preparation. Again and again, people have told me how much they have learned about themselves and others at this time in their lives. Indeed, sometimes people experience a 'remission' of their illness (Christians may wish to call this a 'miracle') and live for much longer than was, at first, predicted.

It is simply a mistake to emphasise the autonomy of the individual, especially at this point. It is relatedness that matters. Rather than seeing themselves as unwanted and alone, people at this stage of life should feel drawn into a circle of love and care where they will be made as comfortable as possible and valued for who they are. It is not necessary always to be independent. Human beings depend upon one another at every stage of life and this one is no different. "Bear one another's burdens and so fulfil the law of Christ", says St. Paul, and this is exactly what the Hospice movement has shown us can be done in the care of the terminally and incurably ill. Thank God for all the wonderful people involved in this work. Another valuable lesson which this movement has taught us is that it is nearly always possible to manage pain and to make sure that patients do not suffer unnecessarily.

Palliative medicine is now highly developed and, whether in hospices or in pain clinics in hospitals, it tries to make sure that science is made to serve the care of people who are seriously ill and relieve them of as much pain as possible. Such relief may, in fact, lengthen the life-span but, even if it has the effect of hastening death, this is quite different from an intervention that intends the death of the patient. One fear that people often have is that they will be 'officiously kept alive' rather than allowed to die peacefully. It should be clear that opposition to assisted suicide, or voluntary euthanasia, is not about keeping people alive at all costs. It is right to respect people's wishes about not wanting medical treatment, the outcomes of which may be uncertain and which may be highly intrusive and uncomfortable. Indeed, in certain cases, competent medical authorities may decide that it is inappropriate to provide medical treatment, though I believe that hydration and feeding should continue unless the means of doing this are judged to be disproportionate to any outcome. We need to remember that those seeking assisted suicide are very few compared to the hundreds of thousands who die each year cared for by their loved ones, with the help of hospices, pain clinics and others in the caring professions.

However, there is a slippery slope. It has been found, for instance, that the withdrawal of treatment in even the most extreme cases of coma, where the prospect of recovery is very remote, has led to such withdrawal when the situation is not so extreme. The Netherlands has not been notable for its success in confining the category of so-called 'eligible' cases for voluntary euthanasia and physician-assisted suicide. In other words, there is 'creep' from terminal and incurable illness to serious disease and, then, perhaps, to ennui or depression, when a person no longer wants to live.

A few years ago, a government paper actually listed as a factor *against* prosecution, the fact that the 'suspect' might be a spouse, partner or close relative of the 'victim'. This flies in the face of evidence that 70 per cent of elder abuse takes place within the family. In factors which carry more weight in favour of prosecution, the document removed the category of belonging to a group, the principal purpose of which is to allow another to commit suicide. There must be questions of public safety at stake here. How are we to avoid undue influence, for personal or ideological reasons, over those who are at a most vulnerable stage in their lives?

There are questions, too, about how intention is to be established. How can we be sure that the person assisting the suicide was 'wholly motivated by compassion'? We should also take account of a ' vulnerable assister' who is told it is their duty of love and care to carry out the wishes of the person seeking to die. The experience of countries which have gone furthest in permitting assisted suicide and voluntary euthanasia does not inspire confidence. Once again, as a society and as individuals, we are poised to cross a bridge which will take us further from the Bible's teaching about the ultimate dignity of human beings which cannot be harmed by other humans, except in the most tightly-controlled circumstances of self-defence or of public order. This is not just about the possibility of making a moral 'mistake' but of moral culpability, of sinning against our neighbour who is, like us, made in God's image.

The Church's task here is not just to guard the consciences of its own members but to point society to its moral and spiritual basis. It is on this that a cohesive view of national life rests, and it is this which will save us from the fragmentation and insularity between different communities which we have seen in recent years. If we do not have a common view about the dignity and sanctity of human life, what else can we have in common?

There is an alternative to the vociferous campaign to legalise assisted suicide and voluntary euthanasia. This involves using all our science to relieve suffering. It means bearing one another's burdens and building a society based, not on atomistic individualism, but on a strong sense of inter-dependence and on the importance of relationships. It requires that we should value the person at every stage of life and be willing, in humility to serve them and to learn from them.

Let us draw back from the brink. Let us not place ourselves in moral jeopardy, and let us continue to protect those who need our protection the most.[1]

Note

[1] For the debate on voluntary euthanasia and physician-assisted death, see Emily Jackson and John Keown, *Debating Euthanasia*, Oxford, Hart Publishing, 2012. For a review of the Christian tradition in the face of contemporary issues, see Nigel Biggar, *Aiming to Kill: the ethics of suicide and Euthanasia,* London, Darton, Longman and Todd, 2004.

Part Four

ISLAMISM'S CHALLENGE TO A CHRISTIAN FUTURE

Western media have, understandably, concentrated on the armed threat which radical Islamism poses to the Western world. There can be no doubt that this threat is real, whether in terms of vulnerable Western-owned targets in the wider world, through infiltration of the West itself or of home-grown extremism and its consequence – terrorism.

There is, however, another threat which is often obscured, and that is to the continuation or emergence of tolerant societies in the Islamic world. One by one, nations in which diversity flourished or was, at least, tolerated have been coerced, through threat of disorder, into enforcing the Islamist versions of Sharī'a, thus reducing fundamental freedoms not only for religious minorities but for women, writers and artists.

Radical Islamists deny, of course, that other kinds of Muslim are Muslim at all. Ṣūfīs, Shī'as, Isma'ilis and 'moderates' are all targeted, but it is often minorities like Christians, Jews, Baha'is and Yazidis who have had to bear the brunt of their attacks.

Some countries, it is true, have resisted the Islamist advance but their stability is not guaranteed and there is relentless pressure on them often from both within and without. They desperately need the support of the international community if they are to survive in their present form. With their survival rests the future of ancient Christian and other communities, as well as that of more modern ones such as the large numbers of expatriate Christians in the Gulf.

Our task is not only to struggle for the survival and freedom of Christians in so many parts of the world, but also to build up their human, spiritual and material resources so that they can not only survive (in often harsh conditions) but also flourish and bear witness to God's gracious work among them.

16

THE ARAB 'SPRING' HAS LED TO A HOT SUMMER: WILL COOLER MINDS PREVAIL NOW AND TEMPERATE LEADERS EMERGE?

There was really no Arab Spring. There was certainly the bursting forth of a pent-up desire amongst the poor for a place at the table. There were protests – even self-immolation – against police brutality attempting to keep the poor out of any productive economic activity. Then there was the jeans-clad and lap-top toting brigade of Westernised youngsters who created an electronic revolution which the world's media mistook for a real one.

If there was a real 'revolution', the revolutionaries were the well-organised, thoroughly trained and sometimes armed cadres of Islamist movements ranging from the 'moderates' of the *Ikhwan Al-Muslimin* (or Muslim Brotherhood) to the *Salafis* and overt or covert affiliates of Al-Qaeda. Surveying the scene, I was irresistibly and repeatedly reminded of Tehran in 1979. At that time also republicans, secular groups, even communists, as well as moderate Islamists, teamed up with those who wished Iran to be a theocracy. The single thing they had in common was to get rid of the Shah and his regime. In this aim they were wholly successful, but as soon as the Shah had been removed the radicals got rid of their erstwhile allies, one by one.

This raises one of the crucial and recurring questions about Islamism and democracy: is it sufficient that a party wins power at the ballot box if this is only a means of replacing one kind of totalitarianism with another – that of the old nationalist despots with Islamist radicalism? How can a plural democracy be introduced in such circumstances? What necessary safeguards and checks and balances need to be put in place to ensure the emergence and flourishing of such a democracy?

The dictators had provided a limited amount of personal and religious freedom in return for strict restrictions on political freedom. That was the bargain. You could have stability and an economy that, more or less, functioned in place of political participation and the possibility of change. These arrangements have broken down irretrievably, and the question is, what is to take their place?

There may not have been an Arab Spring but there certainly has been a long hot summer; whether with the increasing influence of *Salafis* in Tunisia, the continuing atrocities, on every side, in the Syrian Civil War and in the dramatic events in Egypt.

Just as the West is obsessed with seeing only the dictatorial character of the Syrian regime, without paying much attention to the barbarities amongst the rebels and the true agenda of some of them, so also with events in Egypt. The dominant narrative has been that of a military 'coup' which has removed a popularly-elected President and replaced him with puppets of their own. The military is then seen to have moved violently against the 'peaceful' demonstrations of the Muslim Brotherhood.

Such an understanding of the situation is not borne out by expatriates living in Egypt, by diplomatic commentators or by church leaders whose people and buildings have suffered grievously because of the 'peaceful' demonstrations. There seems little awareness that the Egyptian elections, after Hosni Mubarak's removal, took place in a power vacuum when the Muslim Brotherhood was just about the only organised political force in the country. In spite of this, President Morsi's victory was only by the narrowest of margins and, partly because of the system, he was, in fact, elected by a minority of the electorate.

Against this, the movement to have him removed managed to obtain 22 million signatures and was able to bring millions of people out into the streets of Cairo, Alexandria and other cities. Morsi's promise to be inclusive had not translated into action. There was continuous forced Islamisation, the Government was paralysed and the economy was in a shambles. The Brotherhood's slogan that Islam was the answer (*Islam al-hal*) was proving to be pretty hollow. In the absence of a parliament, how was the situation to be remedied and an unpopular president removed?

Egyptians are not proud of what happened after Morsi's removal. The new administration offered the Brotherhood seats in the cabinet but these were turned down. The protestors who had set up camps refused to disperse peacefully and, when repeated attempts at such dispersal had failed, the police, with military backing, began to remove the camps forcibly. There was resistance to this including armed resistance, and large numbers of both protestors and police were killed or injured. Eyewitness accounts tell us that, in some cases, there was indiscriminate firing on residential areas by elements in the protest movement. It is absolutely right to condemn any disproportionate use of force by the security services but, equally, we cannot condone the cold-blooded killing of policemen as there was in Sinai.

Egyptian church leaders, whom I know, are generally patriotic and hopeful (we might say in spite of their experiences). I have never, however, come across such foreboding and fear amongst them as I have with the events that followed the dispersal of the protest camps. Their fears were perfectly justified. Around 50 churches were firebombed, the homes of priests and pastors were attacked, those to be targeted later were marked with a black cross, and even children were killed. Christians were told they had no place in Egyptian society, even though their presence there predates the arrival of Islam by several centuries.

It has been put to me by those who live in the region that, in geo-political terms, the West (and particularly the USA) is now concentrating its energies on the BRICS countries and the Pacific rim, leaving the Middle East to 'moderate' Islamism. If this is so, events in Egypt have shown that 'moderate' Islamism can very quickly reveal another side and, moreover, that freedom-loving sections of society will not always take such a 'handing-over' lying down.

This is also an appropriate moment to ask Islamists what they really believe about the place of women in society, about marriage and divorce law, female education and employment and a host of other matters to do with the welfare of half the population of a country. Furthermore, how do they see national integration especially where non-Muslim religious communities are concerned? What is their view of common citizenship? Without such clarification we could find ourselves back in a situation of virtual *dhimma* for non-Muslims.

Article 18 of the United Nations' Declaration of Human Rights affirms the right to freedom of thought, conscience and religion, the freedom to manifest, in public or privately one's beliefs in teaching, practice, worship and observance and the right to change one's religion or belief. Such rights have been reaffirmed in the International Covenant on Civil and Political Rights of 1966 (ICCPR) and by the UN's Human Rights Committee. It is interesting, in this connection, to note that the prominence of Article 18 in discussions about fundamental freedoms has repeatedly been challenged by Islamic countries, and that an Article 18-like provision is entirely absent in equivalent Islamic declarations of Human Rights. Why is this and can we expect something different in the future? Such a question is important, not only in the context of religious belief, but also to guarantee freedom for artists, authors and journalists. Without such freedom creativity will suffer, imagination will be dimmed and public discussion will ossify. If Article 18 is upheld, naturally, this will mean an end to treating apostasy from Islam as a crime. Punishments for blasphemy would have to cease and only those speeches or acts which incite violence or discrimination against an individual or a group would, as the ICCPR provides, be open to criminal prosecution. Even then, the penalty would have to be commensurate with the crime and not draconian as is the case now.

If by democracy we mean simply the untrammelled rule of

numerical majorities, this will not be enough to conserve the precious values and freedoms mentioned above, which have been agreed internationally. Constitutions, being written now or in the future should, if possible, refer to a state's international obligations. This has, in fact, happened with the new Afghan Constitution but it has been honoured more in the breach than in the observance. The role, if any, that *Sharī'a* will play in the developing jurisprudence of a nation's life should also be set out, along with some broad principles about how it is to relate to the demands of freedom, plural societies and equality. Some hopeful work has been done in this area by Islamic scholars. We should hear more of it.

Democracy also needs checks and balances. One of the features of states in the Middle-East, for example, has been the tyranny of a few, whether nationalist or Islamist. We have to get beyond this to systems where power is shared and where there are proper checks and balances: between president and parliament, in the work of the judiciary, in the encouragement of a free press and in the development of a strong civil society to which government is continually responsive. In some situations, there may have to be something like a Bill of Rights or a Declaration of Citizenship which reiterates the necessity of a common system of law for all, and the equality of all under such law. It would especially note the equality of women and of non-Muslims as far as the state is concerned, whatever the religious law of any community may say. It should have particular regard for conscience and for the accommodation of belief in the public square and at the work place.

Instead of feeling that they are constantly being watched, citizens should feel free in their homes, at their places of worship and on the street. They should be free to display their religious symbols (such as a cross) on their persons or their buildings. Women should be free from harassment if they choose not to wear Islamic dress, and children should be able to study without that 'teaching of hate' which has so set communities against one another. Above all, citizens should feel 'at home' in their own country rather than strangers who are tolerated today, and tomorrow may face persecution or the diminution of their freedom. Although the Kurdistan Regional Government in Northern Iraq still has elements of authoritarianism, it seems to be moving towards a freer society in some of these areas. It is to be hoped that it will retain its autonomy so that it can further develop in such a direction.

Will the hot summer give way to cooler weather when the future can be reassessed with commitment but also dispassionately? Will the region be ruled indefinitely by sectarian conflict or by a vision of inclusiveness, mutual tolerance and justice? It is incumbent upon the friends of countries in the Middle-East not to encourage or sustain sectarianism and extremism in any form but to support progress towards just, participatory and free societies. Neither the Arab Spring nor, as yet, the hot summer has produced such societies. Let us hope and pray that the coming years will lead to a victory for moderation over fanaticism, for belonging over alienation and for freedom over bondage.

17

RADICAL ISLAM AND ITS INVISIBLE VICTIMS

How we read the news is important. As far as the Middle East is concerned, the news is often slanted towards Western interests, whether commercial, military or security-related. It is not, of course, wrong to report and to interpret events in this way but, in doing so, we can miss something crucial that is going on in a nation or a region. It is even possible to say that what is missed could become crucial to international security or trade. That is not my primary concern here which is, rather, to ask what the events mean for the people living in these parts of the world, especially the minorities and the disadvantaged, that is to say the 'invisible' people.

Take Syria, for instance. Under Hafez al-Assad and then his son, Bashar, there was a trade-off: a modicum of social and religious freedom in return for acceptance of restrictions on political freedom. In the minds of the Ba'athist Assad regime this certainly had to do with a fear of radical Islamism but it was also rooted in the authoritarianism of Ba'athism itself. So what has been achieved by upsetting this particular applecart? Western, Saudi and Qatari support for a Sunni-inspired revolt against the Assad regime has led to greater and greater radicalisation, indeed to the birth of ISIS, a movement more extreme even than Al-Qaeda. If the intervention in Iraq was intended to reduce the influence of Iran in the region, it has failed spectacularly because

Iranian support is now crucial to the stabilisation of Iraq after the significant gains made there by ISIS.

Perhaps more than any other country in the region, Syria has been a colourful patchwork of religious, ethnic and linguistic communities: the presence of Alawites and Druze, Eastern-rite Catholics and Orthodox, both Oriental and Chalcedonian, Sephardic Jews and Yazidis, reveals the diversity of religions. As well as Arabic, Kurdish, Aramaic, Turkoman and Armenian are spoken there. Was it not possible to continue to engage with the regime of such a country and to encourage a process of reform, even if that involved setbacks and frustrations? Was it really necessary to support a movement for the overthrow of Assad, a movement which is now known to contain not only the most dubious but the most dangerous Islamists from all over the world? Is the only answer to Ba'athist dictatorship the creation of a monolithic Wahhābī-Salafī state next door to Israel?

And what can we say of Syria's neighbour to the east? Iraq also is home to ancient religious and ethnic communities. There are a number of religions that survive only in Iraq and countries nearby. Many different languages are spoken, reflecting the population's ethnic variety.[1] Under Saddam Hussein, the mutual animosities and hatreds of these communities were kept under strict control on pain of suffering genocide, no less, in order to maintain a unified Iraq. After the American and British-led invasion and Saddam Hussein's fall, the occupying powers dramatically failed to secure civil order and to find a system of governance that would suit Iraq. Given that it is a Western-inspired construct cobbled together from the ruins of the Ottoman Empire, it is doubtful whether Iraq can ever function as a unitary state. The only workable plan seems to be a loose confederation. With the Kurds already effectively independent, some *modus vivendi* needs urgently to be established between *Shī'a* and *Sunni*. Without formal power-sharing agreements, we are likely to see regular eruptions of violence continue, and tactical alliances that include unsavoury extremists like ISIS.

In all of this mayhem, religious minorities have been the most vulnerable. The Christian communities in Iraq, being the largest of these, exhibit the scars of a campaign against them matched only by the violence in Syria. Their churches have been attacked and destroyed, clergy kidnapped and murdered, congregations bombed and machine-gunned while at worship, and they are now expelled by ISIS from their ancient homelands. If any or all of this had happened to any other ethno-religious community there would have been an international outcry long ago. Western-based human rights organisations would have been organising relief and campaigning for international action to protect these communities and their very survival. All credit to the Kurds and to a number of European countries that are accepting refugees, but this is precisely what the extremists intended: to drive these people from land needed for a caliphate centred on Iraq. What is required, rather, is a concerted international effort to secure the future of these and other communities in Iraq. The terrible plight of the Yazidis, who were trapped in the mountains, shows us that those not deemed to be *Ahl al-Kitāb*, or people of the book, are especially vulnerable to genocide. Their future needs securing and should be part of the comprehensive agreement between *Shī'a* and *Sunni* needed to hold Iraq together.

Relief supplies, while meeting the most urgent requirements, are simply not enough. Nor even is arming the Kurds, necessary though that might be. What is also needed is a UN-sponsored and implemented arrangement, with an international and independent force to back it up, to provide safe havens for Christians, Yazidis, Mandaeans and other minorities. This time it is not "no-fly" zones, but "no-go" zones for extremists, that are needed. Such arrangements should be an aspect of any power-sharing agreement between the *Sunni* and the *Shī'a* and should go hand-in-hand with a negotiated end to the civil war in Syria, without preconditions such as Assad's departure.

Iran has a crucial role in securing such an agreement, but it has its own internal problems. Its treatment of its own citizens, especially of minorities, hardly gives room for any confidence that it can mentor a situation of greater tolerance in Iraq. President

Rouhani was elected (by Iranians who wanted greater freedom) as the most suitable candidate of those the *mullahs* allowed to stand. On election, he stated his commitment to human rights and freed a few political and religious prisoners. The hope was that more, much more, would follow. After years of repression, following the brief "spring" under President Khatami, it seemed that we were on the threshold of another "spring".

These hopes have not been fulfilled. Activists such as Shirin Ebadi, the Nobel laureate, remain deeply worried about the situation and there has recently been a marked rise in the arrest of dissidents, members of religious groups, and of public executions. The hardliners are giving a credible impression that they are in charge after all. Although all Christian churches are closely monitored, with informers outside even the Armenian Cathedral in Tehran, it is the Farsi-speaking Christians of the Anglican and evangelical churches who have been singled out for attention. They are told who can attend services and when they can be held, if at all. Their clergy are forbidden to visit parishioners in their homes and are sometimes accused of trying to convert Muslims. The so-called "house churches" are even worse off. The ideologues of the Islamic Revolution regard these small groups of Christians as one of the great dangers to the Islamic state and have done everything they can to eliminate them. More than 30 Christian leaders are behind bars, mostly for the crime of holding a Christian meeting in a home or giving someone a Bible to read.[2]

Among them was Farshid Fathi, who had been sentenced to six years in jail and held in solitary confinement for long periods. Last Easter his foot was fractured when a guard stepped on it. While in prison he had been denied the treatment doctors say he needed for its proper healing. He was an inspiration to his fellow prisoners. He was recently released. Other prisoners include Maryam Zargaran, who is serving four years. Youth groups have been forcibly broken up and women and men are regularly detained as a "warning". Apart from the tightly-controlled situation in four Anglican congregations, all public Christian worship in Farsi is simply forbidden.

The Zoroastrians, followers of the indigenous faith of Iran, are a shadow of their former selves (there are now more of them in India and Pakistan than in Iran), and the ancient Jewish community is a fraction of what it was before the 1979 Islamic Revolution. Non-*Shī'a* Muslims also face discrimination, with restrictions on building mosques and other activities.

The plight of the Bahá'í community is, by all independent accounts, even worse than that of the Zoroastrians, the Jews or the Christians. More than 200 Bahá'ís were executed after the Revolution. Today, more than 120 Bahá'ís are in prison on trumped-up charges — including seven former leaders of the community serving 20-year prison sentences. Their children are often harassed at school, their young people usually barred from university, and adults denied business licences and jobs. Not even their dead are sacrosanct – the ongoing desecration of an historically important cemetery in Shiraz, where 950 Bahá'í are buried, has caused moral outrage all over the world. The Bahá'í question reveals some of Iran's internal tensions. News from the country suggests that public opinion may not be entirely in line with the regime's negative views about the Baha'ís. A prominent Ayatollah has received praise from around the world recently for giving the Bahá'í community a work of calligraphy featuring its own sacred writings. Numerous other public figures have made their own gestures in support of the rights of this community, but the hardliners remain adamant and firmly in control.

It is sometimes said that the persecution of religious minorities in Iran reflects the struggle between hardliners and progressives within the regime. Radical Islamists recently attempted to censor the president's own speech about freedom of expression on the internet after some young people had been severely admonished for making a widely-circulated tribute film to Pharrell Williams's song "Happy". It is clear that some people don't like the president. This may be so, but Rouhani was elected with the blessing of the Supreme Leader, Ayatollah Khamenei, and must be allowed to fulfil the pledges that brought him to office. Iranian leaders cannot continually plead that they have no power over other parts of the state. If Iran is to rejoin the civilised nations of the world, all parts of government need to act together.

For the West, the question is whether a regime that does not treat its own people with respect and represses their fundamental freedoms can be trusted to deliver on the nuclear issue. If the West wants enduring good relations with Iran, it must pursue the cause of freedom for all the people of Iran with as much rigour as it pursues its own safety, and that of Israel, in seeking to limit Iran's nuclear ambitions. A signal that good international relations and domestic respect for freedom are inextricably linked is badly needed. Will the West give such a signal? Among other things, clear support for even the small steps Rouhani is taking would be very welcome and could show the hardliners that he is not alone in his desire for more freedom for the Iranian people.

There have been periods in Iran's long history, such as those of the biblical Cyrus the Great and the Emperor Yazdigard, when it was a beacon of freedom. Will it reclaim this heritage or continue down a totalitarian path? Will Rouhani just prove to be the good cop to Tehran's numerous bad cops, or will he assume the mantle of Cyrus? Much hangs on the answer to this question for Iran's minorities.

Continuing our eastward journey: what can we say of the paradox of Pakistan? On the one hand, we have a parliamentary democracy, flawed certainly but also real with a reasonably free press, an independent (too independent?) judiciary and a fecund civil society. On the other hand, terrorists have free rein over the length and breadth of the country. Some groups, like the Taliban and their allies, such as the notorious Haqqani group, arose during the West's attempt, with Pakistani assistance, to drive the Soviets out of Afghanistan. That plan succeeded not only in its immediate mission but contributed to the eventual unravelling of the Soviet Union itself. Pakistan has considered it as in its interests not to destroy, completely at least, the Afghan Taliban (though it is difficult to know how to separate the Pakistani Taliban from their fellow-extremists). Pakistan's logic is that they serve as an "insurance policy" should an unfriendly regime emerge in Kabul. One definition of "unfriendly" in this context means friendly towards India.

There are other groups that were created by the Pakistan army itself mainly to infiltrate Indian-held Kashmir. Now that this is becoming more difficult, such groups are concentrating on a domestic agenda, i.e. to convert Pakistan into a Wahhābī-Salafi state with no room for *Shī'a*, *Ṣūfīs*, Ahmadiyya, Christians or Hindus — in short, anyone other than themselves.

The only institution capable of tackling these groups is the army. No civilian government, whatever its intentions, can manage on its own. Until recently, the army refused to take decisive action on the grounds that there was "no political consensus" on the issue. Commentators have taken this to mean that some significant politicians support these radical groups. More recently, the army was forced to act after militants "executed" a number of captive soldiers, attacked Karachi airport and killed scores of children at an army-run school. Whether such action will be decisive in ridding the country of the scourge of extremism remains to be seen.

Compared to totalitarian regimes in the area Pakistan feels relatively free, even if sometimes journalists pay a heavy price for their activities. Christians and people of other faiths have freedom to worship, to run their own educational and health institutions and to manifest their faith in public. And yet there have been numerous attacks on churches, temples and other places of worship. Christian villages have been torched and members of the Ahmadiyya community (a heterodox sect) live in fear of their lives. The government always disowns and condemns these acts. Many Muslims have also been shocked by them and some have gone so far as to provide protection for non-Muslim places of worship. This is all very laudable but the blasphemy laws, with mandatory death sentences, remain on the statute books and are a dead hand on freedom of speech, as well as being the means of entrapping numerous Christians and others who then face years in prison (often in solitary confinement for their own protection) before being acquitted by a higher court.[3]

I have made numerous suggestions to successive governments both to ameliorate the force of these laws and to replace them with something more humane. No government, so far, has had the courage to do anything. This is partly because of the fear of extremists but it is also because there has been, as a senior minister once told me, a change in the mind-set of a large segment of the population which has been brought up on the teaching of hatred in textbooks and on ultra-fundamentalist notions about Islam, its Prophet and its laws.

Like other countries, Pakistan has a choice: to sink more and more into an obscurantist Islamism with all that this means for women, religious minorities and even Muslims of traditions different from Wahhabism and Salafism, or to return to the vision of its founders. They did not want to create a theocratic state but one where Islam would inspire the creation of a free, just and compassionate society. As someone who, along with many others, resisted the wrong turn taken 40 years ago, I can only pray that even now the nation will turn back from the brink to which this turning has led it and embark again on the path laid out for it by those who brought it into existence.[4]

To the West, the new regime in Egypt has certainly acted disproportionately in its suppression of the Muslim Brotherhood and in its treatment of a number of journalists. We cannot, however, underestimate the peril that Egypt was facing from an extremist Islamism being imposed on an unwilling population. The massive demonstrations in favour of change have been confirmed by the presidential elections. I was in the country at the time they were held and it seemed to me that, despite reservations, Egypt was now more settled in terms of its future direction.

In an interview on Sky Arabia, President Sisi emphasised a nationalist vision which saw religion as important for society but understood it in an inclusive way. Christians, the media and the intelligentsia are euphoric about what has happened. Some of them are looking forward to one law for all, common citizenship and equality before the law. In some respects, though, they will have to come down to earth. No government can fail to take note of a strong Islamist element in the population and this will continue to influence policy on, for example, the building of churches, the treatment of converts and the freedom of the press. For instance, although the government has eased restrictions on the building of churches, extremists still try and prevent them being built or extended with the threat of violence.

The new constitution guarantees freedom of belief to all the citizens of Egypt, but freedom of *cult* only to 'the People of the Book', i.e. Jews, Christians and Muslims. This means that only the so-called 'heavenly religions' will be able to build places for public worship. Whilst some of its provisions are clearly a welcome advance in accordance with Article 18 of the Universal Declaration of Human Rights, we should press for freedom of belief and its expression, in public and in private, for *all* the citizens of Egypt.

Egypt has, however, taken a turn which countries like Pakistan need to note and, if they do not emulate this, at least it is one from which they can learn valuable lessons for themselves.

Turkey and Tunisia present examples where a certain kind of Islamism itself can become "moderate" and make room for plurality, democracy and some freedom. Will this continue to be the case in each of these countries and will other Islamist movements learn from their example? There seems little sign of it at present, and the Egyptian example shows us that the Turkish and Tunisian experience is not easily transferable.

The region has many endemic social, political and economic problems, but the one question that stands head and shoulders above the others is that of extremist Islamism. What is preventing the emergence of a modern, plural and confederal Iraq? It is Islamism of different kinds. What is the ultimate hindrance in the achievement of a just peace in the Holy Land? It is Islamism again, with its refusal even to acknowledge the existence of Israel. Although Christians have been under pressure because of Israeli policies, more recent emigration has also been caused by

Islamist pressure on Christian businesses, houses and worship, not only in Gaza and the West Bank but in Israel itself. What has led to the horrendous atrocities against communities like the Bahá'í and the Ahmadiyya or turned Afghanistan into a near-failed state? What is preventing the Kashmir issue from being resolved in a pragmatic way so that both Pakistan and India can get on with the task of providing a decent life for their people?

Islamists are fond of saying that "Islam is the solution". In fact, radical Islamism is at the root of the most pressing problems in the Middle East and beyond. I have tried to indicate what can be done about this and what some countries are doing about it. Lessons can and should be learned.

In the end, the question is: does the logic of Islam lead ineluctably to Islamism with closed, regressive and monolithic societies as the radicals desire, or can it also lead to open, free and plural societies? Much of the future of the region, and of areas well beyond it, hinges on how this question is answered by peoples, governments and religious leaders. The world is waiting to hear the answers.

Notes

[1] On diversity, see Gerald Russel, *Heirs to Forgotten Kingdoms*, London, Simon & Schuster, 2014.

[2] See further Rupert Shortt, op. cit., pp45ff and John Allen, op. cit., pp219f.

[3] One collection of evidence is the report, *The Targeting of 'Minority Others' in Pakistan*, British Pakistani Christian Association, London, 2013.

[4] On all of this see two books by distinguished Pakistani Christians: S.M. Burke (and S. Quraishi), *Quaid-i-Azam: His Personality and Politics*, Karachi, OUP, 1997 and George Felix, *Quaid-i-Azam's Vision*, Salford, Agape Press, 2001.

18

ACT NOW TO SAVE THE MIDDLE EAST'S CHRISTIANS – WHY WON'T THE WEST STAND UP FOR THE MOST PERSECUTED MINORITY?

It is hard to believe that at one time nearly the whole of the Middle East and much of North Africa were predominantly Christian. Think of the great Christian cities such as Alexandria, Damascus, Edessa, Constantinople and Carthage. Monasticism, the great civilising force in both the East and West, took its rise to the eastern end of the Mediterranean and some of the Church's greatest theologians came from there.

What changed the picture? In a word, Islam. The arrival of the newly Muslim Arabs disrupted the flow of history in the Middle East and beyond. The Christian cities capitulated one by one. Some communities were destroyed in the conflict, others were dispersed. For those that remained, a system of discrimination was set in place: they had to pay special taxes, wear distinctive dress, they could not build new churches. In due course, they were excluded from holding office. From time to time there were riots and massacres. These, as well as the process of attrition brought about by living under the *dhimma,* progressively reduced the strength of the Christian communities.

In spite of the strictures, Christians were able to maintain their relative strength, in some cases for centuries. In Egypt, the Coptic population did not fall below 50 per cent until after the pogroms of the 14th century. Christians were able to make notable contributions to science, philosophy, government, architecture and the arts. But all the while their mentality, and that of their rulers, were formed by the unequal relationship.

When, under intense Western pressure, the *dhimma* was relaxed in the 19th century, there were still significant Jewish and Christian communities throughout the Ottoman Empire. The creation of the State of Israel in 1948, as well as the wars of 1967 and 1973, meant that the Jewish communities of the Middle East and North Africa migrated to Israel, leaving the Christians as the only substantial minority in many of these countries.[1]

Their new status as fellow citizens with their Muslim compatriots allowed these Christians to make a contribution, out of all proportion to their numbers, to the emergence of nationalist states which were defined not so much by religion as by a shared language, culture and history.[2] Even then, those communities that did not fit in with nationalist aspirations, such as the Armenians and the Greeks in Turkey, faced persecution, execution or exile.

All of this informs the current situation. It has been, however, the rise of radical Islamism from the 1950s onwards that has defined the place and treatment of minorities in the region. The Islamists have been keen to continue the disadvantages suffered by these communities in, for instance, repairing church buildings, and they have pressed for the introduction of fresh restrictions.

The desecration of cemeteries in Libya, the murder of clergy in Iraq and Syria, the attacks on churches in Egypt and their forcible conversion into mosques there and elsewhere, are all contemporary outrages which remind us sadly what mobs and despots have done to these communities in the past.

The changes are not, however, just the doings of an angry mob. In Iran and Pakistan, separate electorates were introduced for non-Muslims so they could vote only for the small number of parliamentary seats allocated to them (Pakistan has since then, to its credit, reintroduced joint electorates). This is a barely disguised attempt to revive the *dhimma*, albeit dressed in 'democratic' clothes. It is well known that the blasphemy laws in Pakistan, Kuwait and elsewhere have had a chilling effect on freedom of speech, and non-Muslims or 'heterodox' Muslims have suffered disproportionately because of these laws. Even when 'apostasy' is not a crime on the statute books, jurists will regularly try people for it under *Sharī'a*. Such a practice completely negates the basic freedoms of belief and expression guaranteed under the United Nations' Universal Declaration of Human Rights (UDHR).

This litany of persecution is long but what, people will ask, can be done about it? There is an urgent need for governments and the UN to promote Article 18 of the UDHR, which guarantees freedom of belief and expression. This element of international law must be brought to the fore, and all states should be expected to adhere to it.

Many are hopeful that the second revolution in Egypt will produce an atmosphere of tolerance. During a recent visit there, I observed a kind of near euphoria among Christians, women and the intelligentsia. But without vigilance the current optimism could evaporate and we could be back to the status quo ante. Christians have many friends in Egypt, but also significant enemies. We must pray that the current trajectory towards greater openness will continue.

In spite of the greater openness to the West since President Rouhani came to office in Iran, there has been no corresponding easing of the situation with regard to minorities. In fact, reports from Tehran suggest a tightening up of controls. This is where the international agenda and the domestic need to be addressed together. A totalitarian Iran will not be a reliable partner globally. Every opportunity must be taken by our leaders to raise the issue of fundamental freedoms with their Iranian counterparts.

The sovereignty of states has, of course, to be respected. But from time to time there have been interventions when there has been danger of genocide, the collapse of state apparatus or unwanted foreign incursion. There have been sanctions, no-fly zones and even 'boots on the ground' to protect ethnic or religious groups from their oppressors – so why not now?

If Muslims need protection in the Balkans, the Kurds in Iraq or indigenous communities in the Americas or Australia, why not give protection to Christians in the Middle East and beyond? Such protection need not always be military or undertaken through the threat of economic sanction. It can often be achieved simply through raising awareness of the situation in which these communities find themselves. It can also be provided through advocacy and campaigning as well as diplomacy and negotiation. But sanctions and military means will sometimes be needed to deter the oppressor and to give confidence to the oppressed. After all, what is sauce for the goose is sauce for the gander.[3]

Notes

[1] See my *Conviction and Conflict: Islam, Christianity and World Order*, London, Continuum, 2006.

[2] Kenneth Cragg, *The Arab Christian: A History in the Middle East,* London, Mowbrays, pp150ff.

[3] On how the notion of the 'Just War' is to be understood and applied in terms of non-conventional conflicts in the 21st Century, see Peter Dixon, *Peacemakers: Building Stability in a Complex World*, Nottingham, IVP, 2009.

19

FREEDOM IN THE FACE OF RESURGENT ISLAM

As I travel so often to the Islamic world my mind turns, naturally, to the role of religion in that part of the world, and particularly to what is happening to Islam there and, conversely, to how it is affecting the political and social situation in these countries and, indeed, more widely than that.

We have so often heard the mantras of "violent extremism", "Islamism" or even "Islamist terrorism" that we are in danger of not noticing that the common element in so much of the turmoil in the Middle East, North Africa, South Asia and West Africa is not extremism or terrorism as such but a resurgent Islam. This manifests itself in a variety of ways: *Sunni*, *Shī'a*, *Salafi*, *Wahhābī* and even *Ṣūfī*. A recent negative example of it was the rioting over Qur'ān burning in Afghanistan and elsewhere when a number of innocent lives were lost. While some forms of resurgent Islam can genuinely be progressively reformist — the names of Anwar Ibrahim and Chandra Muzaffar in Malaysia — the large organisation Nahḍat Al-'Ulema in Indonesia and Asghar Ali Engineer in India come readily to mind — for the most part resurgent Islam is generally backward-looking. That is to say, it is looking back, not just with nostalgia but with political, social and economic programmes in mind, to the origins of the particular tradition to which it belongs. It is usually suspicious of religious plurality and is prepared to countenance the existence of other faiths in only the most restricted circumstances. Because of its

173

missionary nature (which it shares with Islam), Christianity is often viewed with special concern. As a rule, there is a generalised hostility to the West and to Israel which is sometimes expressed in terms of particular grievances such as the West's support for Israel, its armed intervention in various Muslim-majority countries, and its failure to secure justice for Muslims in Palestinian Territories, Kashmir and Chechnya (Bosnia and Kosovo are conveniently forgotten).

Significant movements within this resurgence, like the Muslim Brotherhood (*Ikhwān Al-Muslimīn*) in Egypt and elsewhere or the pietistic *Tablīghī Jamā'at* in South Asia, either claim to be non-violent by nature or at least to have renounced the use of force in the achievement of their aims. Their advocacy of a "pure" Islam, their aversion to any kind of constitutional equality for non-Muslims, their hostility to the West and to Israel and their antipathy towards other forms of Islam can, however, lead their followers to even more extreme forms of Islamism which do not eschew violence. For these reasons extremist Islamism, even when it professes non-violence, cannot be viewed with complacency or approached with that naive engagement which has characterised some of the Establishment's overtures towards it.[1]

In the current situation, joining in the struggle for democracy in the Middle East and elsewhere may enable some of these movements to further what can be a theocratic and pan-Islamic agenda. If their ultimate aim is the restoration of the Caliphate, the recovery of lands lost to Islam and the establishment of a single, worldwide *Ummah*, we must ask: what is the commitment to democracy? Is it to achieve power democratically to fulfil aims which are essentially undemocratic? The acid test for a democratic society is whether a party or a movement is not only willing to take power to govern but whether it is also willing to relinquish it. In this matter, we must say that the jury is out on whether Islamist groups would be willing to give up power. If their success at the ballot box is seen as a "manifest victory" (*fath mubīn*) of their faith, how will this be reconciled with a subsequent defeat at the same box? The world needs to know the answers to such questions.

On its own, of course, democracy is not enough. It could turn out just to be a tyranny of propagandised and radicalised masses unless, and until, it is accompanied by the guarantee of liberty. Such a guarantee must extend to groups like women, non-Muslims and even Muslims who do not belong to the dominant version of Islam in a particular country. It must include not only the freedom to worship but of expression, belief, the ability to manifest one's belief in daily living and the possibility of changing one's belief without fear of legal sanction. In other words, the freedoms guaranteed by the United Nations Universal Declaration of Human Rights. Alongside liberty, we need the will to create and maintain an ordered society based on the rule of law and on equality for all before the law. Without such order, democracy will not mean much to minorities, women and other disadvantaged groups. Only a society based on the rule of law will be able to provide a strong civil society, a free press and an independent judiciary.

There are two false ideas from which we must guard ourselves. The first, prevalent among some diplomats and politicians, is that an improved economic situation will deal with extreme forms of Islamism. While it is true that an adverse economic situation affects the recruitment of the young to radical causes, we must not ignore the ideological bases of such movements. It can also be shown that these arise and flourish as much in oil-rich states as in poorer ones. We need to engage with ideologies themselves in terms of their relationship to Islam's foundational texts, to history, to traditional forms of decision-making and governance and to the present beliefs and values of the international community of nations.

The second false idea, espoused by most Muslims and some Christian leaders involved in dialogue with Islam, is that a true Islamic state will, by its very nature, "protect" non-Muslims. I am sorry to have to say that history does not suggest that such will be the case. There have, undoubtedly, been periods of tolerance when Jews, Christians, Zoroastrians and others have been able to contribute to the Islamic societies in which they have lived. The structured discrimination and injustice of the *dhimma*, however, has always prevented their full participation and has, indeed, led to periodic persecution and violence. We must be very careful about using terms like "protection" in this context as it can be seen as a translation of *dhimma*. Whatever the history, non-Muslims in the Islamic world today wish to be free citizens with equal rights under the law and not *dhimmis*.[2]

It is commendable that Western powers operated a "no-fly" zone against Saddam Hussein to protect the Marsh Arabs in the south and the Kurds in the north of Iraq from the dictator's excesses. A similar situation occurred in Libya where the United Nations authorised the steps necessary to protect people from attack by their own government. But why is the UN or the West unable to tackle the widespread and growing persecution of Christians? In the case of Iraq, why is there so much resistance to a declaration that Christians, Mandaeans, Yazidis and other minorities need to be protected and that, where necessary, their safety in certain zones will be guaranteed by the international community? This does not necessarily mean that they will be unable to live elsewhere in Iraq. They should be able to, and the guarantee of safety for some areas may create confidence about their future everywhere in the country, as they will know they have a fall-back position. At the moment the only option seems to be fleeing the country in large numbers. If the continued presence of these ancient communities is to be safeguarded the international community needs to act now.

In Pakistan, similarly, Christians, Ahmadiyya and other communities continue to suffer not only from prejudice and intolerance but from legal discrimination, enshrined in law based on *Sharī'a*. The abuse of the so-called blasphemy law is an example of blatant intolerance of religious minorities. However, it is not only abuse but the law itself in terms of access to justice, employment, services, etc. which discriminates against non-Muslims. Pakistan is the recipient of massive aid from Western countries. This is to assist with basic services and to prevent the spread of extremism. But why should it not be targeted, first and foremost, at those areas which are most susceptible to extremist influence? It should be used to remove the teaching of hate from textbooks in a variety of disciplines, to reform the educational system, particularly in the madrassas, to strengthen civil society and the role of women and non-Muslims within it and to foster inter-faith dialogue that leads to respect and harmony. Is there any reason why such aid cannot be linked with Pakistan's performance not only in how it deals with its minorities, but how it proposes to review and revise discriminatory legislation itself?

International intervention in Afghanistan has certainly changed the situation dramatically for women and girls, even if much remains still to be done. Alas, this is not so for Christians and other groups. Although the post-Taliban constitution incorporates the Universal Declaration of Human Rights, this has not resulted in freedom of belief and expression in that country. The explanation usually given is that *Sharī'a* will always trump any constitutional guarantees in these areas. This must be a matter of huge concern to the taxpayers in this and other countries who are shouldering a massive burden in the belief that they are promoting freedom in Afghanistan.

In Egypt, which has the largest population of Christians in the Middle East, it is very important that the gains made in the last century or so of equal citizenship are not eroded and that the community is not returned to its ancient *dhimmi* status. The gains of the revolution must include, in addition to democracy, the equality of all before the law, one law for all and the incorporation of fundamental freedoms within the constitution. The new Egyptian Constitution goes some way towards guaranteeing freedom of belief but freedom of worship is still restricted to the so-called 'heavenly religions': Judaism, Christianity and Islam.

I have always thought that Western estimates of the number and importance of the *Shī'a* have not been accurate. This is partly because of the range of *Shī'a* sects, some of which resemble the *Sunni* to a remarkable extent, others appearing more or less outside the pale of Islam altogether. It is also because of the importance of the doctrine of *taqiya*, or of concealment of the faith because of the fear of persecution, that the number of *Shī'a* in a given situation is not appreciated until conditions are favourable to them. We now know that significant numbers of *Shī'a* are to be found not only in Iran and South Asia but in Iraq, Lebanon, Syria, Saudi Arabia, Bahrain, Yemen and Turkey. Many of the features of *Shī'a* resurgence resemble the *Sunni*, for example, their enthusiasm to enact and implement their form of *Sharī'a* in its entirety. In other respects, *Shī'a* are different: much higher store is set by the virtues of martyrdom, for example. Their view of the positive value of suffering is quite unparalleled in *Sunni* Islam. This is linked to another core doctrine which is the concealment and the expected revealing of the True *Imām* or *Mahdī*. In the *Shī'a* resurgence these two characteristics are often seen together. The martyrdom of the faithful in fighting the infidel and seeking justice for believers hastens the 'parousia' of the absent *Imām*. There is, therefore, both an implicit and, at least some of the time, an overt eschatological element to *Shī'a* ` resurgence. The significance of this is that things may be said, or action undertaken, which appear to outsiders as rash or foolhardy but which are designed to hasten the coming of the Imam, the vindication of believers and the establishing of justice here on earth.[3]

We should not imagine that these resurgent forms of Islam or Islamism are present only in Muslim-majority countries. They are affecting, more and more, the lives of people and of nations in many other contexts, whether that is in India, with its Muslim minority as large as the population of some Muslim countries; the Philippines, where there is a long-running conflict with Islamist extremists in Mindanao; China, which worries about the infiltration of radical Islam from its west; or Russia and the situation on its southern flank. In the Western world too these resurgent forms, prone to extremism and adoption of violence, are present and influential. Particularly in isolated and segregated communities of immigrant origin, among the young who may be European or American-born, in universities and prisons, through the internet and on the margins of mosque-life (if not at its centre) and in madrassas, they are ubiquitous as a radicalising and alienating presence.

In such a situation programmatic secularism, with its pale shadow of values derived from the Judaeo-Christian tradition for which it cannot give an account, provides thin gruel for any attempts to check and reverse the trend to radicalisation. On the one hand, it is unable to provide a strong moral and spiritual framework which is needed in addressing a comprehensive social, political and economic ideology explicitly claiming to derive from a particular spiritual tradition. On the other, such secularism may itself (as Peter Hitchens has shown in his book *The Rage Against God*) be unable to resist moving towards totalitarianism in its disregard for conscience (especially of believers), its lack of commitment to the family and to the rights of parents to bring up their children without excessive state intervention, to freedom of belief and the right to manifest one's beliefs in daily work and life.[4]

Russia, India and China have to deal with Islamism within their own borders, but increasingly they will also have to engage with it as it affects their international trade and political relationships. As far as the West is concerned, whilst respecting a proper distinction between Church and State, it is hugely important for it to acknowledge that its value-system is derived from a Judaeo-Christian worldview. Belief in inherent human dignity or equality based on the common origin of all human beings, or liberty as a fundamental right is not arbitrary enlightenment dogma in an irrational world but springs precisely from a cosmos continually being ordered, directed, renewed and redeemed by its Creator. It is not enough for us just to hold these values but, taking account of the challenge from aggressive secularism and radical Islam, we also need to give an account of their origin and importance. Politically correct secularism tends to collapse all of these fundamentals into one mega-value of non-discrimination and extends it, beyond how persons are to be treated, to equal regard for all kinds of attitudes, behaviours and lifestyles.

Because there is little in common to offer that is absolute, secularism has produced doctrines like that of multiculturalism which are content to settle for different religious and ethnic communities to lead their own lives, more or less separately from each other. The business of the state is thus seen not as one of integrating diversity but as providing for separateness in the use of language, housing and education. Such secularism has a strong individualistic focus and concentrates on the safeguarding of individuals, but is weak on the need also to uphold vital social institutions, such as the family. This can lead to the view that everyone who shares a fridge is family, ignoring the importance of what Brenda Almond has called the biological connections so important for nurture, self-awareness and the ability to establish balanced relationships.[5]

At the very time that research is showing us the distinctive way in which children relate to fathers and mothers, there is a determined attempt not only to write marriage out of the picture but fathers as well. Moral relativism has also tended to water down the respect society owes to the person at the earliest stages of life, allowing the embryo to be manipulated, discarded and destroyed in the name of scientific research. This is not far from a eugenicist view of what sort of children it is desirable to have with the gradual elimination of the disabled, those disposed to serious illness later in life or just the weak and the unpretty. At the other end of the lifespan, at the very time that pain caused by terminal disease can be managed (thanks to the Christian-based Hospice movement), we are witnessing an obsessional campaign to make euthanasia and/or assisted suicide legal, even though the dangers of abuse of the elderly and the ill feeling unwanted, and of the deterioration in palliative care provision are well known.[6]

In all of this, we are asked to accept an allegedly value-free system of education. On closer inspection, however, it is found not to be value-free at all but riddled with unexamined secularist assumptions about the world and ourselves which shapes pupils' attitudes towards others, their sense of purpose in life and views on the environment just as much as any religious worldview does. The acknowledgement of the Judaeo-Christian tradition as central to the survival of the West is not necessarily to privilege any particular church or ecclesiastical tradition.

If the challenge of radical ideology, secularist or Islamist, is to be met there must be a strong emphasis on integration and not only in the practical sphere involving the use of a *lingua franca*, policies for mixed housing and schooling and social mobility. These are all very important, but the integration must also take place around a common awareness of history and of a moral and spiritual tradition. Those who have come or will come here are to be welcomed to a society which acknowledges and makes its policy and legislative decisions on the basis of this tradition. Others should, of course, be welcome to make their specific contribution in the development of this tradition, but it should be clear that there is no real or imagined *tabula rasa* from which we proceed to construct society in the image of a so-called progressive constructivism and its exponents. At the moment, things are still topsy-turvy: while it is thought desirable that Muslims and people of other faiths should be involved in policy-making at the highest levels, there is no commensurate involvement of Christians who can clearly articulate a vision for society and an awareness of the importance of its own traditions in this area of life. Such an awareness of a moral and spiritual tradition will lead to a strong affirmation of the natural family as a proper basis for society and the normative context for that social learning which is vital for the wider social interaction which we all need. It will lead to public policies that support marriage not only through the tax system, but in the generous provision for marriage preparation and for assistance in difficult times. The primacy of parents in the nurture and education of their children would be recognised and all apparatus of the state would be strictly ancillary to that. The authorities would not attempt to coerce or to seduce parents back into the workplace if one of them wishes to give priority to the upbringing of children. Rather, such a role would be welcomed and supported.

Awareness of this tradition would lead also to a balancing of autonomy with interdependence. Personal freedom of expression, of belief, in the manifestation of belief and, in many other areas, is hugely important, but the tradition also teaches us that we are relational beings and that even the development of personhood is inescapably relational. This means that the implications of our actions for our near and dear ones, and for wider society, will have to be taken into account. The decision to end one's life, for example, is not just about the person involved but also family and friends and, more widely still, society itself and how it values human life. The termination of a pregnancy, similarly, cannot just be about a woman's right to choose, but must be balanced by a consideration for the unborn, for the woman's partner and the view that society has for the value of human life. We have seen already that the leading values of our nation, derived from the Judaeo-Christian worldview, uphold the uniqueness of human persons, their dignity and freedom. This is not really "speciesism" but signals the special way in which humans are related to the rest of creation: they belong to it but can also alter it, for better or for worse. That is why a proper understanding of the mandate to stewardship in the Bible is so important today. Respect for the rest of creation is necessary not because the earth is a kind of goddess, as in pagan times, nor just for selfish reasons for our survival or that of our descendants, but because creation is itself oriented to purpose, direction and destiny.[7]

Public law in the West has emerged mainly from Christianised Roman Law and the Canon Law of the Church.[8] It has acquired, however, a proper autonomy from particular religious communities. On the one hand, therefore, there has emerged a strong tradition of the equality of all before the law and of one law for all. On the other hand, law has respected the consciences of believers, especially if these have been formed by a recognised spiritual and moral tradition. This is seen, for instance, in the provision for conscientious objection in times of war, and even in the Abortion Act of 1967 which exempts medical personnel from having to participate in procedures which lead to the termination of pregnancy. It is a worrying development, therefore, that recent equality and other legislation does not take account of this important principle, leading religious believers to conflict with the law and to their exclusion from important areas of employment, civic participation and public life.

Religious communities and their members should be free to practise their faith in public and in private without unnecessary hindrance. This principle, however, cannot prevent access to the courts for anyone, nor can it prevent any citizen from asking for police protection for the safeguarding of their freedom. Muslims, for instance, are free to observe the provisions of *Sharī'a* if they wish to do so, but this cannot curtail the liberty or the right to justice under the law of the land or to due protection of the citizen under the law for anyone, including Muslims.[9]

Because the tradition of public law in this country has arisen from the Judaeo-Christian tradition, as refracted by the Enlightenment, it would be a mistake to recognise aspects of *Sharī'a*, which has arisen from quite different assumptions about equality, in terms of public law in the West. It would mean introducing a principle of contradiction in the body of the law. This would be so even for the "softer" aspects of *Sharī'a*, such as its family law. This latter does not recognise equality between men and women in terms of marriage, divorce, the custody of children, inheritance or in the laws of evidence. As can be imagined, this would create huge difficulties in maintaining the principle of equality of all before the law and of one law for all.

Traditionally, the ability to observe *Sharī'a* and to enforce it has been a *sine qua non*, a minimum required for Muslims to continue living in a non-Muslim polity. Demands that *Sharī'a* should be recognised in terms of public law stem from the perception that this is required for Muslims to be able to live in Western and non-Muslim societies.[10] Whether the conditions for Muslims to live in non-Muslim societies are fulfilled is for Muslims to decide in each particular case, but there should be no compromise on upholding the basic principles of public law as it has emerged and developed in the West.

Resurgent forms of Islam, leading to Islamist extremism, pose an international challenge which needs to be tackled in quite specific ways, depending on where it arises and its implications globally. Meanwhile, the domestic challenge must be met with a clear understanding and without compromise on the basic principles on which society is founded and which are needed for day-to-day decision-making. In the West, there is an urgent need for the renewal and the strengthening of the Judaeo-Christian tradition and its role in public life, if the challenges and dangers of extremist ideology are to be addressed effectively.

Notes

[1] On both organisations see Malise Ruthven, *A Fury for God: the Islamist Attack on America*, London, Granta, 2002, pp72ff, 192ff *et al.* On the Tablighi Jama'at see also Ayesha Jalal, *Partisans of Allah: Jihad in South Asia*, Lahore, Sang-E-Meel, 2008, pp267ff.

[2] On the nature and effects of the *Dhimmi*, see Bat Ye'or, The Dhimmi: Jesus and Christians under Islam, London, Associated University Presses, 1985.

[3] Abbas Amanat, *Apocalyptic Islam and Iranian Shi'ism*, London, IB Tauris, 2009, especially ch. 10, pp221ff.

[4] Peter Hitchens, *The Rage against God*, London, Continuum, 2010.

[5] See further my *Triple Jeopardy: Aggressive Secularism, Radical Islamism and Multiculturalism*, London, Bloomsbury, 2012.

[6] For a rehearsal of the arguments see Emily Jackson and John Keoun, *Debating Euthanasia*, Portland, Oregan, Hart, 2012.

[7] On the revival of paganism in the West see Peter Jones, *The Other World View*, Bellingham, WA, Kirkdale Press, 2015.

[8] Peter Stein, *Roman Law in European History*, Cambridge, CUP, 2005.

[9] On this see my 'Islamic Law, Fundamental Freedoms and Social Cohesion', in Rex Ahdar and Nicholas Aroney, *Shari'a in the West*, Oxford, OUP, 2010, pp87f and Denis MacEoin, *Sharia Law or 'One Law for All'?*, London, CIVITAS, 2009.

[10] Steven Gertz, *Permission to Live Under Christian Rule?*, in *The Centre for Muslim-Christian Studies Newsletter* No. 2 Summer 2010, p4.

20

WE CANNOT AVOID THE BATTLE OVER BLASPHEMY

In the aftermath of the killing and maiming in Paris last year, Western politicians and the media studiously ignored the obvious questions about the relationship between this and the general attitudes, derived from *Sharī'a*, to blasphemy and apostasy in the Islamic world. This was, no doubt, for the sake of good community relations and to prevent a backlash against Muslims. These are commendable reasons but, unless we can understand the truth behind these events, we will not be able to deal with the problem of extremism and to prevent further attacks. The issue has, once again, been given the sharpest urgency by the double tragedy in Copenhagen the following month. Facile defences of "free speech" and claims that these are just a handful of deluded terrorists are simply not enough and do not convince a thinking public. We need to investigate thoroughly the hinterland to the minds and acts of the people who carry out these attacks. What has led them to their distorted and dangerous conclusions?

The different schools of Islamic law are unanimous that the punishment for blasphemy is death.[1] It is for this reason that the Federal Shari'at (sic) Court in Pakistan removed the alternative of life imprisonment for blaspheming against the Prophet of Islam and made the death sentence mandatory for this offence. The results of having such a law are well-known. Large numbers of Christians, Ahmadis (members of a heterodox sect) and even Muslims have been accused of blasphemy, tried and sentenced to death. Even people with a history of mental illness have not escaped the rigours of this law and recently the Lahore High Court rejected the appeal of Asia Bibi, a poor peasant woman, against the sentence of capital punishment imposed on her for allegedly blaspheming in the course of witnessing to her Christian faith.

The law has been widely misused to settle personal scores and to gain an advantage in matters like property disputes. Once a charge is made the accused's fate is sealed. Both police and judiciary are intimidated by extremists and, at least in the lower courts, there can be only one result: conviction and the death sentence. In the case of Asia Bibi, the worrying development is that the higher courts too now seem to have been intimidated. It is concerning also that Pakistan's example is being followed by other nations. The case of Raif Badawi, who was convicted to 10 years in prison and 1,000 lashes for insulting Islam in Saudi Arabia, is but one example of this tendency.

An important feature of the general atmosphere created by this law is a sharp increase in mob violence against those accused of blasphemy and this extends to their family, their home and even the village or community in which they live. There have been numerous attacks on places of worship, schools and Christian and Ahmadi communities because someone within these is alleged to have blasphemed. Mobs can be incited by someone with a personal grudge and mosque loudspeakers are used to gather crowds which are then encouraged to mete out "rough justice".

Article 18 of the United Nations Universal Declaration of Human Rights guarantees the freedom of thought, conscience and religion and also the right to manifest our beliefs in teaching, practice, worship and observance. It also guarantees our right to change our beliefs. Although most Muslim countries have adopted this and other declarations, it has often been with a declared or mental reservation insofar as they are consistent with *Sharī'a*. This has led to various restrictions ranging from those on free speech to restriction and even prohibition of worship. It is interesting to note, in this connection, that Islamic declarations on human rights, such as the Cairo Declaration (1990) made by the Organisation of the Islamic Conference, either omit Article 18 altogether or significantly alter its content to bring it closer to the requirements of *Sharī'a*.

The Organisation of the Islamic Conference (OIC) has long campaigned, with near-success, to have defamation of religion made an internationally recognised offence. It is only gradually that non-Muslim states have seen the implications of such a law for freedom of speech and of the press. There has also been pressure by various Islamic organisations in the West to bring in legislation against "hate speech", which would restrict freedom to criticise or satirise religious beliefs. In Britain, an attempt by the Labour government to bring in such legislation forbidding "hate speech" was only qualified by last-minute amendments in the House of Lords safeguarding academic discussion, preaching and propagation of secular and religious beliefs which might otherwise have been construed as hate speech against a particular religion or lifestyle. This has not prevented over-zealous police or other officials from trying to stop Christian evangelism in "Muslim areas", forbidding the display of biblical texts in public places or arresting street preachers who were thought to be "offending" this or that pressure group.

In an important intervention in the *Daily Telegraph*, Dr Tim Winter (aka Shaykh Abdal Hakim Murad), a senior Muslim theologian at Cambridge University, points out that image-making is itself an offence in Islam but then goes on to claim that what has immeasurably compounded this offence for Muslims is that *Charlie Hebdo* (and the Danish cartoons before that) intended to "mock, deride and wound". He goes on to say that to laugh at the Prophet cannot be understood as free speech but does not say whether academic discussion of him, or apologetic by polemical secularists or Christians, would be or could be. Using the by now well-known tactic of gaining domination through claiming victimhood, he appeals to Muslim lawyers in Britain to use existing hate speech, slander and libel legislation to trigger a series of complex cases which would lead to the protection of Muslims from "abuse". As with the OIC's exertions regarding the defamation of religion on the international stage, is this a thinly-veiled attempt to have some kind of blasphemy law recognised nationally?[2]

What is the difference between Asia Bibi and numerous others on death row, having been convicted on blasphemy charges, and the killings on the streets of Paris and Copenhagen? Is judicial execution different from these extra and anti-judicial atrocities? Why does the international community tolerate one but not the other? Is it because Westerners are involved in one but not the other?

We can no longer avoid a serious discussion about blaspheming in Islam, and the culture around it, if we are to understand and to prevent both judicial execution and extra-judicial murders. As with apostasy, the Qur'ān seems not to provide for any punishments in this life for blasphemy against God and the Prophet though, as with apostasy, various unrelated verses are pressed into service by those who would find such a punishment in their scripture. The most the Qur'ān does is to say that such people are cursed in this life and in the next where God will mete out to them "a humiliating punishment" (33:57). It is claimed that the execution of poets, such as Ka'b ibn al-Ashraf in 624AD, for insulting the Prophet, sets a precedent for executing blasphemers today. Others say that these poets were executed for inciting sedition and not merely for blasphemy.

Also, there are well-known stories of the Prophet forgiving some who had insulted him. It is incumbent on Muslims to follow the Sunnah, or practice, of their Prophet. Which aspect will they follow today? A great deal depends on what answer is given to this question.[3]

Some scholars have suggested that there should be a high bar set for entertaining allegations of blasphemy. Those who make such accusations must themselves be pious Muslims and, if a false accusation is made, the penalty for this must be the same as for the offence of blasphemy itself. From time to time, proposals are put forward which will make it procedurally more difficult for such allegations to be brought, but the fundamental questions remain that of free speech and the balance to be struck between this and civility in society, as well as the need for public order. Are there any limits on freedom of expression?

The UN Declaration itself provides for the possibility of restrictions for the purpose of securing due recognition for the right and the freedom of others, and for meeting the just requirements of "morality, public order and the general welfare". What does this mean? Do the limitations have to do only with law and can we include custom and convention in public life and the media?

In this sense the events in Paris which have highlighted the role of satirical magazines like *Charlie Hebdo* have also obscured the serious discussion which needs to take place about the authenticity of the extremists' claim that they represent "true Islam". Such a discussion needs to take place not only among Muslims but with all those who have to live in Muslim lands or who have Muslims as neighbours, colleagues and fellow-citizens. How are the Qur'ān and the Sunnah to be interpreted and whose interpretation is correct? To what sources are the extremists appealing and can such appeals be countered?

In a free world the founders of all major religions will come under scrutiny: Moses, Muhammad and Jesus are not excluded from such study. What was their message? What were their aims? What kind of people were they? These are legitimate areas for serious discussion. It is a pity that they have been short-circuited, for the time being, by the tongue-in-cheek activities of satirists though, it is to be hoped, not for good.

Should religious believers seek any protection under the law from insult to their precious beliefs? People are protected from false statements being made about them either orally or in print. Article 20 of the International Covenant on Civil and Political Rights (ICCPR) also prohibits advocacy of religious hatred that leads to discrimination, hostility or violence against an individual or community. That is to say, the intention is to protect individuals and communities, not articles or systems of belief as such. If a belief is attacked, surely its best defence is a reasoned response rather than violence or legal sanction?

The British in India sought to prevent the propagation of religious hatred as a means of promoting social harmony and maintaining public order. In certain contexts, this may be a legitimate aim but, if it is given legal form, it must be hedged about with safeguards for free expression. To put it another way, freedom of speech must be the presumption and any limitations would need to be justified on a case-by-case basis.

Any penalties for breaches of such limitations must be commensurate with the offence. One of the problems with laws concerning apostasy and blasphemy in some Islamic nations is their draconian nature and lack of flexibility and judicial discretion. It cannot only be Muslims who are thus protected. In the Islamic world the urgent need is to protect Christians, Yazidis, Baha'is and Ahmadis from the hatred engendered by textbooks, extremist sermons and pamphleteering.

The tragedies in Paris and Copenhagen should lead us to face these and other issues squarely, not to avoid them simply to maintain social cohesion within our societies or friendly relations with our trading partners. If they are not faced, domestic and international peace will be short-lived.

Notes

[1] See my 'Islamic Law, Fundamental Freedoms and Social Cohesion', in Rex Ahdar and Nicholas Aroney (eds) *Shari'a in the West*, Oxford, OUP, pp78f.

[2] See Abdal Hakim Murad, *Scorning the Prophet goes beyond free speech – it's an act of violence,* [online]. Available at: http://www.telegraph.co.uk/news/religion/11351280/Scorning-the-Prophet-goes-beyond-free-speech-its-an-act-of-violence.html [accessed on 21 Aug 2015], London, Telegraph, 17 Jan 2015.

[3] On those who were forgiven and those who were not, see Ibn Ishaq's *Sirat Rasūl Allah*, English Trans, *The Life of Muhammad* (Tr. A. Guillaume), Karachi, OUP, 1967, pp.540ff. See also Mirza Tahir Ahmad, *Murder in the Name of Allah*, Cambridge, Lutterworth, 1989.

21

THE GLOBAL RESURGENCE OF ISLAMISM

The revelation that 'Jihadi John' was, in reality, a young Londoner, the departure of three young women from another part of London to serve ISIS in Syria and the poll showing that a significant minority of Muslims in this country believe that those who attacked and killed the *Charlie Hebdo* journalists had some justification for taking the law into their own hands, raises urgent questions about the alienation of young Muslims in this country.[1] What is leading them to turn their backs on the country where many of them have been born, and where all of them have been brought up and educated?

The background here is surely the global resurgence of Islamism, which seeks Muslim identity through a rejection of the modern world in favour of the culture and society which existed at the time of the Prophet of Islam, Mohammed, and his companions. This leads many also to reject, too, how Islamic civilisation developed in the course of history, and the accommodation which it had to make with non-Muslim neighbours and the extent to which *Sharī'a* was modified to meet the needs of the times.

At first, this resurgence was conveyed to the young in the isolated communities of British cities and towns by radicalised *Imāms*, who usually come from abroad, through the teaching of hate in some textbooks and in centres established to propagate visions of radical Islam. More recently this has increasingly been usurped by the electronic revolution. ISIS is but the latest extremist movement to use sophisticated new media to spread its message of fear and terror.[2]

Universities remain another location where, through voluntary societies, students are pressurised to conform to Islamic demands on gender segregation, dress, food etc. They are also exposed to speakers and materials which may lead to further radicalisation.[3] Likewise, radicalisation is likely to occur in prisons, where the numbers of Muslims is disproportionate to their percentage in the population at large.[4]

For many, it is a question of identity. Rather than identifying with Britain as a nation, with a plural and diverse society and with moderate Islam, whether in *Ṣūfī*, *Sunni* or *Shī'a* forms, they are increasingly identifying with a supra-national and extremist version of their faith. Here the priority is for the *Ummah*, or the world-wide community of the faith, and *Sharī'a*, in its most uncompromising form, as a panacea for all of society's ills and for the recovery of lands lost to the infidel.

Radicalisation involves a leap from a personal and social faith to a comprehensive political, social, economic and spiritual ideology. As such, it can be compared to other manifestations of totalitarianism such as Marxism or National Socialism, hence the term Islamo-fascism used by some. It is true, of course, that belief in an extremist ideology does not necessarily involve engagement in violence but, as we have seen, it can lead to it. Both the ideologues and their disciples claim inspiration from the fundamental sources, history and teaching of Islam. If they are wrong to do so, this has to be clearly demonstrated to them and to the public generally.

For many years I have been arguing that religious leaders of any faith, if they come here to work, should be vetted as to the origin and authenticity of their qualification, their knowledge of English and their awareness of the culture and values of this country. We must make sure that British taxpayers are not, inadvertently, subsidising the teaching of hate in text books published here or imported from overseas. On the one hand, new media can be used to raise awareness of the variety in Islamic tradition and teaching. On the other, there has to be close monitoring and control of websites which advocate violence or discrimination against people of a different faith or view.

Whilst universities and colleges have a duty to uphold free speech, they also have a responsibility to prevent students being encouraged to break the law or, indeed, deny freedom of speech or movement to others. Universities should be places where people of different kinds can mix. Ghettoisation of every kind must be avoided. In prisons, any association or privilege that goes beyond legitimate religious observance has to be discouraged, as does the dissemination of extremist propaganda.

Socially, there has to be an end to misguided policies of 'multiculturalism' which have encouraged some communities to become segregated in housing, education and other activities. This has lessened a sense of national belonging, of common citizenship and of a shared language, precisely where this is most needed. It is good that some progress has been made in this area but much more needs to be done.

Extremist Islamism is a global phenomenon. We cannot support or tolerate it elsewhere while we fight it at home merely because it is perceived by some as being in the 'national interest'. Educational aid programmes, for instance, need to make sure that we are not, unwittingly, supporting the teaching of hate in schools. We have seen that giving refuge to those engaged in extremist ideology and terrorism elsewhere has immediate implications for our own security. Our resolve against terror internationally will also deter those who plan for it on our streets.

Finally, mistakenly or not, radical Islamism claims to have spiritual foundations and inspiration. It cannot effectively be opposed without reaffirming the Christian foundations and values of this nation which gave us Magna Carta and the liberties which flowed from it. As we have celebrated, it is the 800th anniversary year of this great document, let the faith which inspired its writers inspire us too, as we face the challenges of our age and our world.[5]

Notes

[1] See BBC Radio 4 Today, Muslim Poll, [online]. Available at: http://comres. co.uk/polls/bbc-radio-4-today-muslim-poll/ [accessed 14 Sept 2015], London, ComRes, 25 Feb 2015.

[2] See further James Brandon, *Virtual Caliphate: Islamic extremists and their websites*, London, Centre for Social Cohesion, 2008.

[3] John Thorne and Hannah Stuart, *Islam on Campus: A survey of UK student opinions*, London, Centre for Social Cohesion, 2008.

[4] Patrick Sookhdeo, *Faith, Power and Territory: A Handbook of British Islam*, McLean VA, Isaac Publishing, 2008, pp64f.

[5] The Baroness Cox, Bishop Michael Nazir-Ali (et. al.), *Magna Carta Unravelled*, London, Wilberforce Publications, 2015.

22

RESOURCES FOR CHRISTIAN LEADERSHIP
IN THE MIDDLE EAST

I was delighted to deliver the Michael Prior Memorial Lecture in 2011. First of all, because of Fr. Michael Prior, his inspirational personality, his leadership and indeed his friendship, and I'm so glad that this lecture has been endowed so that his work will continue to be remembered and commented upon in one way or another. But also because of the work in bringing to people's attention, particularly the churches and also more widely, the questions facing Christians under pressure, whether in Palestinian Territories or more widely in the Middle East or all over the world. This is a valuable ministry. I know it is a struggle because the media don't want to know, people on the streets don't want to know, but nevertheless there is a prophetic element to it and we need to remain committed to what we have been called to do.

So many of the contexts of my meetings (as of so many others with Fr. Michael) had to do with either Israel, Palestinian Territories or with the Middle East generally. I did want to say at the outset that we must get the message across that the Christian faith has its origins in the Middle East, and that there are significant communities of Christians that remain in the Middle East. There are lots of problems with that, but the fact that they are there cannot be denied. Events in the Middle East, again and again, alert us both to how ancient these communities are but also to the peril in which so many now live.

Christian Witness

My point of departure has to do with the origins of the Christian churches and of the Christian faith in the Middle East. If we depart with that in view, the first thing to note is what Bishop Younan Munib, the Lutheran bishop in Jerusalem, has called the story of *marturia* – the story of witness in one way or another. He is referring to Christians in Palestinian Territories, but the same can be said of Christians generally in the Middle East. The story of *marturia* can be described in three senses, I think. First, in the ordinary sense of the *martyrdom* of suffering. Here is a church that has had an almost continuous history of suffering under one kind of rule or another. The Copts often say that they were first persecuted by the Romans, and the story goes on and on. The same can be said of many other churches in that area.[1] But *marturia* is not just about martyrdom, it has a more positive meaning than that.

The second aspect of the Christian story in the Middle East is that of witness in the sense of *apologetic,* of actually giving an account of the Christian faith in a particular situation, and this has been so from the earliest of times. Justin Martyr, after all, came from a town called Flavia Neapolis, which is now the modern Nablus in the West Bank, and his other great successor, Clement of Alexandria, came from Alexandria in Egypt as the name itself tells us. Justin and Clement symbolise to me the necessity for Christians always to be able to give an account of their faith to those who are not Christians. Justin and Clement did that, not only in relationship to the Jewish communities around them (Alexandria was a great Jewish centre at the time), but also to the Pagans. The apologies to the emperors and to the Roman Senate said: "Don't be afraid of Christianity. It is a perfectly reasonable thing to believe, this is why we believe the things that we do".[2] This aspect of *marturia* is very important for Christians today in the Middle East because it is possible in the situation at the moment to think of *marturia* as simply martyrdom and to be resigned to a life of suffering without the positive aspect of understanding and giving an account of one's faith.

But the third aspect of *marturia* in the context of the Middle East is the rise of *monasticism*. At the very time when the Church itself had to be told that it needed to turn away from worldly involvement, from corruption, that it needed to turn away from the temptation of power, it was the women and the men who went out into the deserts who gave their witness in that way. Pope Benedict gave that very famous lecture (which became notorious in some circles for all sorts of wrong reasons) in which he explored how Christianity came to be identified with the destiny of Europe. In many ways that is true, but he went on to say, "except for some significant developments in the East". Well, what were those significant developments in the East? One of them certainly was monasticism which (because of the providential nature of Athanasius' exile because of the Arians) arrived in the West and has given, and continues to give inspiration to churches in both the East and West, and indeed now in the South.[3] Indeed, how important is this work in the Middle East today?

In Iraq I have met with many Christians and Muslims. One of the things I did was to go to the House of Love (*Dār al Mahabba*) in the middle of Baghdad which is run by the Sisters of Charity, who are Mother Theresa's sisters mainly from India and Bangladesh, and they look after children who were born deformed because of Saddam Hussein's chemical attacks in Halabja and other places. That is their apostolate and it is a wonderful work in bringing up these children, looking after them and encouraging their faith. There is evangelism, social action, incarnational ministry – all of those things there and we cannot, therefore, ignore that work. But monasticism, or giving of one's life to Christ in that way, is an important aspect of *marturia* that we must learn from the story of the churches in the Middle East. It is very sad to see empty monasteries and nunneries in some parts of the Middle East but not in Egypt. The monasteries in Egypt are full to overflowing with monks and nuns of the highest calibre who have left their professions (e.g. medicine and engineering) and entered these communities. So we are delighted that that story of the desert in Mesopotamia, Syria and Egypt also continues today.

Theological Method

The second point, going on from *marturia,* is the way in which the Middle East churches gave us *theological methodology* – how to do theology. People who use these methodologies are sometimes not aware of the background, but it is part of education to be aware of the background to the way in which we use our education. In all the story of the Christian churches there are two main ways of doing theology, and both of them came from the Middle East. One is what you might call the Antiochene, found in many other parts of the Middle East at the time. There were some people who were Antiochene in their theology who were not regarded later as orthodox, but some who were: Theodore of Mopsuestia and John Chrysostom come to mind. The theology of Antioch was first of all biblical: its point of departure was the Bible: God's revelation and the story of salvation in the Bible. It was historical: it took history seriously; not only the history that we find in the Bible, but also the story of the church. And it was exegetical. Throughout the centuries we have found people whose theological methodology, whether they knew it or not, has been the method of Antioch. It has many important things to teach us today, indeed, also the church in the Middle East.

But the other great strain was of course the Alexandrian. The Alexandrian method is quite different from the Antiochene; it is philosophical, it is systematic; some people might say it is speculative, and it is certainly spiritual. A different way of doing theology is to read Origen or Clement of Alexandria, for example. How they tried to make sense of the Christian faith for themselves and tried to make sense of it for others is quite different from the sermons of St John Chrysostom or his commentaries on the Bible. The point is that the worldwide Church owes these two main theological methodologies to the churches in the Middle East. The churches in the Middle East need to, if I may say so humbly, once again take seriously these methodologies, and to work with them and not simply to be content with tradition as it might have been passed down, or worse, to be content with imported theologies from the West which are now becoming so freely available.[4]

Dhimma, Dialogue and Development

However we look at the 7th century, there was a very great disruption and it cannot be minimised. It completely changed the map of the Middle East because we forget that the centre of the Christian world until then was the Middle East. The great Christian cities were there: Alexandria, Damascus, Jerusalem, Constantinople and Edessa. But the arrival of the Muslim Arabs changed things; sometimes suddenly, sometimes gradually, but change things it did. And as far as the churches in the Middle East are concerned, there are some aspects about what happened to them that must be mentioned.

One of them is the emergence of the *dhimma*. This was the condition under which Christians could now survive in the Middle East. The fact that they could survive as Christians or Jews, later on, Zoroastrians, is a positive thing. But the conditions were very onerous: they could keep their churches but to repair them they had to seek permission; they could not build new churches. Still the cause of riots so often in Egypt, for example, is the desire for Christians to build a new church or even a church hall. Since the revolution in Iran, no new churches have been built in that country.

When I was Bishop in Pakistan we were given a piece of land in a very nice, quite affluent area and the people of that area, all educated people, came to me and said: "Bishop, we know you've been given a piece of land here; please don't build a church here". In another area, where we did build a church, the present bishop tells me that still, about a quarter of a century since I left, the Muslims around them have not allowed the building to be used for worship.

Jizya has been mentioned and is now putting in a sinister

re-appearance, something that was a reality for Christians for centuries. The pain of the poll tax had to be endured simply because people were Christians or Jews, and in the 18th century the Ottoman delegate would arrive in Jerusalem and people would be forced to pay tax, the *Jizya*. If they couldn't pay they were imprisoned and then the community had to ransom them. They could not show any external symbols of their faith, wear a cross or a crucifix or whatever it was. Their homes had to be humbler than Muslim homes, they could ride donkeys but not horses (that's maybe appropriate for those who follow the Bible, Jesus arrived on a donkey in Jerusalem. Nevertheless, it was meant as humiliation). When the *Jizya* was paid it had to be paid with a sign of humiliation to fulfil the verse in the Quran which says that when they pay the tax they must feel small (Qur'ān 9, 29).[5]

Now I say all these things because the *dhimma* has actually formed the mentality of many of the Christian communities in the Middle East, how could it not? That is to say in relation to the majority, to one another and to the outside powers. After the Ottomans introduced the *Tanzimāt* (reforms more in line with Western ways) many of the *dhimmi* communities did not want to lose their *dhimmi* status because they didn't know what equal citizenship would mean, when it came.[6]

Nevertheless, in spite of this quite severe curtailment of their freedom, the Christian communities, and also the Jewish, did engage in what we might call dialogue with those around them and particularly with Muslims. As far as Christians are concerned, this dialogue that the Christians in the Muslim world had with the Muslims was of a quite different character to the sorts of things that were being said about Islam in Byzantium, or indeed Western Europe, because Byzantium and Western Europe saw Islam and Muslims simply as adversaries. There was a military situation quite often but this was not how the Christians in the Muslim world saw it and, just in the first few centuries, Jean-Marie Gaudeul, the great student of Muslim-Christian dialogue, counts nine Christian apologists of the first rank. One of those was St. John of Damascus. We sing his hymns; he belonged to the family al-Mansur, which was the family that opened the gates of Damascus for the Muslims after the Byzantines had deserted it. That's the kind of family he came from. In his *De Fide Orthodoxa*, his magnum opus, St. John speaks of Islam as a kind of Christian heresy. What is not so well known is that there is dialogue between a Christian and a Saracen (as St. John calls him) that survives in John's work. You may say there's nothing very remarkable about this dialogue, but what is remarkable is that John uses the Qur'ān, is aware of the Arabic of the Qur'ān, and in his argument he is not afraid to refer to the Qur'ān in defence of Christian beliefs.[7]

For example, in the argument about Jesus being the Word of God, and whether the Word of God is eternal, that is a matter of discussion both in Islam and in Christianity. If the Word is eternal, as Muslims believe, John says the Word must be God, otherwise you would have two eternals and would, therefore, be guilty of *Shirk,* of associating partners with God, which is the worst sin in Islam. Muslims believe the Qur'ān to be the eternal word of God but have never claimed it to be God! Jesus is also called the Word of God (Kalimatohu) in Qur'ān 4:171, and Christians have always believed him to be God incarnate.

Then we have other apologists like Bishop Theodore Abu Qurra, the Bishop of Haran, who did not actually use either the Bible or the Quran but simply used logic (syllogism) in his discussion with Muslims. Another person worth mentioning is the Patriarch Timothy of Baghdad. Timothy's dialogues were with the Caliph himself, not an ordinary Muslim or even a Muslim divine, but with the Caliph Al-Mahdi, the father of Harun Al-Rashīd and Mā'mūa Al-Rashīd, the great Abbaside Caliphs. The dialogue takes place in a friendly atmosphere; the Patriarch enters the Caliph's presence, he blesses the Caliph who then predictably asks him difficult questions about the Trinity, the Incarnation, the virgin birth, and so on. For example, in one of his answers about the Trinity, Timothy says that it is like the sun with its light and its heat. Eventually the Caliph indicates that the interview is finished and Timothy then prays for the Caliph and withdraws. Now that was the kind of dialogue that was even then possible, and as always we must ask the question: "What do we learn from this tradition that comes from the churches of the Middle East and comes from a very early age in the engagement with Islam?"[8]

There is another side to the dialogue which appears in the emergence of the Islamic Mysticism of Sufism. Margaret Smith, a great scholar of Sufism, did remarkable work on the interaction between the monks of the deserts of Syria and Egypt and the early Ṣūfīs. It is right to say that there is something in Sufism which comes from the Qur'ān itself, which comes maybe from the prophet of Islam's own religious experience, and the Ṣūfīs themselves point to verses like the 'Light' verse in the Qur'ān (24:35) or the 'Throne' verse in the *Surat Al Baqarah* (2:255). This much is true, and there is no reason for us to deny that Sufism has its origins in the religious experience of Islam. But it is undoubtedly the case that the Ṣūfīs admired the monks. Muhammad Iqbāl, one of the founders of Pakistan, gives six reasons for the rise of Sufism. One of them, interestingly, is very similar to that associated with the rise of the Christian Monasticism, which is the growing worldliness of the Abbasides and the desire of people to withdraw from it, the corruption of the rulers and the legalism of the *fuqaha* (the *Sharī'a* lawyers). But one of the reasons that he gives is the living example of Christian monks. This is Muslim testimony not Christian testimony from a leading Muslim thinker of the 20th century. And what the Muslim *Ṣūfīs* admired about the Christian monks was their asceticism, the fact that they had given up everything for God, and this is why Jesus himself became a pattern for the *Ṣūfīs*. The worship of the monks (even in the Qur'ān this may be referred to, but certainly the *Ṣūfīs* were very aware of it), the all night vigils, the regular offices that monks were assigned to – these point to a different kind of dialogue, a spiritual dialogue not a theological one like that of John of Damascus or Timothy of Baghdad.[9]

Another aspect that has to be mentioned about the Christian

presence after the arrival of Islam is the role that the Christians played in the development of what has come to be called Islamic civilisation. The question people have often asked is: "How did these people who came from the desert suddenly, or almost suddenly, develop this huge material, intellectual and spiritual civilisation?" Well, one answer to this is that they wanted to, but the other is that it would not have been possible without the active participation of the Christians and the Jews. The patterns of government, certainly from the Abbasid centuries, were borrowed from the old pre-Islamic Persian Empire. As to the architecture, poetry, literature and so on, the original inhabitants of these lands contributed a great deal to the abundance of what came to be called Islamic civilisation. Just one example, however, needs to be given and that has to do with the intellectual emergence of this civilisation. It is often said in Western universities that the West received back much of Hellenistic learning from the Muslims, and that is true, but the question is "how did the Muslims get it?" and that is not often spoken of. The Muslims got it because Christian clergy (they do have their uses) translated the Greek corpus: philosophical, theological, scientific, literary, either directly from the Greek into Arabic, or from Greek into Syriac into Arabic. The most well-known example of this is the father and son team; Hunayn Ibn Ishaq and Ishaq Ibn Hunayn. They were Nestorian Christians. The father knew better Greek so he translated from Greek into Syriac; the son knew better Arabic so he translated from Syriac into Arabic, and between them they translated the whole of the Greek medical corpus into Arabic. This was received by the West and was the basis, I understand, of the Oxford medical syllabus right up to the 18th century.[10]

How did the West get it? Well, it got it in two ways. It got it through Jewish traders (this is how the Jews got involved in this process) and this is shown by the fact that Arabic or Islamic names in Western languages are quite often in an Hebraic form so, for example, Avicenna, is Ibn Sina the great Persian chemist and Averroes is Ibn Rushd. So you can see how that process of transmission went on.

The other route was the Arabic-speaking Christian communities of the West (not of the Middle East, not of the East,
but of the West). Who and where were they? These were the
Mozarabs (Mozarab comes from the word *Musta'rab* - those
who have become Arabicised) of the Iberian peninsula. We still
have a Mozarabic liturgy. In fact, there is a church in Portugal,
the Lusitanian church, which still uses the Mozarabic liturgy.
These Arabic speaking communities transmitted some of this
learning to the monasteries and the emerging places of learning
in Western Europe. [11]

One of the things that Dr. Kenneth Bailey, who is a very
important name in this matter, has drawn to our attention is
the tradition of biblical translation and exegesis that went on
throughout this Muslim 'period'. I am so sad when I see Middle
Eastern ordinands, or ordinands in other Islamic countries,
reading only Western commentators. I went to a seminary in
Egypt and it was full of Bible commentary by Westerners. This
is good, but you have people like Ibn Al' Assāl, you have the
Iraqi Ibn Al-Tayyib, medieval Christian commentators on the
Bible. Where are their notes, what are we doing with them? Dr
Kenneth Bailey claims that Arabic, after Latin and Greek, has
the most Christian literature that still survives. Arabic is the third
language after Latin and Greek. Nevertheless, whether it is or
not, there is a great deal still to be done to edit, to publish, and
to comment on. [12]

Arab Renewal

The *Dhimma* had many undesirable features. Certainly the
leaders of the Christian communities became very involved in
worldly affairs, in running courts, in administering the various
aspects of law that fell to them in terms of their own communities
and this still happens. When opportunities were given to them
to be equal citizens under the Ottomans, many of them didn't
want this because they were quite happy with the way things
were. This is not just a matter of historical interest but also of
interest today. For example, in Egypt, will there be a tradition of

one law for all, of equality for all before the law, or will we sink back into a situation where the Muslims had the *Sharī'a* and the Christians are allowed their own law and no common identity of citizenship therefore emerges? This is a lively question in Egypt and other countries today.

After the *Tanzimat* were published at the beginning of the *Nahḍa* (or renaissance), the first *Nahda* of Arab nationalism, what role did the Christian Arabs play? Bishop Kenneth Cragg in his very interesting and influential book called *The Arab Christian* points out that, for one reason or another, the Christian Arab communities played a disproportionate part in the leadership of the *Nahḍa,* and in the articulation of the concept of Arab nationalism. He mentions a number of people: Constantine Zurayq, Farah Autun, Butros Ghali (the ancestor of the present Eyptian politician Butros-Butros Ghali) and Michel Aflak, the founder of the Ba'ath party. This is perhaps the reason why Arab nationalism, whilst it recognised Islam as one of the products of the Arab genius, did not over-emphasise the role of Islam. It took culture, language and history much more seriously.[13] The demise of nationalism and the rise of Islamism which has led to the difficulties we are familiar with have to be discussed: why did Arab nationalism decline and why did a different vision begin to replace it, and are we now on the verge of new kinds of nationalism?

In the light of all of this, what we have to say to those who are involved in the emergence of leadership in the churches of the Middle East is, first of all, that the tradition points us to a deep engagement with the Bible, that the formation of leaders must be biblical and the school of Antioch gives us the biblical, spiritual and historical resources that we need for such a renewal of biblical leadership.

Secondly, the spiritual: that the inheritance of these churches is not so much to be found in the hierarchies and the formal structure, but in the monasteries. This is from where the renewal of the church will come and, as far as the Coptic Orthodox church in Egypt is concerned, it is how it has happened. It was the renewal of the monasteries that brought renewal of the Coptic church in so many parts of Egypt and overseas as well.

It also has to be historical, that is to say it has to be engaged with the questions that history has left with the Christian communities in the Middle East, and which need now to be addressed and to be resolved. In this connection some Palestinian theologians have done very useful work on the nature of this engagement, including how it can most constructively take place. Many of them, and some foreign observers, mention the importance of indigenisation, inculturation and contextualisation and we turn to these next.

Indigenisation, Inculturation and Contextualisation

Middle Eastern church leaders sometimes express surprise at those talking about the Middle East and their ignorance of an indigenous church and indigenous leadership. This is very often true, but it is also true, in some parts of the Middle East, that the indigenous churches are not truly indigenous. Their leadership is not indigenous, the way in which money is received and spent and accounted for is not indigenous, and this has led generally to a spiritual crisis in some of these churches which is very dangerous for their future. *Indigenisation* must include addressing all of those issues, but it must also be about the involvement of women and men in the life of the church, whatever you decide about the present and future ministry of women. Indigenisation cannot mean simply the indigenisation of the hierarchy; it must be wider than that if there is to be true renewal in the church. It includes what role clergy and laity should play together, what structure should be produced for them to interact fruitfully together in some churches in Palestine, perhaps some of the biggest churches. A great alienation has to be overcome between the laity and the clergy because of the lack of indigenisation.

Secondly, there is the question of *inculturation*. In one sense, as has been said again and again, these churches are churches of the land; they use the language of the people or at least the language that used to be of the people. Nevertheless, the question of inculturation remains important in terms of how worship and witness is to be expressed in the culture today, not yesterday or the day before yesterday. In this some very good work has been done by Middle Eastern Christians themselves. I am thinking, for instance, of the work early in the 20th century by Abraham Rihbany, *The Syrian Christ*. Dr Kenneth Bailey (although the name sounds American – and, of course, he is an American – he is actually more Middle Eastern than many people within the Middle East) has shown how crucial it is to our understanding of the Bible that we take the culture in the Middle East seriously. Without taking account of the culture of the Middle East, past and present, we cannot truly in fact understand the Bible itself. And then most recently the Syrian follower of Christ, as he refers to himself, Mazhar Mallouhi, who has given his lifetime to publishing the Gospels and other parts of the Bible in a way that Muslims understand. So his Eastern reading of St. Luke's Gospel, for example, is very widely admired in the Muslim world, and he has now published a *Ṣūfī* reading of St. John's Gospel, a very fine attempt at reading St. John's Gospel through *Ṣūfī* eyes. That is just one example of inculturation, but there are many others.

Thirdly, *contextualisation*; and I distinguish inculturation from contextualisation because I think contextualisation is more about the political, the social and the economic contexts in which people live, rather than the traditional culture which makes up their spiritual and moral values. In the Palestinian cultures, the attempt at contextualisation must take into account the situation in which the Palestinian people find themselves, a situation of not only great destruction but of great deprivation for them, having lost their traditional homes and their lands, sometimes finding themselves as refugees in their own land, and sometimes refugees outside their land. All of this must be taken into account in any attempt to contextualise the Christian faith into their own situation.

Liberation Justice and Mercy

Canon Naim Ateek, the Director of the Sabeel Ecumenical Centre, has tried to do this in his book *Justice and Only Justice,* and in his other work. It is true of course that the trajectory of liberation that he identifies must be one that the Palestinian people read from the Bible. I can't see how a people like them can read the Bible without taking the story of Exodus in the way that Ateek takes it. But liberation, he makes quite clear, has to follow the recognition of justice both by those who have oppressed the Palestinian people, and the Palestinian people themselves. Justice is a central category in the Bible not only in terms of justice between one human being and another, but justice as something that shows us what God is like; divine justice is where we get our notions of justice.

Nevertheless, I have been very interested to know that Ateek does not only talk about justice but he also goes on to mercy. This is very important to say, particularly in Muslim contexts where *Sharī'a* has such an important influence. Mercy of course for Palestinians, but Ateek actually goes further and says mercy also for the Jews. He identifies the Holocaust as something that must be taken into account by the Palestinians, as something that has happened to the Jews for which they deserve mercy and, therefore, hospitality. They deserve a place in the land, not at the expense of justice for the Palestinians but because justice and mercy stand together. The only point that I will add to what Ateek says is that mercy is not simply because of the Holocaust but it is also because of how the Jewish people were treated in the Islamic world. That is a very important point to make. In Baghdad in 1948 approximately 20% of the population were Jews, and the same can be said of Egypt, of Syria, of Yemen and so forth, and where are they all now? So, with Ateek we can say liberation, justice and mercy should be aspects of a Middle Eastern contextualisation of the Gospel for our time.[14]

Forming Leaders Today

How is the formation of leadership to be organised today in the Middle East? I am involved very much in this and it seems to me that in some places it is not possible to do this conventionally. In Iran, for instance, all the Church's property was confiscated, so to have a residential facility, like the Alexandria School of Theology, is no longer possible. The only way in which it can be done is through theological education by extension. But that may be something again that is a divine overruling; that what we see as a misfortune for a church may actually turn out to be an opportunity for training people very much in the place where they are contextually, and lay people as well as clergy, so that theological education does not remain an interest for a small group of people but becomes much more widespread than that. One of the things that the Iranian government has recently given permission to church leaders in Iran for is a centre for interfaith dialogue. They said to me: "What is a centre for interfaith dialogue?" and I said, it is whatever you make it. Whatever you do you can always be taken truthfully as preparing people for interfaith dialogue because that is the context in which they live.

Where there are residential facilities and more conventional theological education, we have to re-shape theological education so that it takes the Islamic milieu seriously and is not simply imported methodology from the West. So many of our seminaries and theological colleges have simply taken what the West was doing before the Second World War, and carried on with it. That never was appropriate and it certainly is not today. This situation is now seriously being addressed in countries like Egypt and Pakistan. The result will surely be pastors, evangelists and teachers who are truly grounded in the culture and context.

Next, we come to a system of mentoring. I came across this in Central Asia actually, in the mainly Muslim former Soviet republics. The system of mentoring is important there because the churches grew so rapidly, and the people who became the pastors of these churches were not really theologically educated (and not educated at all in many cases). So what was developed was a system of people, in this case, going in from outside (but not always from the West) and mentoring these new pastors so that they grew in the job that they were doing. This needs to happen on a much wider scale in the region.

We have seen how leadership has been exercised in the tumultuous history of the churches in the Middle East, how people have reflected theologically on their situation, what they have given the world-wide Church and what needs to be done if there is to be effective leadership in these churches today. Such leadership is crucial for the future of these churches and for Christians in their own lands, in relationship with the worldwide church.

Notes

[1] Henry Hill (ed), *Light from the East: A Symposium on the Oriental Orthodox and Assyrian Churches,* Toronto, Anglican Book Centre, 1988; Iris H. El Masry, *Introduction to the Coptic Church,* Dar El Alam El Arabi, 1977, pp20f; Shawky F. Karas, *The Copts since the Arab Invasion: Strangers in their Land,* Jersey City NJ, 1986.

[2] On this, see Robert D. Sider, *The Gospel and its Proclamation: Message of the Fathers of the Church,* Washington, Delaware, 1983.

[3] *Faith, Reason and the University: Lecture of the Holy Father at Regensberg,* Vatican Library, 2006; Benedicta Ward SLG, *The Sayings of the Desert Fathers,* London, Mowbray, 1981 and Laura Swan, *The Forgotten Desert Mothers,* New York, Paulist Press, 2001.

[4] See further Henry Chadwick, *The Early Church,* Harmondsworth, Penguin, 1969, pp184ff and Robert B. Eno, SS, *Teaching Authority in the Early Church: Message of the Fathers of the Church,* Wilmington, Del, Michael Glazier, 1984, pp77ff, 103ff.

[5] For the detail see Bat Ye'or, *The Dhimmi: Jews and Christians under Islam,* London, Associated University Presses, 1985.

[6] Kenneth Cragg, *The Arab Christian: A History in the Middle East,* London, Mowbray, pp141ff.

[7] Gaudeul, *Encounters & Clashes: Islam and Christianity in History,* 2 Vols,

Rome, Pontifical Institute for Study of Arabic and Islam, 1984; D.J. Sahas, *John of Damascus on Islam,* Leiden, Brill, 1972.

[8] William Young, *Patriarch, Shah and Caliph,* Rawalpindi, Christian Study Centre, pp197ff.

[9] Margaret Smith, *Studies in Early Mysticism in the Near and Middle East,* UK, Kessinger, and, Muhammad Iqbal, *The Development of Metaphysics in Persia,* Lahore, Bazm-i-Iqbal, 1964, pp76ff and Tarif Khalidi, *The Muslim Jesus,* Cambridge, Mass, Harvard University Press, 2001.

[10] For further information, see Michael Nazir-Ali, *Conviction and Conflict: Islam, Christianity and World Order,* London, Continuum, 2006, pp69f.

[11] See Thomas E. Burman, *Tathlīth Al-Wahdāhīyah,* in John Toolan (ed), *Medieval Christian Perceptions of Islam,* New York, Routledge, 2000, pp109ff.

[12] Kenneth Bailey, *Poet and Peasant and through Peasant Eyes: A Literary-cultural Approach to the Parables of Luke,* Grand Rapids, Eerdmans, 1976 and *Jesus Through Middle Eastern Eyes: Cultural Studies in the Gospels,* London SPCK, 2008.

[13] *The Arab Christian,* op.cit., pp153ff.

[14] *Justice, and only Justice: A Palestinian Theology of Liberation,* Maryknoll, NY, Orbis, 1989.

Part Five

CHURCH IN CRISIS

Whilst global Pentecostalism booms and independency emerges, especially in Africa, as a force to be reckoned with, the mainline denominations are facing a crisis, not only of numerical decline, but of faith and morals which may prove to be terminal. The Anglican Communion, and particularly its member churches in the West, is an example of this situation.

There are numerous factors which have led us to where we find ourselves, but chief among them has been the attitude to the Bible. Rather than a respectful reading of a privileged text, bearing witness to God's mighty acts, we have had a 'hermeneutic of suspicion' of reading against the 'grain' of the text, of seeking to deconstruct it and to reduce its relevance for us. Those who wish to read it in its plain and canonical sense, mindful of the Church's historic and consensual reading, and yet also to respond to its invitation to explore all of its depths, are labelled 'fundamentalists' or 'literalists'. Such attitudes, naturally, lead to a crisis of confidence in the very foundations of the faith. This can be especially true of those in ministry whose training may have taught them to deconstruct the biblical text, but who have been given nothing by way of reconstruction so that they have little to preach about.

There has also been an emphasis on the individual, on autonomy, rather than interdependence and this has led to a weak understanding of the Church, in its different manifestations, and in the authority of the community to which the Christian must pay close attention, rather than constantly seeking to reinvent the wheel.

Buying into a false, progressivist anthropology has led to a baptising of things as they are, to an emphasis on acceptance and inclusion and to an overly optimistic view of cultural change as tending to be for the better. A more realistic view would have taken more seriously what is wrong with human nature and how it can be put right by the coming of the Gospel.

The following chapters attempt to diagnose the disease and also to discover what steps need to be taken to find a cure and to reverse the direction towards decline, fragmentation and ultimately, death. I believe that faithful, biblical and historic Anglicanism still has a place in God's purposes. Our task is to restore it to its proper place so that, once again, it can bear effective witness to the good news of Jesus Christ, as it has received it.

23

THE NATURE AND FUTURE OF
THE ANGLICAN COMMUNION

It is a great privilege indeed to be part of this miracle of the renewal of Anglican Christians through the Global South, GAFCON and other orthodox movements. It really is a miracle how many people have tried to prevent it but it has not been prevented because it is part of God's purposes for our Church. And it is about those purposes that I wish to speak - the nature and the future of the Anglican Communion. And indeed the one belongs to the other. The future of the Anglican Communion is to be found in its authentic nature, not recently invented innovations and explanations, but what actually belongs to the Church as we have always known it.

So let us first think about the Church and the churches. The New Testament speaks of the Church, as you know, in many different ways. There is the church of the household: of Priscilla and Aquila, of Nympha, of Lydia – how many women there have you noticed? Of the church at Troas – again, the church of the household and we know that the household in New Testament times was not the nuclear family of the West. It was rather like the family that many of us know but extended with servants and employees and all sorts of other hangers-on. The church of the household is very important in the New Testament. It is the church of those who are in some way like one another. It has to do with likeness or homogeneity.[1]

But then there is another way in which the New Testament

speaks of church, and that is of the church in a particular city or town – Ephesus, Corinth, Rome, Antioch or Jerusalem. This is where people who are unlike one another come together. So if you read the instruction about the supper of the Lord in 1 Corinthians 11 or, indeed, about the Christian assembly in James 2, it is about the rich and the poor, the old and the young; in 1 Peter 5 and in Galatians 3, men and women, Jew and Gentile, all having come together to get on with one another in service to the Lord. There is the church of the household, the church in a particular city or town, and then the church in an area or region. Much of the New Testament is addressed to the church in a particular area, whether it's Galatia, or Asia, or the churches in Judea or Macedonia, wherever it may be. Finally, there's the worldwide Church of God which is described by St. Paul in the letter to the Galatians as 'Jerusalem our mother that is above' and, in the letter to the Colossians and the Ephesians, as the body of which Christ is the head. The worldwide Church is the church from which all our churches derive, and to which we have to remain faithful, and all our churches also make up that worldwide Church of God throughout all the ages and everywhere in the world.[2]

Now what, you say, has this to do with Anglicans? Well, at the Anglican Reformation the Church was expressed in two main ways. There was the parish church, which had a responsibility for everyone in the community. So the church was incarnate in every community with a ministry to every person and every home. Then there was the idea of the national church. At that time Western Europe was coming to a sense of people being in nation states and so it was natural that the life of the church should also be expressed in that way, as a national church. What about the church of the household? Well, perhaps it survived in the family – family prayers, being Christian in the family, passing on the faith, that sort of thing. And Callum Brown has rightly said, I think, that the demise of Christianity as a public religion in Britain dates from the time when it ceased to be passed on in the family, from the parents. Don't blame anyone else. Of course, the national church reflects to some extent the provincial idea already found in germ in the New Testament in the churches addressed in a particular region, and also promoted by the churches of Africa, and by Cyprian in his relationship with Rome and the other churches.[3]

The idea of the Church as being a universal reality certainly suffered at the Reformation. But it survived in three main ways. First, it survived in the appeal to Scripture. That is to say, every church to determine its authenticity needs to appeal to Scripture as the final authority. Secondly, it survived in the universal appeal to antiquity; the Church of England was not doing anything new but was simply continuing with the ancient church of the Fathers and the Councils. And thirdly, it survived in the hope of a general Council which might gather together to settle differences among Christians (we mustn't forget that there were Protestants at the Council of Trent, even if the differences could not be reconciled at the time).

We are facing a changing situation where people want to be "church" with those who are like them. We find this in Africa, with people wanting to be church in the context of their own tribes. We find it in Asia, and now we find it with the affinity model churches, the network churches for instance, or the virtual churches in the Northern Hemisphere. And that will no doubt spread to the south as well. I used to be quite hostile to people wanting to be church with others who are like them because it could encourage caste-based churches; it could encourage people from one religious background who become Christians to want to stick with one another. But looking at the church of the household and the idea that it is possible for people who are like one another to be church has led me to modify my views a little. I now feel that it is permissible for people to be churches in this sort of way, networked in terms of their profession or their leisure or where they live or whatever else you can think of – their expertise in IT, for instance.[4]

But there is one condition, and that is that this cannot be the only way of being church. If you want to be church with those who are like you, you also have to be church with those who are unlike you. You have to maintain that tension which is found in the New Testament between the church of the household and the church set in the wider community. The emergence under God of the Anglican Communion as a fellowship of churches has raised again for us now, in a very sharp way, the question of universality. How do we make the universal church an effective fellowship of believers and of churches? Historically the various instruments have developed to do this: Lambeth Conference, the office of the Archbishop of Canterbury, the Primates' Meeting, and the Anglican Consultative Council. But in the crisis that is facing us at this time we have found these not to be enough because, in the end, they were based on English good manners of restraint and mutual consultation. And we have found that in our world, English good manners are simply not enough. So we have to find another way while respecting the need for good manners. So, there is the Church and the churches, and secondly, communication and culture. Professor Lamin Sanneh is perhaps the greatest authority on the relationship between the communication of the Gospel and culture in our generation. His work on the translatability of the Gospel reflected on the translation of the Bible into African languages and the impact that translation had had on African societies, an impact which those who actually did the translation could not have foreseen. But he has pointed out that the question about translatability is not just about the translation of the Bible into different languages, valuable as that is, but it has to do with the nature of the Christian faith itself. That is to say that the good news of Jesus Christ is intrinsically translatable from one culture to another. And he points out that even the fact that the New Testament was first written in Greek and not in the Aramaic or the Hebrew of Jesus' time, is itself a fact of translation. You begin with translation.[5] It was not for another 100 years or so that the New Testament was translated back into Syriac or Aramaic. This is in contrast to other worldwide religions like Islam. Islam is also universal; you'll find it in many different parts of the world. But wherever you go, and whatever the local manifestations, there is a certain 'Arabicness' about the Qur'ān, about the prayer, about the call to prayer, which cannot be translated. But the Gospel can be, and has been throughout the ages.

Pope Benedict in his very important address at Regensburg, which drew attention because of what he said about the relationship between Christians and Muslims, addressed the question of the relationship between Gospel and culture - perhaps a more important aspect of the lecture. In this lecture, Pope Benedict said that there was a providential encounter between the Gospel and Hellenistic culture which provided the Church with the vocabulary to engage with the Hellenistic world. And he refers to the vision that St. Paul received of people calling him to Macedonia, of the vocation to Europe, therefore, as one aspect of this providential encounter. I doubt personally whether Acts 16 will bear the sort of weight that he puts on it, but we can agree that the encounter was providential and, at the same time, that there were many other encounters going on.[6]

I have for long been interested in the story of the church in the Persian Empire, the other great superpower besides Rome at that time. It's a very similar history.[7] Armenia was the first country, the first nation, to call itself Christian. Ethiopia became a huge Christian empire at about the time of the rise of Islam. And no one can accuse the Ethiopian church of Hellenism! So, there have been all these providential encounters and we thank God for them, and we have to ask what lessons we can learn from them for ourselves today. When we consider the Anglican situation, the translation of the Bible by William Tyndale into English is a landmark not only in the story of the English church but of the English nation and of the English language.[8] It is impossible to think of a Shakespeare or a Milton or a Donne without a Tyndale. And the translation, the rendering into the vernacular of the liturgy of the Book of Common Prayer, of worship in a language understood by the people, is all part of this process of translation. This is wealth that we cannot easily give up – translatability belongs to the very nature of Anglicanism.

In the preface to the Book of Common Prayer, and the Articles of Religion, it is said that every church has a responsibility to render the Good News in terms of its culture. There is, of course, a downside to this, and that is that it is possible for the Gospel to become so identified with a particular culture that it becomes captive to it. And Anglicanism has been exposed to this danger of capitulation to culture from the very beginning. Wherever we are, in whatever culture we find ourselves, we must be aware of this danger of captivity and capitulation.[9] Moreover, while our foundational documents may speak of relating the Gospel to culture, we have in fact often failed to do so. And so Anglican Christian churches have not been able to look at African or Asian or South American culture in the way that they should.

That brings me then to the question of constancy and change. What is it in this situation of flux that must remain constant? It is to my mind the passing on, and the receiving and the passing on again, of the apostolic teaching. That is how the Church lives, that is how the Church derives its strength and that is how the Church grows. In every culture, in every age, people notice things in that apostolic teaching which others have not noticed or which have been forgotten, or neglected, and so this or that aspect of the apostolic teaching can be recovered. It should not surprise us, therefore, that slaves in America rediscovered the liberation trajectory in the Bible or that women are today rediscovering what the Bible says about the proper role for women in the Church and in the world. For many years I worked with the Human Fertilization and Embryology Authority as Chair of its Ethics and Law Committee. This brought me into contact with a body of new knowledge that I had to make sense of. It is also true, then, that the Church is faced with new knowledge, so how do we relate the unchanging apostolic teaching to new knowledge? We now know far more about the early embryo, for instance, than people did fifty years ago, or even thirty years ago, and so we must have a healthy view of relating this apostolic teaching to change; there must be the possibility of development in terms of our doctrine. However, what I would want to say is that this development has to be principled. As John Henry Newman pointed out in his thinking on this issue, any development of this kind must have a conservative action on the past. It must conserve the vigour of the Gospel, it must represent a continuity of principles, and it must provide a basis for change that is not simply laxity and 'giving in'.[10]

When any question arises as to whether something is an authentic expression of the apostolic teaching or not, in such changing circumstances, we have to test it against the Bible, because the Bible is the norm by which we appreciate what is authentically apostolic. That is the reason for the Bible being the ultimate final authority for us in our faith and our life, and this is the reason Anglicans have taken the study of the Bible so seriously.

You study something because you regard it as important, not because you regard it as unimportant. In study there are a number of aspects to it, to which I want to draw your attention. The first is the study of what lies *behind* the text. Why was a particular text put together? What were the purposes of those who were writing it? What were the oral traditions that lay behind it? We are all used to studying the Bible in that way. We study what is behind the text, what is *in* the text, the grammar, the literary value of the books of the Bible, and then what is *in front* of the text. That is, how we relate the Bible to our circumstances, our culture, our context, our situation. This process of inculturation must go on, but there are two important things to be said about it.

First of all, there are limits to this process. They can't just take place anyhow. And the limits have to do first of all with the nature of the Gospel itself. Whatever the process of inculturation does or does not do, it cannot compromise how God has revealed his purposes to us, how Jesus Christ has come in the flesh, what he has done, who he is – all of that cannot be obscured by the process of inculturation.

Secondly, the process should not in any way impair the fellowship that there is between Christians. So my inculturation cannot be such that you fail to recognise the authentic Gospel in my church, and vice versa. We can talk about inculturation also in terms of rendering the mind of Christ, or the mind of the Scriptures, in terms of a particular culture or people, to make something intelligible to people, inspiring for them, authoritative for them, so that they may live their lives by it.

And so we come to the question of how fellowship is maintained – how it is enhanced and not impaired, and to the question of communion and conflict. Unity is a very precious thing indeed. What a good and joyful thing it is when brothers and sisters live together in unity, the Bible tells us. And we must seek to maintain that unity and that peace which builds unity. And there must be unity in diversity. We are not all the same. We are all different. You remember the story about the great Archbishop of Cape Town, who was a single man and very shy, who was asked to address the Mothers' Union. So when he got up to speak he wanted to put the Mothers' Union at ease - and also himself so, he said, "Ladies, I would like you to know that beneath this cassock you and I are exactly the same!"

But it's not like that, is it? We are all different, and this unity is a unity in diversity. It has to be – and this is something that is a matter for discussion – it has to be legitimate diversity, not just any kind of diversity. I asked John Stott once, "You told us many years ago to stay in the Anglican Church because it is comprehensive. What do you say now?" He said, "I've always believed in principled comprehensiveness." And that is another good phrase, 'principled comprehensiveness'. William Reed Huntington, the American Episcopalian theologian – and yes there were some, and I hope there are some still – distinguished between what he called the Anglican principle and what he called the Anglican system. Well, the Anglican system we're all aware of: spires and fluttering surplices and choirs singing, archdeacons and, you might say, bishops! If that's the system, what's the principle? It is the responsibility and the privilege of the local church to be, and become, the catholic church in that place and that means every local church. But Huntington was a good enough ecumenist in his day in the 19th Century to know that the local church could not be the catholic church in its place without being in relationship with all the other local churches. He anticipated the World Council of Churches' New Delhi Statement by about 100 years. How then is local church to be the catholic church in relationship with all other local churches so they can also be the catholic church in that place? That is the question.[11]

Huntington, attempted to answer this by developing what has now come to be called the Chicago-Lambeth Quadrilateral. That is to say, there were at least four things that were necessary for us to recognise the church in one another: the supreme authority of the Scriptures, the Catholic Creeds, the Sacraments instituted by Christ himself, and the historic ministry of the church. And that Quadrilateral has been hugely important in Anglican discussion with other Christians. Many of the plans for church union, not least in India, Pakistan, and Ceylon, as it was then, could not have been conceived without the Quadrilateral playing a major part in this.[12]

But apart from it being significant ecumenically, it was also good shorthand for Anglican identity. Anglicans have tended to say when people ask the often justifiable question "What are you about?": "This is what we're about: the Quadrilateral". But again, the Quadrilateral has not proved enough in our circumstances. I have spoken already about the instruments of communion, of the necessity of why they arose, and of their inadequacy now.[13]

So what else do we need to do to make sure that we continue to live in communion and do not perpetuate conflict that is unnecessary in the church? I do believe there are some things that need attention. The first is that we have to be clear we are a *confessing* church. Some people have the mistaken idea that Anglicans can believe anything – or sometimes even that Anglicans believe nothing. I don't know which is more serious. We have to be clear that we are a confessing church articulating the Gospel in terms of our own tradition. Secondly, to be a confessing church effectively we need to be a *conciliar* church. That is to say we need to have councils at every level, including worldwide, that are authoritative, and that can make decisions that stick. In the last few years I've been frustrated by decision after decision after decision that has not stuck, and we cannot have this for the future for a healthy church. And then thirdly, we need to be in our councils *consistorial*. That is to say the councils themselves, or through their representatives, need to exercise the authority of a teaching office. In particular circumstances – not every day, nor promiscuously, but in particular circumstances – the faith has to be articulated clearly for the sake of people's spiritual health and for the sake of mission.

There is both the need for continuity and the need to recognise context. Successive Lambeth conferences have said that the Anglican Church is willing to disappear in the cause of the greater unity of Christ's church, to make that sacrifice. We should continue to affirm that. If it is necessary for the Anglican Communion to die so the Gospel may live then so be it. [14] But before we jump to too many conclusions about this, we have also to acknowledge there are things in the Anglican tradition that we can offer as a service and as a gift to the worldwide church: the vernacular liturgy and its beauty, the way in which we think theologically, the way in which the people are formed, the musical traditions of the church, the way in which catholic order has been expressed, particularly in an Anglican form. We would not like to lose these things, but to offer them to the wider church as indeed we have done ecumenically for the last 100 years or more. [15]

But there is also the context. And whilst we value the continuity, we also have to be clear that the church and its life needs to be expressed effectively in a plural world, in a globalised world, where private deals cannot carry credibility indefinitely and where we have to be clear with our neighbours what Gospel it is that we have. People quickly rumble what we are trying to do, if we're trying to deceive them with something that is not the Gospel of Christ. So continuity and a changing context have to be held together.

And then, finally, to the commission and the coming days. If we are about anything we should be about mission – the

Great Commission and its continuing validity for the church. A journalist rang me up the other day and he asked, "Bishop, do you believe in witnessing to people of other faiths?" I said, "Of course I do". He said, "Does that include Muslims?", and I said, "Of course it does". And the headline the next day was "Bishop wants to convert Muslims"! Well fair enough, though that's not the only thing I want to do with Muslims; there is, for example, service and dialogue. But I have an obligation – an obligation to witness to all that God has done in Jesus Christ for me, for you, for the world, even for Muslims – praise the Lord – and I am not apologetic about it.

The Great Commission has to be carried out in every context, and perhaps the greatest challenge we have is that of militant secularism, which is creating a double jeopardy for Western cultures; the West is losing the Christian discourse at the very time when it needs it most. Well, let us pray that we are able to recover our Christian nerve in the West, and to make sure that the Gospel is not lost. All that is of value, of positive value, in Western culture largely depends on its Judeo-Christian heritage and this will serve as a way of enhancing and prospering persons and communities and renewing them once again.

But in every context mission remains important as we seek to serve people, as we are present with them, as we identify with them, as we challenge them, as we have dialogue with them. But this mission has to take place from within movements of renewal. One of the things we really need to be aware of is the over-institutionalising of the Church because it is that which has led to this present crisis. People are in love with the institution and the structures of the Church rather than the Lord himself.

There have been in Christian history moments of renewal, e.g. the monastic movement; when the Church had become lax and corrupt and rich, the monks went out into the deserts of Egypt, Syria and Mesopotamia to purify and to renew the Church. What a great renewal that was! Pope Benedict said at Regensburg that important things in Christian history had happened in Europe except, for some significant developments in the East. Well, one of them was monasticism which Athanasius, when he came to exile in the West, brought with him. Another example is the great missionary societies, notably, the Church Mission Society (CMS), of which I was the General Secretary, and which was formed over 200 years ago. It took the Archbishop of Canterbury two years to even reply to their letter asking for permission to be set up. But that did not prevent God's work, and CMS, under God's providence, was responsible for so many who are upholding the faith within the Anglican Communion. Today also we seek such movements of renewal for the sake of mission and, if the present unrest leads to a renewal of mission-mindedness in our churches, then the pain and the sacrifices will have been worth it.

Notes

[1] See further R. Campbell, *The Elders: Seniority within Earliest Christianity*, Edinburgh, T & T Clark, 1994.

[2] On all of this, see the discussion in *The Church as Communion*, Rome, Congregation for the Doctrine of the Faith, 1992.

[3] In Robert B. Eno, SS, *Teaching Authority in the Early Church (Message of the Fathers of the Church)*, 14, Wilmington, Delaware, Michael Glazier, 1984, pp 84ff.

[4] See further *The Pasadena Consultation – Homogenous Unit Principle*, Wheaton, IL, Lausanne Committee, 1978.

[5] Lamin Sanneh, *Translating the Message: The Missionary Impact on Culture*, Maryknoll, NY, Orbis, 1989 and 2009.

[6] Benedict XVI, *Faith, Reason and the University: Memories and Reflections*, Vatican Library, 2006.

[7] See William Young, *Patriarch, Shah and Caliph*, Rawalpindi, Christian Study Centre, 1974.

[8] Brian Moynahan, *William Tyndale: If God Spare My Life*, London, Abacus, 2002.

[9] On this see particularly, Ephraim Radner and Philip Turner, *The Fate of Communion, the Agony of Anglicanism and the Future of a Global Church*, Grand Rapids, Eerdmans, 2006.

[10] J. H. Newman, *An Essay on the Development of Christian Doctrine*, Notre Dame, Indiana, University of Notre Dame Press, 2010.

[11] William Reed Huntington, *The Church-Idea: An Essay towards Unity*, 4th Edn, New York, Charles Scribner's Sons, 1899.

[12] See W. J. Marshall, *Faith and Order in the North India/Pakistan Unity Plan*, London, 1978

[13] See the debate in Robert Wright (ed), *Quadrilateral at One Hundred*, Cincinnati Ohio, Forward Movement, 1988.

[14] *An Appeal to all Christian People*, Lambeth Conference, 1920 and the 1930 Conference's Encyclical in Gillian Evans and Robert Wright (eds), *The Anglican Tradition: A Handbook of Sources*, London, SPCK, 1991, pp 377, 389f and *The Emmaus Report: Anglican Ecumenical Consultation 1987*, London, ACC, 1987, pp 9ff.

[15] *An Appeal to all Christian People*, Lambeth Conference, 1920 and the 1930 Conference's Encyclical in Gillian Evans and Robert Wright (eds).

24

JESUS, LORD OF HIS CHURCH AND
OF THE CHURCH'S MISSION

I want to put before you three very short passages from the letter to the Ephesians, which is a companion letter to Colossians. There are many similarities in thought and in context, and in even the people to whom these letters are addressed.[1]

The first passage is from Ephesians 2:19–21, which speaks of the Church as the household of God, built upon the foundation of the apostles and prophets, Christ Jesus himself being the key cornerstone (or perhaps it could be *capstone*), in whom the full structure (perhaps it could be *every building*) is joined together and grows into a holy temple in the Lord.

So the Church is built on the foundation of the apostolic testimony, mission and teaching. Some people may think that this contradicts what the Apostle had said in 1 Corinthians 3:11 that it was Jesus Christ who is the foundation, but actually there is no contradiction because the apostolic testimony itself is about Jesus. The apostolic testimony by the work of the Spirit points always to Jesus, reminds the Church of Jesus, glorifies Jesus, brings to our mind all that Jesus has done, and said, and is. 'The foundation of the apostles and prophets, Christ Jesus himself being the cornerstone....' Now the cornerstone is what aligns the whole wall, as it were each brick to another. That is one understanding of the word that is used here – a very rare word by the way – or it may mean *capstone*, the capstone of the pillars; that's the other sense in which the Greek translators of the Old Testament, the Septuagint, use the word; something that caps what has already been put together. So Jesus Christ, I think we can say fairly, is both foundation and capstone: the beginning and the end, Alpha and Omega.

The second passage that I had in mind is from Ephesians 1:23. It is quite an amazing statement about the Church, and it says about Jesus that "God has put all things under his feet and has made him the Head over all things for the Church, which is his Body, the fullness of him who fills all in all".

So Jesus Christ is the head of the church in all things, not just in spiritual matters, not just in matters of doctrine or worship, but in everything he is the Head of the Church. There is no 'vacancy' for such a Head – that is always, eternally filled – because Jesus is the Head of the Church and we cannot, therefore, look to merely human authority, to human rulers, as claiming any part of that Headship. I think it is very important for Anglicans to understand this, and that I, as someone who has been a diocesan bishop in the Church of England, say it. The other point here is that however we might interpret *plērōma* or 'fullness', the Church is seen as sharing in the fullness which is properly Christ's.

The third passage that I had in mind about the Church in this wonderful letter is from Ephesians 3:11, where the Apostle says that it is "through the Church that the manifold wisdom of God is made known to the principalities and the powers...." Through the Church God's wisdom is made known to the 'principalities and powers', and what are they? They are the assumptions and the prejudices and the principles by which human institutions and indeed the supernatural world are ordered and governed, or perhaps we can say disordered as well. To say that through the Church God's wisdom is made known is to declare, in the highest sense, the Church's mission: to make known God's message, to speak truth to power.

Now when we read these exalted statements about the Church, naturally we ask: to what or to whom does this apply? And there are several senses of the word 'church', both in these letters and more generally, that I wish to draw to your attention. First of all, the Church – elect in Jesus Christ, which has existed from all ages – is God's people throughout the ages and throughout the world as a result of God's gracious purposes for his creation. St. Paul calls this in the letter to the Galatians 4:26 "Jerusalem our mother which is above". That is the Church that is meant, not simply a human institution, but of and from the divine plan. But St. Paul is very capable of coming down to earth, so in the letter to the Colossians certainly there is this sense of God's eternal purposes being worked out among his people, but there are also references to local churches. St. Paul speaks of the church of God at Corinth, or we might say at Laodicea or Rome or Ephesus or wherever it may be. This is the church, in a particular town or a particular city, as it is gathered together by God's will and the work of the Spirit in the life of the believer. It is a very important manifestation of the Church, and so much of what is said in the New Testament is addressed to churches such as these.

But there is another sense in which the word 'church' is used in the New Testament. In his letters to churches in various towns – Romans, for example, or Colossians – Paul often remembers the church that is in people's homes (Romans 16:5; Colossians 4:15). The early church did often meet anyway all together in someone's home, but I think this usage is different. This means a part of the church in Laodicea that is at Nympha's house, or a part of the Church in Rome which is to be found in Priscilla's and Aquila's home, or part of the church in the home of Lydia or Chloe (it is interesting to see how many women are mentioned in this context). Each of these is properly called God's church. The church in someone's home clearly shares a likeness – people are like one another, it is a family representation – and this also allows us to express church where people are like one another, in interest or profession or ethnicity perhaps, or language. As I said before, I used to be rather hostile to people speaking of the church in this way, where the church is characterised by homogeneity, but I now see from a more careful reading of the New Testament, that there is a valid understanding of the church here that is possible. A church like that of fresh expressions – so many of the fresh expressions in this country are characterised by homogeneity – is fine, but a church like that is not enough. It has to be balanced by other things. One of them is the diversity of the church in the wider community. In the New Testament it is a town: Rome or Ephesus or Corinth or Laodicea, wherever it might be. These churches in the town – I suppose our parishes are not unlike this church – are now characterised not by homogeneity but by diversity. It is here that we note, both in St. Paul and in the Letter of James, instruction given about poor and rich together, for instance, people of different social status. Many of these cities were cosmopolitan centres, with people of different races and languages – Jews, Greeks and others. So when we speak of the church, we have to keep all of this in mind.[2]

When can we say in this situation that the Church of God, that the Church of Christ, is present to a sufficient extent that the Lord is among his people? Article XIX (of the Church of England's 'Articles of Religion'), which is appropriately titled 'Of the Church', says that 'The Church of Christ is a congregation of faithful men in which the pure Word of God is preached and the sacraments duly administered'. I think each of those phrases is important: congregations ('congregation' is nearly a translation of *ekklēsia*) of faithful men, however that may be expressed – in a household or town-wide in a parish church; 'faithfulness' – faithful men, faithful people (that is important), people who have come to know the Lord are people who are committed to the following of Jesus Christ and then in which the pure Word of God is preached. How often we are told here in the Church of England: "Vicar, you are going to keep to seven minutes, aren't you?" I think it is possible to preach the pure Word of God in six or seven minutes, but it is not desirable. And so 'sermonettes lead to Christianettes', as is so often said. The whole counsel of God has to be brought out. 'The pure Word is preached and the sacraments duly ministered, according to Christ's ordinance'. What makes the church is not a sociological understanding of community (though this may be useful to have), not an understanding that relies purely on venerable tradition and place

(I'm not saying those are unimportant), but faithful people, the preaching of the pure Word of God, and the sacraments. Without these things there may be denominations, there may be ancient traditions and churches, but are they any more the church of Christ? Or has the glory departed?

I was once at a very grand assembly of a denomination in the West – let's put it like that. It was very grand, very awe-inspiring. But in the middle of it, I had this sense that they had the form of godliness but not the power thereof (2 Tim 3:5). What makes the Church, that is to say, everything that the Church needs in its ministry – its life together, its preaching, the celebration of the sacraments – comes about because of the nature of the Gospel itself. In other words, how we are church is not different from what the Gospel is. The Gospel produces what is authentically church. This is a lesson we must learn again and again if the *ecclesia* is to be *semper reformanda*. Again and again we should check how we are church against the Gospel, and you would be surprised at how much resistance there is to such an idea in some circles, if you put it forward.

God provides for every church in every place all that the church needs for its ministry and its mission. That's the miracle of the work of God's grace. But it is also true that no church can be fully and wholly the church of Christ in a particular place without being in fellowship with all the other churches of Christ in all the different places. Jerusalem, which is our mother above, is that transcendent reality of the Church in which, by God's grace, we all participate. The local church is gathered together in the presence of the Lord, which is a primary reality of the church, but the relationship between churches – those in Judea and the Gentile churches, for instance, the churches of Macedonia, the churches of Asia – these are also mentioned as somehow participating in the reality of becoming God's people and are, therefore, being 'church'.

At the time of the Reformation some traditions, rightly because of abuse, emphasised the absolute importance of the sacred deposit, the Word of God in Scripture; others emphasised the importance of the sacred ministry. I think that it was something of a miracle in the Anglican Reformation that we were able to keep both together – sacred deposit and sacred ministry – because the Church needs both. We need that deposit of the Word of God once for all given to the saints; but we need also the authentic teachers called and commissioned and empowered by God, to bring that Word alive to our people, to make sure the Word bears fruit in people's lives and to share that Word with the world. The sacred ministry is not on the same level as the sacred deposit. That misunderstanding can be ruled out at once. As is said in the Articles [Article XX], the Church is the keeper of Holy Writ, a witness to it, a steward of it, but always the Church and its ministers are servants of the Word and not its masters.

It is true that we have to bring the lordship of Christ and the sovereignty of his Word to bear on our mission in the world, and this means taking account of the world – and knowledge of the world (philosophy, science if you like, is mentioned in the Letter to the Colossians) – and to make serious attempts at relating God's Word to what the world has known in the past or is coming to know now, and what it may come to know in the future. It means also refuting what falsely claims to be knowledge, whether old or new. Anglicans have been distinguished in trying to relate God's Word to new knowledge, and we must continue to do this. However, we do need to say that revelation is about confirming reason. The priority of revelation must be maintained particularly when it relates, for example, to purpose in our world, to the meaning of creation, to human destiny, to human freedom given by God, and what has gone so wrong because of us.

Any interpretation of the world – of the origins of human life, of the coming of consciousness and self-consciousness – that does not take account of why the world has been made, what it is for, and what our destiny is, must be judged inadequate because it does not fit in with the revelation that God has given us about his purpose for us and our destiny, therefore, in him. If we are going to understand how the Church is and how the Church relates to the world around it, understood in these different ways which I have tried very briefly to explain, what should the Church be doing to be the Church? There are certain things that are absolutely essential for the Church, in every aspect of its manifestation, to be and to do.

First of all, it must be possible for God's people to gather. To be a lone Christian is to be a 'dead' Christian. We must gather together to hear God's Word, to celebrate the sacraments, to learn from one another, to pray for one another – the list is long. Any failure at any level for Christians to gather together around the Gospel is a serious failure and weakens the witness of the Body of Christ. Gathering is so important, but gathering must be, first of all, for the sake of praying. How encouraging it is for us to be able to pray together, to celebrate the Supper of the Lord together. It shouldn't really be remarkable for Christians to celebrate the Lord's Supper together, but in our Communion in recent years it has become a problem. Gathering together, praying together, learning from God's Word and from one another together. The learning has to be not just from one another, not just an affair that has to do with us, however careful the listening and however exalting '*indaba*' might be – I've no personal experience of it – it has to be around God's Word, that is absolutely essential.

And then teaching together. The Church has to say from time to time something about how the world is, what issues are faced by a nation or a community or the world. From time to time, it has to declare what God's Word is saying in this situation or that. The Lambeth Conferences have never been perfect – I have been closely involved with some – but until the last one it was possible for Anglican bishops gathered together in solemn assembly to speak authoritatively about a variety of matters. These included our relations with other churches, what we thought of other faiths, the need for Christian unity, our self-understanding as Anglicans at the 1930 Conference, the coming into being of the Church of South India in 1948, the family in 1958 and, then, in 1998 human sexuality. The Lambeth Conferences were able to say with spiritual and moral authority, even if not legal, what the Church's faith was. But that has become impossible now. This is a serious injury to the Body and an inability to keep together. The keeping together comes about not only as a result of consulting and learning together, but of deciding together. In the 'Appeal to All Christian People' in 1920, the Church decided together – the bishops together decided – on what terms Anglicans would be willing to talk about unity with other Christians, and that became useful not just for Anglicans but for all sorts of other Christians as well. In 1998 the bishops gathered together and, by a huge majority, an overwhelming majority, decided together that they would teach in their own dioceses and provinces what they had discerned to be God's will in terms of human sexual behaviour, knowing how important that is for our life together.

But then there is the will to discipline, which arises out of the common decision-making and the common teaching that the Church is able to declare in the world. There was a big debate at the time of the Reformation about what place discipline should have in the Church, and the Reformers were rightly wary of the excessive discipline of the medieval church. But the Anglican Reformers, as is well set out in the Second Book of Homilies [Book 2, Homily 16 for Whitsunday], make it quite clear that the Anglican tradition is for effective discipline in the Church. It is not that the Church cannot exist without discipline, but that the church's good, the church's spiritual good, comes about through effective discipline in the Body. This ought to be obvious; any institution, even human institutions, cannot function without discipline. How do we expect the Church of God, so diverse, with people from so many different backgrounds and issues and gifts, to function without discipline? This discipline has to be about both right belief and godly life, even when the two can be separated.

If that is the case, what should we be saying about our Anglican Communion today? It has been said already that the so-called 'Instruments of Communion' that have developed over the last fifty years or so have all failed in one way or another. Even the Lambeth Conference, which has existed for a much longer period than that, has been found not to be effective in setting forth the teaching of God's Word as we understand it in the situations that men and women face in their particular contexts. In this I don't think the Instruments can be given artificial respiration and somehow revived. It's been tried, and it may even be worth trying again, but it hasn't worked. I am sad about that, but I think we do need to find new ways of association, of coming together, not just to be 'warm and well-filled', but to do the essential tasks. It was successive Lambeth Conferences up to 2008, but excluding 2008, that said that the heads of the churches, the Primates, have a particular role in maintaining the unity of the Church.[3] Both Lambeth 2008, the Anglican Consultative Council, and the progressive watering down of the Covenant have reduced, almost eliminated, the Primates from this particular role that other Lambeth Conferences were saying it was necessary for them to fulfil. I think that is a tragedy, because at one stroke it has made decision-making impossible. But, in addition to the Primates' meeting – in a way the Primates' meeting arises from what I am going to say next – what we need to be doing is to have a meeting of bishops, clergy and lay people who come together for consultation and for prayer and to identify the issues and the opportunities that we have in our world. They would come together *synodally* (I'm not saying "synodically") with the intention of walking together, walking in the way of the Lord, walking together in God's way for God's work according to God's Word.

But within such a synodal and missional gathering, there must be a gathering of those who have oversight. I'm purposely avoiding the word bishops here, because it would be easy for me to say such a gathering should be a gathering of bishops. Bishops should certainly be included, but I think we've got to move beyond that to a gathering of people who, in addition to the bishops, also exercise one kind of oversight or another. That may be in the formation of people for Christian ministry; it may be people who are rectors of churches that are crucial to the future of our Communion. (Some rectors of churches exercise enormous oversight and have very large staff which can be compared to what happens in a diocese. Why should they be excluded from such a gathering?) It may be leaders in church planting ministries. This will certainly need a reform of *episcopē* in the Church, perhaps even of the episcopate. I know what I am saying is radical, and there will be natural Anglican resistance to it, even in my own mind some resistance, but I think in all fairness I must say it. I believe that associating in these ways will make us more attuned to what actually God is saying to the churches – the local churches, the clusters of churches, you can call them that if you want – and how God wants to glorify His church, the church as she is in His eternal plan and eternal sovereignty.

How do we go about it? I think it is here that movements like GAFCON or the Global South have a splendid opportunity to model this in our own life together as it emerges. That is to say, we do not have to wait forever for non-existent instruments of decision-making to make decisions that they will never make. But how long will this carry on? We have got to start doing this in our own life. So I'm hoping that we will begin to show how the Church is to gather, how to pray together, how to decide together, what to teach and also how we include people and also sometimes sadly have to exclude, for the sake of discipline. Exclusion, by the way, is real in the New Testament but always for the sake of restoration.

How then are we to model what we are commending to the wider church? Practically, I think what this will mean is to have a mechanism that brings together people with oversight. I am quite willing to talk about how that may happen, how difficulties might be overcome, who would be included and who wouldn't or who shouldn't be, and all that can be talked about, but we shouldn't miss this opportunity because, in addition to the bishops, there are other people who can contribute to our gathering, praying, deciding and teaching, which is so important for us. What is more, when they go back to wherever they are exercising oversight they can make it real. We must make sure that this takes place in the wider context of the Church gathered. I've always thought that Acts 15 is a very good example of how the Church should gather. The whole Church gathers, the apostles speak, the apostles and the elders set out what the decisions of the Church are, and then the whole Church sends out the message that it wants to send out to the world.

There must be a wide gathering of fellowship, of listening to God's Word together, of praying together, consulting together, but in that context those with oversight must have a special responsibility for setting out what we believe to be necessary for the future. And the Primates in their meetings will enable us to gather, to do these things and, later on, to implement what decisions have been made.

I am not saying that this should happen as a replacement for the Anglican Communion, but I am saying that this should be a model, a lesson that can be learnt by the wider church.

Finally, we must of course remain a dynamic movement, a movement that is committed to the Jerusalem Declaration.[4] Some structures are necessary even for movements. Living beings move, and there are some very simple living beings that don't have very much of a structure, but a lively, developed and progressive movement needs some structure. However, we must not forget that we are a movement in mission, and this may necessitate the inclusion of some people in our common life who do not belong to the structure, who are not people who are exercising oversight, who are not bishops or Primates or rectors of churches, or principals of theological colleges, but who are leaders in mission.

In my time as a bishop both in Pakistan and England I have emphasised the voluntary principle in the life of the Church. There are some things that the church must do officially, but the growing edge of the Church, the spread of the Gospel, the coming of people to faith, their growth and their nurture in the faith, often comes about from people who have been called to fulfil a particular vocation. Sometimes it means recognition and commissioning by the Church, but sometimes it just goes on, and we have to safeguard this voluntary principle. We must be praying that God will produce, as indeed he has, movements in our Anglican Communion, in our local churches, in our national churches, for bringing people to faith, for renewal in the life of the Church, for leadership in worship. We should not be suspicious of these movements, as if they were harmful for the institutions, but celebrate them as God's gift to us today. Effective leadership – effective *episcope* if you like, exercised by Primates and other bishops – must in the future involve the recognition, enabling and empowering of this voluntary principle. Once again, we can learn from our past.

We can be confident of Christ's lordship in a Church which is faithful to his Word and which seeks to bring this Word to bear on the needs, aspirations, fears and hopes of the world to which it has been sent as an ambassador. Let us humbly, but properly, recover our confidence in the transforming power of God's Word.

Notes

[1] For discussions of the relations between these two letters see C. F. D. Moule, *The Epistles to the Colossians and Philemon,* Cambridge, CUP, 1980. See also Francis Foulkes, *Ephesians,* Leicester, IVP, 1983 and John Muddiman, *The Epistle to the Ephesians,* London, Continuum, 2001.

[2] On all of this, see my *Shapes of the Church to Come,* Eastbourne, Kingsway, 2001, pp71ff.

[3] See, for instance, Res 18 of the 1988 Lambeth Conference in its Report *The Truth Shall Make You Free,* London, ACC, 1988, p216 and Res III: 6 of the 1998 Conference in The Official Report of the Lambeth Conference 1998, Harrisburg, PA, 1999, p396.

[4] As agreed by acclamation at the 1st GAFCON in 2008, see *Being Faithful: the Shape of Historic Anglicanism Today,* London, Latimer, 2009, pp6f.

25

THE ANGLICAN COMMUNION AND
ECUMENICAL RELATIONS

It has often been said that Anglicanism is but an expression of the Western, Latin tradition of Christianity.[1] Indeed, the formularies of the Church of England, the foundation documents of Anglicanism, explicitly lay claim to continuing with the medieval church, where this could be done without endorsing unnecessary accretion and corruption.[2] This continuity was affirmed not only in diverse Primers and Catechisms but also in piety and devotion.[3] There was, however, innovation as well as continuity. If the first Prayer Book reflected continuity with the Old Sarum rite, the second clearly showed the influence of Martin Bucer and other continental reformers. On the one hand, Anglicans like Richard Hooker refused to unchurch Roman Catholics even if they engaged in controversy with them; on the other, they recognised the reformed churches of the continent as truly churches, even though they lacked the three-fold ministry of bishop, priest and deacon.[4]

Although the pattern of theological thought, forms of ministry and of ecclesiastical life in the Church of England remained that of the Western type, the Reformation and its aftermath brought more contact with the Eastern churches. This is shown already in Cranmer's use of the Liturgy of St. Basil in the 1549 Eucharistic rite and in Lancelot Andrewes' borrowing from liturgies of SS Chrysostom and James.[5] Whilst the Articles declare that the Eastern churches have erred, early Anglican theologians, like

Richard Field, are not prepared to unchurch them or to say that they have been deprived of the Gospel of Salvation. Rather, their separation from Rome is evidence that communion with that See cannot be a necessary sign of belonging to the Catholic Church.[6]

The first sustained ecumenical contact with the Orthodox churches came, however, with the Non-Jurors. The Non-Jurors were bishops and clergy who could not conscientiously take the Oaths of Allegiance and of Supremacy to the newly-arrived William and Mary after the Glorious Revolution of 1688, because they had already taken such oaths to the exiled James II. They became, in effect, an *ecclesiola,* surviving in one way or another, for over a hundred years. Because they were a relatively small body, they sought wider fellowship and although, through James, they had contact with Rome, their attention was really focused on the Eastern churches. For nearly ten years they were engaged in negotiations with the various Patriarchs of the Eastern churches, addressing several 'humble supplications' to them and receiving, in reply, some very haughty letters making a number of demands of them.

In the end, the negotiations proved abortive for reasons which bear rehearsal as they have some contemporary significance. The Non-Jurors were mostly High-Church Anglicans who believed the Church to be a spiritual society with its own laws and who emphasised the importance of liturgical worship in the life of the Church. In this, they provide the link between the Caroline divines of the 17th Century and the Tractarians of the 19th. In spite of their High-Church tendencies, they could not accept patriarchal demands that they should put tradition on the same level of authority as the Holy Scriptures. Whilst they honoured Mary the Blessed *Theotokos*, they were afraid of excessive Marian cults in Orthodoxy as much as in Rome. Again, although they believed firmly in the communion of saints, they had scruples about the necessity of invoking them. They readily acknowledged the presence of Christ in the Eucharist but were wary of cults of Eucharistic adoration and, finally, they could not agree to the worship of icons as a matter of faith. To this we might add the grand question, as Hooker puts it, that hangs between Rome and Anglicans: the doctrine of justification by faith alone. The issue was raised by Cyril Lucar, Patriarch of Constantinople in the 17th Century and others within the Orthodox Church. But while Roman Catholic-Lutheran and, to some extent, Anglican-Roman Catholic dialogue has directly tackled this question, it is difficult to find evidence of direct discussion in this area as far as Anglican-Orthodox dialogue is concerned, especially in view of the often-repeated Orthodox insistence on 'free cooperation with God's grace' and working for our salvation.[7]

The 18th century was also the beginning of the Evangelical Revival which radically altered many of the landmarks in church life, including the uneasy, and sometimes down-right hostile, relationship between Anglicans and Dissenters or Nonconformists. As the historian of Evangelicalism D.W. Bebbington, has shown, all of this was changed by the Revival. Evangelicals were prepared not only to lower denominational barriers to intercommunion, for instance, but also to join with one another in a common cause and to establish organisations for its fulfilment. Thus the British and Foreign Bible Society was created for the better dissemination of the Scriptures at home and abroad and the London Missionary Society for cooperation in overseas mission – another favourite object of the Evangelicals and one which was to produce significant challenge as well as opportunity for ecumenism.[8]

Across the Atlantic, a vision for unity would arise in a very different context. Already in the second half of the 19th century an Episcopal priest, William Reed Huntington, had formed a local clergy fellowship along with the local Roman Catholic priest. It was here that his ideas about church unity in the USA developed. These can be found most conveniently in his book *The Church-Idea: An Essay Towards Unity*, first published in 1870. Huntington distinguished between the Anglican system and the Anglican principle. The latter had become obscured by the former which included surplices, spires, choirs, important-sounding titles for church officials and the like. For Huntington, it also included the Church of England's relationship to the state which, in his opinion, compromised its adherence to the Anglican principle. According to him, the Anglican Principle could be articulated in terms of a common adherence to four principles: Scripture as the Word of God, the Catholic Creeds as the Rule of Faith, the Sacraments ordained by Christ himself (i.e. Baptism and Holy Communion), and the Episcopate as a means of, and a focus for, unity. This was the first public airing of the now famous Quadrilateral, which has been so influential in ecumenical discussions including Anglicans – and, indeed, beyond that.[9]

For Huntington, the principle involved the right and the duty of every local church to be and to become the catholic church in that place. There is here both the pole of locality and that of catholicity. The local church must take its own culture and context seriously; for Huntington this meant that the situation in the USA was markedly different from that of the Elizabethan Settlement in England. Proposals for the greater unity of Christians could, for example, be better explored because there was no pressure in terms of the Church's relationship to the state. At the same time, Huntington knew well enough that the local church could only be truly catholic in relationship with all the other local churches. In this he can be said to have anticipated the World Council of Churches (WCC), New Delhi Assembly's call for unity which involves "all in each place united with all in every place".

Huntington's somewhat intra-American and pan-Protestant vision was adapted and given a more 'Catholic' direction by the House of Bishops at the 1886 Chicago Convention of the Episcopal Church. It was, more or less, in this form that the Quadrilateral was adopted by the 1888 Lambeth Conference, although that conference sought to bring it into greater conformity with the Articles of Religion.[10]

Even the 1888 Lambeth Conference, however, saw the Quadrilateral not in fully Catholic terms but only as applying to 'Home Reunion' or to 'the English-speaking peoples'. It was not until the 1920 conference's *Appeal to All Christian People* that its remit was extended to the whole world. Since then it has been hugely influential in negotiations for church unity on a regional or national basis. The many schemes of union that mushroomed in different parts of the world could not have been imagined without the Quadrilateral. Certainly, the ones that came to fruition – those of South India, North India and Pakistan – owe a great deal to the vision of the Church as set out in the Chicago-Lambeth Quadrilateral. The influence of the Chicago-Lambeth Quadrilateral on the so-called 'Lima Text' or the WCC's Faith and Order agreement on Baptism, Eucharist and Ministry is also apparent and has been noted.[11]

The Quadrilateral has, however, been criticised for being minimalist and anti-confessional and even non-liturgical. The charge of minimalism was met already by the American House of Bishops in 1886 when they not only deepened its content, but also declared that it was a basis for serious study rather than being sufficient for unity as such. The various plans for union also had to flesh out the theological and ecclesiological implications of organic unity among the churches. As to being anti-confessional, Huntington was certainly not a fan of the 39 Articles. Whether Anglicanism is confessional or not has been a subject of debate for many years, not least at this time of fresh challenges to its unity. On the one hand, it does not possess the great confessions of the churches of the Reformation, such as the Westminster for the Presbyterians or the Augsburg for the Lutherans. On the other, it is most emphatically a credal church with all three of the catholic creeds: the Apostles', Nicene and Athanasian, being regularly used in the liturgical worship of the Church. This is, of course, recognised in the Quadrilateral.

We have noted above the ecumenical significance of the Quadrilateral but it was also, from almost the beginning, seen as being related to Anglican identity, to what was regarded as essential for the Church's faithfulness. At this time of crisis in the Anglican Communion, it cannot be said too strongly that the bare bones of the Quadrilateral are not only insufficient for pursuing an ecumenical vocation but also for our self-understanding as Anglicans. Both the wider Global South movement and GAFCON have shown interest in developing a 'confessing', if not 'confessional' aspect to Anglicanism which is based on its traditional formularies: the Book of Common Prayer, the Ordinal and the Articles of Religion.[12]

The Quadrilateral does not mention the concern, for example, of the 1930 Lambeth Conference about the nature of the Church's unity and how this unity is to be maintained. The so-called Instruments of Unity (i.e. the office of the Archbishop of Canterbury, the Lambeth Conference of Bishops and its Standing Committee which evolved into the Primates' Meeting and the Anglican Consultative Council) were seen as maintaining and promoting this unity. In the current crisis all have, however, proved unequal to the task, as set out by the 1930 Lambeth Conference, of sustaining mutual loyalty through the common counsel of bishops in conference. Successive Lambeth Conferences have guided the communion in important ecumenical, moral and doctrinal areas, but the last Conference (a) could not gather all the bishops and (b) did not produce any resolutions or teaching documents, relying on the so-called 'Indaba' process for continuing deliberations on difficult questions in the Communion. Again, both the 1988 and 1998 Conferences asked for an enhanced role for the Primates in resolving communion-threatening problems. Such a role was certainly envisaged in the earlier drafts of the Anglican Covenant, proposed by the Windsor Report, but has been progressively marginalised in the subsequent drafts. The last draft had an excellent theological and ecclesiological preamble, but the section on the implementation of any covenant has been rendered virtually toothless by outlining a process of consultation which is unlikely to lead to a decision that is effective: Even this has now been rejected by the very churches for whom it was drafted.[13]

Alongside the Quadrilateral then, there is a need to develop the credal, confessing aspect of Anglicanism as well as its need for a functioning conciliarity which, on the one hand, acknowledges the Anglican genius for a synodality which gathers together representatives of the whole *laos* of God but, on the other, provides for a differentiated understanding of how responsibilities are exercised in such gatherings, according to biblical and historic patterns found in the Church. These steps are necessary not only for Anglicanism's own self-understanding and proper functioning but also for ecumenical credibility, so that our partners can have confidence in our rootedness in the Scriptures and the Apostolic Tradition.

If the Quadrilateral was one kind of encouragement towards seeking greater unity with Christians of other traditions, the different arrangements for co-operation amongst mission agencies in Africa and Asia was certainly another. In Kenya and India, for example, various kinds of 'comity' agreements had emerged which recognised the mission agencies of different denominations as having particular spheres of influence. Such arrangements were undoubtedly instrumental in bringing about, for example, the Kikuyu Conference in Kenya which went beyond co-operation in missionary work and proposed steps towards a united Church. This led to a fully developed scheme of church union modelled on that for the Church of South India. Although it did not result in the uniting of the churches, it laid the foundations for greater co-operation in matters of social and political justice, for instance, and to the emergence of the National Council of Churches in Kenya (NCCK) which has been of some significance in the national life of that country.[14] Since then, there have been many schemes for church union in which Anglicans have been involved. Apart from the schemes in South Asia, none of the others has come to fruition. Although church union schemes have continued to emerge (for example, the Welsh scheme in the 1980s), the failure of the Anglican-Methodist Scheme in 1970 marks a watershed for Anglican involvement in this model for unity.[15]

The entry of the Roman Catholic Church, following the Second Vatican Council, into the Ecumenical Movement has changed the entire topography of ecumenical relations. From this time on, the emphasis has been on bilateral dialogue between world communions rather than between denominational expressions within a particular country or region. The aim, then, is not so much united churches at this level but, rather, reconciliation at the universal level although, of course, with local implications. The bilateralism of this approach has, however, been complemented by multilateral work, for example, in the preparation of the World Council of Churches Faith and Order Commission's Report, with full Roman Catholic participation, on Baptism, Eucharist and Ministry and on a common confession of the Apostolic faith.[16]

Before we enter into a detailed discussion of Anglican-Roman Catholic relations, however, we must return to relations with the Orthodox, both Eastern and Oriental or, if you like, Chalcedonian and non-Chalcedonian, and with the Assyrian Church of the East.

The 1920 Lambeth *Appeal to All Christian People* coincided with an Encyclical from the Ecumenical Patriarch regarding Christian unity. Two years later, the Patriarch and his Holy Synod set out a statement on the validity of Anglican Orders which is notable for its clarity and charity. This led to the well-known visit by an Orthodox delegation to the 1930 Lambeth Conference and to a positive resolution requesting further dialogue on doctrinal issues which unite or divide the two communions. Other Orthodox churches such as Alexandria, Jerusalem, Cyprus and Romania, agreed with the judgement of Constantinople on the recognition of Anglican Orders. There was an air of optimism about Anglican-Orthodox relationships throughout the 1930s and '40s but, from 1948 there was increasing recognition that serious obstacles remained to inter-communion between the two families of churches. For example, as Bishop Kallistos Ware points out, whilst Anglicans thought that the judgement on Orders had to do with the *present* status of Anglican clergy, the Orthodox view had more to do with what would happen if Anglicans and Orthodox reached sufficient doctrinal agreement to warrant the restoration of communion.[17]

After Archbishop Michael Ramsey's visit to the Ecumenical Patriarch Athenagoras I, there was a new 'spring' in relations between Anglicans and Orthodox with the coming into being of the joint Anglican-Orthodox Doctrinal Commission. However, no sooner had the Commission issued its first agreed statement (Moscow 1976) than it was plunged into a first-class row over the ordination of women in some parts of the Anglican Communion.

Some Orthodox churches and theologians, in the light of this development, wished to downgrade the dialogue to an educational exercise which no longer aimed at mutual recognition and organic union. In the end, however, and partly as a result of efforts by Robert Runcie, the then Anglican Co-Chairman of the dialogue, it was decided to continue the dialogue as before, though with a fresh realisation of the disagreements and obstacles in the way of unity.[18] Whilst the consecration of women to the episcopate in some Anglican provinces did not cause quite the furore among the Orthodox that some were expecting, the consecration of an active and partnered homosexual to the episcopate in the Episcopal Church once again brought Anglican-Orthodox relations to a point of crisis. A number of Orthodox churches have declared that they are unable to continue dialogue with the Anglican Communion. An example of such unease is the frank speech delivered by Metropolitan Hilarion Alfeyev to the Church of England's Nikean Club, which promotes ecumenical relations. In this, he declared that the dialogue is doomed to closure if the unrestrained liberalisation of Christian values continues in many communities of the Anglican world. Given that Metropolitan Hilarion is the head of the Moscow Patriarchate's Department for External Relations, this has been recognised as a serious declaration indeed.[19]

On the other hand, the Anglican-Orthodox International Commission was able to publish an agreed statement on the *Church of the Triune God* which explores ecclesiological and cultural issues at some length, but does not directly address a number of the concerns raised by Metropolitan Hilarion in his speech.

Anglican contact with the Ancient Oriental Churches dates, in the main, from the 19th century as commerce, empire and missionary activity brought these churches to Anglican attention. Within the Ottoman domains, these communities had long lived as *dhimmis*, or protected minorities, with all the disabilities that entailed. British diplomats, scholars and travellers often found them living in parlous conditions. Their reports back home created pressure for the Church of England to come to the assistance of these beleaguered Christians.[20]

In India, the situation was different. At the dawn of the 19th century, the East India Company did not permit Christian Mission in British territories. (It was compelled to change this policy as the century progressed.) This meant that Anglican and other mission agencies, such as the Society for the Propagation of the Gospel (SPG) and the Church Mission Society (CMS), were forced to locate either in territories held by other European powers or even to operate in the areas still ruled by native princes. CMS thus found itself in the state of Travancore on a 'mission of help' to the Syrian Orthodox Church there. This expression was to characterise much Anglican involvement with the oriental churches. As distinct from Roman Catholic or other Protestant efforts, it was felt that the emphasis should not be on converting local Christians to Anglicanism and establishing an Anglican church, but on the revitalisation of the existing church and its members. Among the 'St Thomas Christians' of South India this took the form of encouraging theological education, assistance with the translation of the Bible into Malayalam, since the liturgy of the Church remained in Syriac, and in education more generally. The early missionaries were discreet and patient, but some of the later ones wanted change in the Church at a faster pace. The result of this was increasing friction between the hierarchy and the missionaries, eventually bringing CMS involvement to an end, but not before some of the Syrian Christians had separated themselves into an Anglican Syrian Church. Ultimately, this led to the formation of the Anglican diocese of Travancore and Cochin. The impetus for reform did not cease, however, within the ancient church and the reforming party was able to secure the consecration of a bishop by the

Patriarch of Antioch. After years of litigation and dispute, the result was the emergence of the Mar Thoma Syrian Church, an oriental church in liturgy and church order but reformed along Anglican lines. The churches of the Anglican Communion, including the United Churches of South Asia, are in communion with this church and its bishops attend representative Anglican gatherings.[21]

The dispute within the Church in South India had brought the Patriarch of Antioch, Peter III, to Britain in hope that the Church of England might mediate between the two sides. This was not to be as the Archbishop of Canterbury clearly supported the reforming party and its bishop, Mar Athanasius. The visit did result, however, in an educational 'mission of help' for the Syrian Orthodox Church's schools in Turkey. Because of the tension in India, it was not as significant as the work among the Assyrians. George Badger's work amongst the Assyrians (also called the Church of the East and, erroneously, the Nestorians) led to the Archbishop of Canterbury's mission to the Assyrians. This was largely an educational initiative run by a number of clergy and the Sisters of Bethany. Not only did they establish schools and a seminary, they were also responsible for much scholarship on the language, manuscripts and liturgy of this ancient church.

In Ethiopia also, Anglican missionaries from largely evangelical mission agencies, such as the Bible Churchmen's Missionary Society (BCMS, now Crosslinks) and the Church's Ministry among the Jews (CMJ), have refused to proselytise amongst Orthodox Christians. They have sought to assist in the renewal of the Ethiopian Orthodox Church and to integrate any converts, resulting from their work, into the Ethiopian Church. With Armenians, likewise, there have been warm relations with cooperation in education, especially theological education. Anglicans have, for long, supported the Armenian people in their search for justice and security in their homeland and in the diaspora. There has also been collaboration in pastoral care and the sharing of church buildings.[22]

As with the Chalcedonian Orthodox, recognition of Anglicans

as perhaps the nearest amongst Western-type Christians to the Oriental churches has been seriously affected by the ordination of women to the priesthood and the episcopate and, even more seriously, by the decision in some provinces of the Anglican Communion to permit the blessing of same-sex unions and the ordination of active homophiles to the priesthood and the episcopate.

A very significant development has been the *rapprochement* between the Chalcedonian Orthodox and the non-Chalcedonian. Under the auspices of the World Council of Churches, these ecclesial families have now produced agreements on the Christological questions which have divided them since the fifth century. This, in turn, has led to ecumenical cooperation in the areas of mission, liturgy, the life of women in the church and the development of spirituality. The Roman Catholic Church has also come to important agreements with the Oriental Orthodox and the Assyrians on Christological issues.[23]

It is clear that some effort is required to restore the confidence of the ancient oriental churches in the apostolicity and orthodoxy of the Anglican Communion. This is also true, of course, of the Chalcedonian churches and of the Roman Catholic Church to which we now turn.

Pope Pius the Fifth's excommunication of Elizabeth I, and his releasing of her English subjects from any allegiance to her, set the tone for Anglican-Roman Catholic relations in the latter part of the 16th century. In such a situation of open hostility, where recusant Catholics were regarded *ipso facto* as traitors, any discussions could only be polemical and adversarial. It was not until the next century that any positive evaluation could be made and influence acknowledged which was beyond mere controversy.[24] There were, of course, friendlier contacts such as those that William Wake, Archbishop of Canterbury in the 18th century, had with the Gallicans and through his wider writing on the nature and status of the Roman Catholic Churches. The Tractarian revival, which sought a recovery of the Church of England's 'Catholic' heritage, also brought renewed contact and fresh interest on both sides which could not be dampened by Leo XIII's negative judgement on Anglican Orders in *Apostolicae Curae* (1896) and the '*Responsio*' by the Archbishops of Canterbury and York known as *Saepius Officio*.[25] In the end, this interest led to the abortive Malines Conversations which did, nevertheless, provide the groundwork for the future.

The present state of Anglican-Roman Catholic dialogue can be traced back to the historic meeting between Michael Ramsey, Archbishop of Canterbury, and Pope Paul VI in 1966 which followed the 2nd Vatican Council's recognition, in the Decree on Ecumenism, that elements of Catholic faith and order (*fidem et structuram ecclesiasticam*) continued to exist within the Anglican Communion. The two leaders' joint declaration agreed a dialogue based on 'the Gospels and on the ancient common traditions'. A preparatory commission then, with remarkable speed, issued the Malta Report which resulted in the appointment by the two churches of the first Anglican-Roman Catholic International Commission (ARCIC). In just over a decade it completed ground-breaking agreements on the Eucharist, Ministry and Authority. These were then submitted to the authorities of the churches for reception. It is interesting, in this connection, to note that while the Church of England and the Anglican Communion (in the shape of the 1988 Lambeth Conference) were able to recognise the agreements 'as consonant in substance with the faith of Anglicans', the Roman Catholic Church's Congregation for the Doctrine of the Faith (CDF) could only give it a warm, but qualified, welcome.[26] Perhaps some of the emerging fault lines could already be seen. The Roman Catholic bishops of England and Wales wished to see a stronger evangelical voice in the dialogue, especially on the doctrine of justification by faith and the importance of the Word of God for the Church. The CDF's response raised the question about the ordination of women and pointed out that correspondence with the Archbishop of Canterbury had mentioned this point in the context of any Roman Catholic re-evaluation of the question about Anglican Orders in the light of the agreement on ministry.[27]

As if in response to the Catholic Bishops Conference of England and Wales, the second ARCIC began its work with a consideration of the doctrine of justification. Here they themselves acknowledge the work already being done on this subject by the Lutheran-Roman Catholic dialogue. It is clear that the Anglican-RC agreement, *Salvation and the Church,* must be read in the light of the subsequent Lutheran-Roman Catholic Declaration which makes this doctrine a touchstone or measure of the Christian faith and a criterion which orientates all the Church's teaching and practice to Christ.[28]

The Commission continued its work with *The Church as Communion, Life in Christ: Morals, Communion and the Church, The Gift of Authority,* and *Mary: Grace and Hope in Christ.* Although there have been debates and discussions about these reports in different provinces in the Anglican Communion and the Roman Catholic Church has responded to some of this work, there has not been the kind of authoritative response which was seen in respect of ARCIC I. This may well be because of the changed relationship between the communions and the lower expectations that they now have of one another. The final phase of ARCIC II's work was seriously affected by developments in the Anglican Communion following the ordination of a partnered and active homosexual to the episcopate in the USA.

In spite of the serious difficulties already looming, Anglican and Roman Catholic bishops meeting together at Mississauga in Canada in 2000 felt sufficiently optimistic to call for a new commission of bishops which would be able to implement the ARCIC agreement in different parts of the world. As it points out, however, the work of the new commission (known as the International Anglican-Roman Catholic Commission for Unity and Mission, or IARCCUM) was affected by the situation in the Anglican Communion almost from the beginning, and it felt unable to take the two churches on to another stage in their relationship. In the end, it contented itself with summarising the ARCIC agreements and commenting on them, as well as setting out some more practical areas for ecumenical cooperation.[29]

A number of Anglican groups have felt that the Bishop of Rome alone can guarantee their continuance in historic orthodoxy and have petitioned the Vatican for some kind of 'corporate union'. This has led Rome to provide for Ordinariates which recognise Anglican liturgical, theological and pastoral 'patrimony' to some extent. Such concessions seem based on the recognition by Paul VI, at the canonisation of the English Martyrs in 1970, that when the Roman Catholic Church is able to embrace her ever-beloved sister, the Anglican Communion, in the fullness of unity, 'there will be no seeking to lessen the legitimate prestige and worthy patrimony of piety and usage proper to the Anglican Church'.[30] There is also some provision for the continuing ordination of married men even if the norm of clerical celibacy is upheld, and for special formation for all candidates for Holy Orders in the Ordinariates.

Whilst much of this can be welcome, there are important ecclesiological and practical questions which remain: the ecclesial form of the Ordinariate is 'presbyterian' in the sense that it does not provide for a bishop. It is strange that one episcopally-ordered church should provide for the reception of those from another episcopally-ordered church in this way. It seems also to go against the spirit of the teaching in *Sacerdotalis Caelibatus* that sacred ministers from other churches, who are received into the communion of the Catholic Church, may be able to continue the exercise of their ministry. There is the danger, as has happened with many Eastern Catholic churches, of the Ordinariate gradually being latinised, in this case because of a necessary recourse to a Latin episcopate. Again, whilst the continuing ordination of married men is welcome, will the 'objective criteria' required of it include the Anglican experience of married clergy or will they just be about matters like 'scarcity'? The provisions for formation also could lead to latinisation unless there is robust attention given to distinctive programmes and institutions for the transmission of Anglican patrimony. At best then, it seems the Ordinariates are only a step along the ecumenical path and not the final fruit of Anglican-

Roman Catholic dialogue.[31]

The serious setbacks in the last few years have not brought the dialogue to an end. There is a new ARCIC and it has been charged with the very subject which has gripped the Anglican Communion over the last decade: how moral aspects of living the Christian life relate to communion. Because of the severity of the difficulties, however, there seems to be a sense, as with the Anglican-Orthodox dialogue noted earlier, that the dialogue is about the better understanding of each church's beliefs and practices and, therefore, of difference rather than being a focussed endeavour to achieve the restoration of communion. It may be that God, in his mercy, will overrule and the churches will, once again, be able to return to a common quest for that unity in faith and life for which Christ prayed.

At the same time, it must be noted that just as relations with the historic churches of the East and with the Roman Catholics have encountered new obstacles, Anglicans have, in different ways, become closer to the mainline Protestant denominations. One of the expressions of this must be the far-reaching agreement between the British and Irish Anglican churches on the one hand, and the Nordic and Baltic churches on the other. The so-called Porvoo Declaration, building on past agreements between, for example, the Church of England and the Church of Sweden or the Church of Finland creates, in effect, a communion of churches in Northern Europe. This has happened without full agreement about the nature of episcopal ministry and whether those churches which lost the historic line of succession (perhaps for good reason) were willing to regain it within the new context created by the agreement. It is interesting that this declaration did not create any of the sharp disagreements which occurred when the Church of South India was inaugurated, with the incorporation of non-episcopally ordained ministers in an episcopally ordered church. There was a guarantee then that future ordinations would all be episcopal by bishops in historic succession. Such a guarantee was not forthcoming at the time of the Porvoo agreement, only that ordinations would be carried out in an overall episcopal context and with episcopal authority. Although the Anglican Communion was asked to comment on the statement after it was issued, the 1998 Lambeth Conference welcomed it in fulsome terms.[32]

Since then, new obstacles have emerged even in this communion of churches with the removal of reference to gender in the marriage service of the Swedish Church and the election of a same-sex partnered female bishop in that church. Once again, there was nothing like the anguish caused by similar developments within the Anglican Communion. This raises the question as to whether the agreement is of sufficient "thickness" to warrant the grand title of 'Communion of Churches' given to those who are a party to it.

The Lutheran theologian, Professor Michael Root, has pointed out the similarities and differences between the Porvoo process and the attempts at a closer relationship between the Episcopal Church in the USA (TEC) and the Evangelical Lutheran Church of America (ELCA). He notes that whilst the Porvoo churches share a history of establishment in Europe, the American churches are part of the great denominational mix of American Christianity. The other big difference is the absence of episcopacy in the American Lutheran churches until fairly recent times. Even when it was introduced, there was no claim, as in Europe, to stand in some kind of historic succession. Historic episcopacy would then gradually be absorbed by the ELCA as TEC bishops participated in the consecration of its bishops (as Lutheran bishops would in the consecration of TEC bishops). In the meantime, and despite the frequent description of the relationship as one of 'full communion', there would be inevitable restrictions on the complete interchangeability of ministries.[33]

In England, the collapse of the Anglican-Methodist scheme of union in 1972 was a shock to ecumenists and was, particularly, regarded by the Methodists as their having been left at the altar. This, undoubtedly, created a crisis of trust between Anglicans and Methodists, at least in Great Britain. International dialogue between the two communions has continued, nevertheless, and those who had opposed the scheme, mainly Anglo-Catholics and Evangelicals, were quick to set out their own views on how a union could be achieved which was theologically coherent, locally driven and gradual.[34]

Since 1995, conversations have resumed between the Church of England and the Methodist Church, leading to a covenant for unity. Once again, it is unclear whether there is a real agreement on matters like the place of the Bible in the life of the Church, the Sacraments and Ministry. From the point of view of some conservative Evangelicals, the Methodist doctrine of 'perfection', i.e. the possibility that sin can be eradicated from a believer's life, has continued to cause problems of conscience.[35]

We have seen how Anglicans came to be in communion with the Mar Thoma Church, an oriental church in the Syrian tradition. They have also established communion with Old Catholic churches, which emerged from 18th and 19th century movements against papal supremacy in the Roman Catholic Church, and with the Philippines Independent Catholic Church, which has roots in the war of independence against Spanish rule in that country. As in other cases already noted, some of these relationships have been threatened either by developments in the Anglican Communion or, indeed, within these churches themselves. The Lambeth Conference of 1998 recommended that ways should be found of taking counsel and making decisions together. As with the Anglican Communion itself, it is doubtful whether, without a coherent ecclesiology and an effective ecclesial structure, such relationships can flourish.[36]

There have been many other significant ecumenical encounters and agreements in which Anglicans have been involved, not least, of course, the structures and instruments of the ecumenical movement itself. Since the Edinburgh Missionary Conference of 1910, Anglicans have been involved in the Mission, Faith and Order, and Life and Work aspects of the movement. The *Appeal to all Christian People* of the 1920 Lambeth Conference gave the movement a much needed impetus. Anglican relationships with the Orthodox contributed to the eventual participation of the Orthodox in the ecumenical movement. Faith and Order and Life and Work were, in due course, merged into the World Council of Churches (WCC) which was inaugurated in 1948. Anglicans have always participated vigorously, if sometimes critically, in the life and institutions of the WCC. They have also been active in local and regional expressions of ecumenism. In some cases, as in Britain and Ireland, and in the Middle East, they have worked towards more comprehensive councils that could include the Catholic, Orthodox, Protestant and Pentecostal families of churches.[37]

Since 1978 at least, the Anglican Communion has been aware, as have other churches, of the emergence and growth of a whole spectrum of newer churches. Some of these are so-called African Independent churches. Two Anglicans in particular, David Barrett and John Padwick, have been at the forefront of bringing their extent and their importance to the attention of mainline Christianity. There has also been a veritable explosion of Pentecostalism in South America, the Caribbean, Africa and East Asia, with Pentecostals now numbering some 400 million and, claiming large sections of the population in countries like Brazil and Korea, they cannot be ignored. Another Anglican, the sociologist David Martin, has shown how Pentecostalism is changing the social and economic, as well as the spiritual, situation in a number of countries on different continents. Timothy and Rebecca Samuel Shah have been researching how Christian faith, including its Pentecostal expressions, is affecting communities in terms of changing their social status and economic standing.[38]

All of the above means not only that the Anglican Communion, as such, and the various provinces need to engage with Pentecostalism and independency in terms of dialogue, but also that local, regional and international structures will have to be found which can accommodate such traditions without undue obstruction from those with vested interests in keeping them out. The ecumenical process, *Not Strangers but Pilgrims,* of the churches in Britain and Ireland set out to be as inclusive as possible in the establishing of new ecumenical instruments for the nations involved, and proposals at the WCC's 8th Assembly in Harare envisaged the development of a 'forum' which would include churches and other bodies that could not, for the time being, belong to the WCC. The question remains, of course, why a new ecumenical instrument should not emerge at the world level in ways similar to the emergence of such instruments at regional or local levels which would replace the WCC, rather than being in addition to it. From experience and conviction, Anglicans have an important contribution to make in the re-forming of ecumenical instruments at this and other levels.

On the one hand, Anglicans have always claimed to be *part* of the One, Holy, Catholic and Apostolic Church and, on the other, they have sought a greater and deeper expression of its unity. Again and again, they have claimed that Anglicans have no distinct doctrine or theology but they have also themselves wished to preserve that patrimony of which Pope Paul VI spoke so warmly. If asked about the specific content of this patrimony, they might say that whilst Anglicans have no distinct doctrine, they *do* have distinctive methods and approaches to the doing of theology and of interpreting the Christian Tradition in all its richness. There is a rich liturgical, literary and devotional tradition which is admired, sometimes by non-Anglicans, and sometimes even by non-Christians. Approaches to pastoral work, a commitment to the wider community, local or national, and involvement of clergy and laypeople in decision-making are other features of a distinctive Anglicanism.[39]

Anglicans have been wont to say that Anglicanism is 'provisional' in the sense that Anglicans are prepared for a distinct Anglican Church to disappear in the greater cause of Christian Unity – for its churches to be less and less Anglican so they could be more and more catholic. This has, at least partially, been demonstrated in the united churches where Anglicans have united with Christians of other traditions. At the same time, there has been a sense that Anglicans also have certain gifts to bring to the wider unity which they seek.

The tension is seen clearly in the *Appeal to all Christian People* of the 1920 Lambeth Conference and an encyclical of the same conference, as well as in the well-known Resolution of the 1930 Conference on the Anglican Communion.[40]

As we have seen, however, a more fundamental question has arisen recently about Anglican identity itself. It is vital for Anglicans to know who they are and to have effective instruments to sustain their fellowship, one with another. It is clear that previous Lambeth Conferences have emphasised, as Archbishop Robert Runcie put it in his opening address at the 1988 Lambeth Conference, *interdependence* rather than independence.[41] Their understanding of the autonomy of particular or national churches has been called 'autonomy in communion' by the Windsor Report of the Lambeth Commission on Communion.[42] The report points out that, as long ago as the 1920 Lambeth Conference, it was said that churches were not free to deny the truth or to ignore the fellowship.[43] The 1930 Conference declared that, as in antiquity, Councils of Bishops were the proper instrument to maintain the Church's unity.[44] The 1988 and 1998 Conferences both requested that the Primates of the Communion be given "enhanced responsibility in offering guidance on doctrinal, moral and pastoral matters".[45] It is crucial that Anglican structures should reflect such an understanding of the Communion for the sake of Anglican identity itself, and so that our ecumenical partners may be clear what kind of ecclesial body they are dealing with. Anglican involvement in the search for unity has mostly been honourable and principled. Let us keep it that way.

Notes

[1] See, for example, S. Platten (ed), *Anglicanism and the Western Christian Tradition*, Norwich, Canterbury Press, 2003.

[2] The Prefaces and the sections 'of Ceremonies' in the *First and Second Prayer Books of King Edward VI,* London, J. M. Dent, 1968, pp3f, 286f, 292, 321f,

438. See also Article 34 of the *Articles of Religion*.

[3] See further M. Nazir-Ali and N. Sagovsky, *The Virgin Mary in the Anglican Tradition in the 16th and 17th Centuries*, in A Denaux and N Sagovsky (eds), *Studying Mary: The Virgin Mary in Anglican and Roman Catholic Theology and Devotion*, London, T & T Clark, 2007, pp131ff.

[4] On this see P Avis, *Anglicanism and the Christian Church*, Edinburgh, T & T Clark, 1989, pp31ff, 51ff and *passim*.

[5] Further M. Nazir-Ali and N. Sagovsky, op. cit., pp136f; see also D Harrison, Introduction to *The First and Second Prayer Books of Edward VI*, op. lit, px.

[6] Avis, op. cit., p71f.

[7] M. Nazir-Ali, *Scripture in Ecumenical Dialogue*, in John Stott and others, *The Anglican Communion and Scripture*, Oxford, Regnum/EFAC, 1996, pp87f. See also Anglican-Orthodox Dialogue, the Dublin Agreed Statement, London, SPCK, 1984; *The Church of the Triune God*: the Cyprus Agreed Statement, London, ACO, 2006; *Joint Declaration on the Doctrine of Justification*, LWF and RCC, Grand Rapids, Eerdmans, 2000; *Salvation and the Church*, ARCIC II, CHP/CTS, London, 1987; T. Ware, *The Orthodox Church*, Middlesex, UK, Penguin, 1973, pp226f.

[8] D. W. Bebbington, *Evangelicalism in Modern Britain*, London, Unwin Hyman, 1989, p66.

[9] W. Reed Huntington, *The Church-Idea: An Essay Towards Unity*, New York, Scribner & Sons, 1989.

[10] J. R. Wright (ed), *Quadrilateral at One Hundred*, Cincinnati, Forward Movement, 1988, pp8ff. See also M Nazir-Ali, *The Vocation of Anglicanism*, Anvil Vol 6 no 2, 1989 pp117f.

[11] *Baptism, Eucharist and Ministry*, Geneva, WCC, 1985. See also Wright, op. cit, p13.

[12] See, for example, D. W. Gomez and M. W. Sinclair (eds), *To Mend the Net*: Anglican Faith and Order for Renewed Mission, Carrollton, Texas, Ekklesia, 2001 and the Jerusalem Declaration in gafcon.org

[13] *The Truth Shall Make You Free*, Report of the 1988 Lambeth Conference, London, CHP, 1988, Res 18:2a, p216; *The Official Report of the Lambeth Conference 1998*, Harrisburg, Morehouse, 1999, Res III:6b, pp396f. See also the draft of The Covenant.

[14] See further Stephen Neill, *Anglicanism*, Harmondsworth, Penguin, 1960, pp379ff, and Gordon Hewitt, *The Problems of Success: A History of the Church*

Missionary Society 1919-1942, London, SCM, 1971, pp142ff.

[15] *The Emmaus Report: A Report of the Anglican Ecumenical Consultation 1987*, London, CHP, 1987, and C.O. Buchanan, E. L. Mascall et al, *Growing into Unity: Proposals for forming a United Church in England*, London, SPCK, 1970.

[16] *Baptism, Eucharist and Ministry*, op. cit., and *Towards a Common Confession of the Apostolic Faith*, *Confessing the One Faith*, Faith and Order Paper NO153, Geneva, WCC, 1991, and *Towards Sharing the One Faith*, Faith and Order Paper NO153, Geneva, WCC, 1996.

[17] See further S. Neill, *Anglicanism*, op.cit., pp370f; Alan Stephenson, *Anglicanism and the Lambeth Conferences*, London, SPCK, 1978, pp166f cf. Resolution 33 of the 1930 Lambeth Conference, in R Coleman (ed), *Resolutions of the Twelve Lambeth Conferences 1867–1988*, Toronto, Anglican Book Centre, 1992, pp77f; and Timothy Ware, *The Orthodox Church*, Harmondsworth, Penguin, 1973, pp324f.

[18] On this see *The Emmaus Report: A Report of the Anglican Ecumenical Consultation*, London, ACC, CHP, 1987, pp89ff, and *Anglican-Orthodox Dialogue: the Dublin agreed statement*, London, SPCK, 1984, pp1ff.

[19] See www.mospat.ru/en/2010/09/10/news25819

[20] Henry Hill (ed), *Light from the East: A Symposium on the Oriental Orthodox and Assyrian Churches*, Toronto, Anglican Book Centre, 1988.

[21] Ibid, pp82f; Alexander Mar Thoma, *The Mar Thoma Church*: Heritage and Mission, Kottayam, 1986.

[22] On Anglican relationships with the Oriental churches see Michael Nazir-Ali, *From Everywhere to Everywhere: A World View of Christian Mission*, London, Collins, 1990, pp57ff.

[23] Paulos Gregorios, W.H. Lazareth and N.A. Nissiotis (eds), *Does Chalcedon Divide or Unite?*, Geneva, WCC, 1981, and Thomas Fitzgerald and Peter Boutenoff (eds), *Turn to God Rejoice in Hope: Orthodox Reflections on the Way to Harare*, Geneva, WCC, 1998. See also the Information Service of the Pontifical Council for Promoting Christian Unity for progress in dialogue between the Roman Catholic and the Oriental Churches, e.g., Nos 76, 90, 117, 127.

[24] See further Owen Chadwick, *The Reformation*, London, Penguin, 1990, pp286f, and Avis, op. cit., pp23ff.

[25] Texts can be found conveniently in *Anglican Theological Review:Anglican Orders; A century of Apostolicae Curae*, vol LXXVIII, No 1 Winter 1996,

Evanson, 111, pp127ff.

[26] See Christopher Hill and Edward Yarnold (eds), *Anglicans and Roman Catholics: the Search for Unity*, London, SPCK/CTS, 1994, pp12ff, 111ff, 153ff, and 156ff.

[27] Ibid, pp109, 163f.

[28] *Salvation and the Church*, London, ACC/RC Secretariat for Promoting Christian Unity, 1987 and *Joint Declaration on the Doctrine of Justification*, Grand Rapids, Eerdmans, 1999.

[29] On this see *Growing Together in Unity and Mission: An Agreed Statement of IARCCUM*, London, SPCK, 2007.

[30] See Hill & Yarnold, op. cit., p148. It is noteworthy that what had been said about the reconciliation of two communions is now being used to receive individuals and groups from one communion to the other.

[31] Apostolic Constitution *Anglicanorum Coetibus* along with its Complementary Norms, hf_ben_XVI_ape_20091104_anglicanorum_coetibus_en.html.

[32] *Together in Mission and Ministry: The Porvoo Common Statement with Essays on Church and Ministry in Northern Europe*, London, CHP, 1993; *The Official Report of Lambeth Conference 1998*, op. cit., Res IV:16, pp411f. See also Synodical Opinion of the Bishop of Rochester at his Diocesan Synod, 11 February 1995.

[33] Michael Root, in *A Commentary on the Concordat of Agreement*, J. Eniffiss and D. Meitosen, Minneapolis, Augsburg, 1994, pp138ff.

[34] On international dialogue see, for instance, *Sharing the Apostolic Communion*, North Carolina, World Methodist Council, 1996. On the English situation see C.O. Buchanan, E. L. Mascall, J. I. Packer and G. Leonard, *Growing into Union: Proposals for forming a united church in England*, London, SPCK, 1970.

[35] On the Methodist doctrine of perfection see D W Bebbington, op. cit., pp153f. On the conversations and the problems involved, see *An Anglican-Methodist Covenant*, Peterborough, Methodist Publishing House, 2001.

[36] *The Emmaus Report*, op. cit., pp38ff, and Lambeth 1998, Res IV.6, pp407f.

[37] On the Ecumenical movement and its various bodies see further *Dictionary of the Ecumenical Movement* (N. Lossky, J. M. Bonino, J. S. Pobee, T..F. Stransky, G. Wainwright and P. Webb [eds]), Geneva, WCC, 1991. On Anglican perspectives on ecumenism see G R Evans and J R Wright, *The Anglican Tradition: A Handbook of Sources*, London, SPCK and Minneapolis, Fortress, 1991. Also see the *Emmaus Report*, op. cit.

[38] *The Report of the Lambeth Conference 1978*, London, Church Information Office, 1978, pp111f, the Report of the 1988 Lambeth Conference, op. cit., Res ii, p 213, and *The Report of the 1998 Lambeth Conference*, op. cit., Res IV:21, p415, *The Emmaus Report*, op. cit., pp142f. See also David Barrett and John Padwick, *Rise up and Walk! Conciliarism and the African Indigenous Churches 1815-1987*, Nairobi, OUP, 1989, and David Martin, *Pentecostalism: The World Their Parish*, Oxford, Biblelands, 2002.

[39] See further Paul Avis, *Anglicanism and the Christian Church*, op. cit., pp36ff and G. R. Evans and J. R. Wright, *The Anglican Tradition*.

[40] See Evans & Wright, op. cit., pp377f, 380f and 380f. Also, R. Coleman (ed), *Resolutions of the 12 Lambeth Conferences 1867 – 1988*, Toronto, Anglican Book Centre, 1992, pp45f, 83f.

[41] *The Truth Shall Make You Free: Report of the 1988 Lambeth Conference*, op. cit., p 15.

[42] *The Windsor Report 2004*, London, ACO, 2004, pp81ff.

[43] Ibid, p 51.

[44] Evans & Wright, op. cit., pp389f, Coleman, op. cit., pp83f.

[45] *Report of the 1988 Conference*, Resolution 18 and of 1998 Resolution III.6.

26

THINKING AND ACTING MORALLY

"If a thing is worth doing, it is worth doing badly", said G. K. Chesterton and it is in that spirit that I have approached this subject, recognising its importance and complexity, but also my modest ability in tackling it.

In our rapidly changing world, not only are we faced with moral choices more frequently, the choices before us are increasingly complex. At the same time, there is a tendency to populism; that is to say to the view that what is morally acceptable in a given society must be determined by public opinion even if the reasons for holding such views are not terribly strong. On the other hand, there are influential sections of the community who stand to gain commercially or in other ways, and who wish to promote a particular technology or way of viewing the human person, society or the world at large. In such a situation, if we are to hold our own, we need to be clear about the basis for our thinking and acting morally.

In this chapter, we shall consider the nature of moral decisions and the scope of morality, whether it can be held to be universal but also what could be specific to a culture or a time. We shall look at the relationship between natural law and revelation as found in the Anglican tradition, and ask whether knowledge of what is naturally right can be attained naturally. In the light of this tradition, we shall consider some sharp moral questions as they arise today, particularly in the field of reproductive medicine, euthanasia and medical ethics generally. Finally we shall consider, very briefly, the relationship of morality to religion and to law.

Morality, universal and relative

First of all, in moral decision-making, we need to ask how we arrive at particular moral decisions. It is important here to emphasise the place of both reflection and deliberation in the process. Reflection is primarily thought about who we are and what the world is, while deliberation is, as the term suggests, a 'weighing up' of choices regarding how we should act, based on our reflection of how things are and how they ought to be. From this emerge the so-called generic moral rules, e.g., "All killing is wrong." Such rules may be more or less specific, depending on the extent of our reflection and the scope of circumstances we have in mind e.g., "All killing is wrong except in the cause of defending the weak from aggression." However specific such rules may be, they are not particular moral judgements. In themselves these latter are spontaneous acts of recognition that a particular way of behaving is wrong but they need to be informed by reflective and deliberative moral reasoning which has led to the framing of moral rules. A particular moral judgement, therefore, may take the form, "This killing is wrong because it is an instance of the kind of thing we meant when we said, 'All killing is wrong except in the cause of defending the weak from aggression.'"

While particular judgements are, of course, related to specific situations, moral rules are universal in scope. To say, "All killing is wrong", even when the rule is modified by exceptions, is obviously to make a statement that is supposed to be true of all times and all places. Such universality of moral rules is, naturally, incompatible with radical moral relativism which denies that there are fundamental moral rules which, in principle, apply to all human beings and all human societies. It may, however, be compatible with a cultural relativism which holds, for example, that people are not to be blamed if they act according to their conscience in the light of cultural values, or if cultural circumstances are such that a moral rule applies in a particular way in that culture. Thus in a polygamous society, a man who behaves honourably towards his wives should not be accused of offending against the dignity of women since he knows no better. Also, in such a society the application of the rule about the equality of women may have to be applied differently, at least for a time. History is full of examples of zealous efforts by missionaries and others to impose monogamy suddenly on traditionally polygamous societies with disastrous results, not least for the women themselves. It may be that equality of opportunity in education and employment, participation in political life and equality in law will bring about the desired result. Ultimately recognition of the dignity and equality of women will also lead to an acknowledgement of monogamy as fundamental to an adequate anthropology. This is, in fact, what is happening with the Christianising of many societies, for example, in Africa. Even with cultural relativism, however, it should be possible to challenge people with the demands of a moral law, written on their hearts and of which they have some awareness.

Any outright denial of the universal scope of morality would leave unexplained the very general agreement among human societies, for instance, about murder, lying, stealing and betrayal. In a rapidly shrinking and 'globalising' world, where people from different cultural and religious backgrounds daily rub shoulders, moral agreement is of crucial importance. Hans Küng has pioneered the search for a global ethic and has related it closely to his work on dialogue between the different religions of the world. For him, not only peace but justice and the protection of the created order depend on this dialogue and the common ethical values that will arise from it.[1] Even a polemical and polarising writer like the political scientist, Samuel P. Huntington, recognises that people of all civilisations need to identify common values, institutions and practices. Only then will a universal civilisation emerge.[2]

It is clear that questions about human dignity and of respect for the environment, so fundamental to the identification of common values, cannot be answered on a purely utilitarian or consequentialist basis, but must take account of the nature of humanity and of the world as well as of our sense of duty, regardless of consequences, in these matters.

A universal moral order?

It is fundamental to Christian faith that decisions are moral because they respond to the reality which confronts us and, above all, to the ultimate reality of God himself. 'Teleological order' in creation is of immediate significance to us if we are to understand creation and to act in relation to it.[3] The unity and 'purposed' character of the universe, of which we are part and in which we are agents, lies behind the Christian 'Natural Law' tradition which is itself grounded in the 'Eternal Law' of God's will and wisdom. If creation as a whole, and creatures within it, have been created in particular ways and for certain ends, this implies that we as agents will have to behave in such a manner as to respect this teleological character of the created order, ourselves included. Such 'ends' need not be seen as fixed and immutable – a common objection to teleology. As James Ward saw, teleology can be understood as that purposiveness in creatures which leads them to develop 'epigenetically', achieving ends in keeping with their nature but not predetermined from the outset.[4] The scientific method of observation, abstraction and discovery of new relationships between objects is not in itself inimical to teleology. In fact, teleology may be an ally if it posits regularity in nature and also helps in the integration of the sciences into a coherent worldview.

Considerations such as these have led to the view that a universal moral order is embedded in universal structures of human interaction with the world, and in social interaction. This is shown, for example, in the way different cultures show respect for the environment and in the acknowledgement of the need for social structures which will promote justice. Such a view about a universal moral order does not deny the need for moral development in individuals whether in terms of the internalisation of ideals or through learned behaviour. Nor does it deny the need to move from heteronomy to autonomy and from there to a social morality of mutual care and connectedness. In fact, if there is a universal moral order, it is necessary for both individuals and society to develop in increasing recognition of its claims.

Christians affirm, therefore, the original goodness of creation and perceive an order in it which displays the wisdom of the Creator. While human ignorance, wilfulness and rebellion obscure something of the order in nature and in society, there continues to be some common recognition of good and bad, right and wrong, virtue and vice in otherwise widely diverse human societies. On the one hand, the universalisability of moral principles is both embedded in, and leads to, the recognition of a common order and, on the other, institutions such as marriage and family, are universally recognised as vital for social survival, even if they have been misunderstood and abused in practice.[5]

Some moral theologians, whilst acknowledging the authority of the natural order, hold, nevertheless, that such an authority is not merely a matter of discovery but must rely on God's revelation, especially in Jesus Christ, if it is to make a full impact on our understanding and conduct. Even if this is so, we must allow some natural discernment of such an authority and some such discernment in the various religious traditions, if any project for a global ethic is to get off the ground. At the same time, we can agree that the recognition of such authority receives its definitiveness from God's revelation in Christ.[6]

Anglican moral tradition
Anglican moral theology, in particular, has seen the sources of moral decision-making in the access which human reason has to Natural Law as a manifestation of the Eternal Law of God's own being and also in the divine positive law revealed in the Bible, without which sinful humans could not fulfil God's will for them.[7] The two sources are not, however, discrete and

unconnected. The divine positive law affirms, corrects, confirms and clarifies what we know already of the world's teleological structures and the demands of a universal moral order. It is a guide in the necessary development of conscience and, indeed, in the correction of an erroneous conscience. Our contemporary tendency to respect conscience is entirely laudable but such respect cannot be at the expense of that social and ecological flourishing which comes only from a recognition of, and an acting upon, those moral principles which are derived from the 'deep structures' of the universe and of human society. Early Anglican moralists had a tendency to emphasise the seriousness of moral obligation both in terms of social responsibility but also of the individual believer's path to holiness of life. In this endeavour, we are to be guided by both Natural Law and the positive divine law so that we may safely attain to life eternal.[8]

Stewardship and creation

The discernment of law and order in the universe (which is, after all, what makes science possible) should not, however, lead to the so-called naturalistic (or empirical) fallacy, that is, deriving 'ought' from 'is'. Although the world is ordered, it is not perfect and while human societies have laws, they can also be characterised by injustice, tyranny and a lack of compassion. Whatever the circumstances, we should attempt to do our duty rather than succumb to them or try to tailor our duty to them. This would, indeed, be a sign of moral weakness. Some religious traditions, moreover, see the role of humans as exercising 'dominion' or 'stewardship' over creation. That implies that it is not to be left exactly as we find it but that we can alter it for the greater good of humanity and, perhaps, creation itself. In the Judaeo-Christian tradition such a view is rooted in the first chapter of the Book of Genesis where man and woman are created together in the image (*selem*) of God. The significance of such language is that it was used for the image of rulers in places where they could not be personally present. In the same way, humans are God's visible emblems or representatives on earth.[9] Somewhat differently, the *Qur'ān* speaks of human beings as God's representatives (*khalifah*) on earth (2.30) avoiding the language of *imago dei*. Both the Bible and the *Qur'ān*, however, see human beings as creative in producing conditions and life suitable for themselves. In both Islam and Christianity a 'Promethean' motif emerges which sees humanity as 'building' on God's creation itself. Muhammad Iqbāl's famous Persian work the *Payam-i-Mashriq* (Message of the East) puts it in this way:

> You made the night, and I the lamp
> You the clay and I the cup,
> You, desert, mountain-peak, and vale,
> I, flower-bed, park and orchard,
> I, who grind a mirror out of stone,
> Who brew from poison, honey-drink.[10]

In the dialogue, the deity has accused humans of destroying the original goodness of creation and of ecological and social irresponsibility. This is the human reply to the divine charge. Interestingly it does not deny that there has been environmental and social damage but points, rather, to what has been achieved by humanity in very adverse conditions. Iqbāl's mentor at Cambridge, James Ward, sums up Christian thinking in this area thus:

> ...this metamorphosis of nature by human art and industry, though it exceeds the wildest dreams of Fairyland, is yet throughout natural insofar as no new forces or elements are involved in its several processes and products, and the laws of nature are everywhere observed and obeyed. Yet we know that it is throughout the work of men, not the work of nature, in the sense of requiring ceaseless guidance and control.[11]

How far should we go?

Our own situation is, however, vastly different from the world of Ward and Iqbāl. The question now is not so much whether we should seek to 'build' on nature but how far should we go.

The identification of our genetic make-up and particular genes which may cause or predispose certain people to disease is, perhaps, uncontroversial especially when these people can be helped either through direct medical intervention or through counselling about life-style. Interference with the genetic structure of plants and animals without taking into account wider ecological factors is more problematic. The development of sophisticated reproductive medicine, moreover, has made it possible for the characteristics of offspring to be more and more minutely specified. This immediately raises the spectre of eugenics. To put it at its sharpest, are children ends in themselves or merely the means of parents enjoying yet another product of our technological age? Similar issues arise, for example, with xenotransplantation: should animals be produced solely for this purpose and made to live in quarantine for the whole of their lives? What is the risk of transmitting new viruses to human individuals and communities? To what extent is it permissible to use treatment that requires high levels of immuno-suppressive drugs and life-long monitoring? Are there alternatives, such as growing tissue from the patient, for certain kinds of treatment?

Developments in technology, emphasis on autonomy and the value given to public opinion have all conspired to raise particularly acute questions about the beginning and end of life. It is generally agreed that human gametes, while living human material, are not accorded any specific status in terms of sanctity of life. Is there then a human person at the moment of conception, when the gametes come together, or is 'personhood' something which develops as the embryo is embedded in the womb, grows into a foetus and is, eventually, born into a community? Christian tradition has, for long, distinguished between the 'formed' and the 'unformed' foetus (based on the Septuagintal translation of Ex 21:22). This allowed a distinction between the abortion of a formed foetus, which was regarded as homicide, and that of an unformed foetus, which was seen as gravely sinful but not as homicidal.[12]

Respect and personhood

Such distinctions also allowed the later development of ideas of 'ensoulment'. For St Thomas Aquinas, for example, this occurred at about forty days after conception (Aquinas also distinguished between male and female, and the time it takes for the respective ensoulment of each, but that is not relevant for our present purposes). He saw ensoulment as the emergence of organisational and directional principles in the foetus. It is interesting that this is also, approximately, the time when scientists expect to see the establishment of a functioning nerve net and the beginning of brain activity. In law, it appears that the foetus begins to be treated as an individual person when it is deemed capable of extra-uterine survival. As technology develops this period changes, standing at the moment at 22-24 weeks of gestation.

Clearly there are watersheds in the long journey to birth: conception, implantation, the beginning of brain activity, viability outside the womb, all of these are important and have led some to take the view that we must remain agnostic about the precise time that we have a human person. This should, however, lead to increased respect for the embryo and foetus, as we do not know exactly when personhood commences.[13]

The Human Fertilisation and Embryology Act's limit on embryonic research is fourteen days or until the appearance of 'the primitive streak' (when the cells that form the foetus separate from those that form the placenta), whichever is sooner. Before this, the developing embryo is not distinct and the possibility of identical twins, for instance, cannot be discounted. For some, however, even such a conservative limit is not conservative enough. They would reject the view that because there is considerable natural wastage in the earlier stages of gestation, there can be little harm in using for research material much of which would be discarded anyway. They would argue also that the deliberate creation of embryos for research is quite different from natural wastage. Even if the early embryo is not fully developed, it has the potential of personhood and should, therefore, be treated with respect. From the Christian point of view, the Bible certainly speaks of the foetus in personal terms, and even as capable of being filled with the Holy Spirit (Ps 139:13–16; Jer 1:5; Lk 1:15, 39–45; Gal 1:15).

Respect for the dying and the dead

At the other end of life, there are a host of sharp questions about 'the right to die', the role of medical practitioners in assisting death and the question of 'non-voluntary' euthanasia, where the patient is not competent to give consent. The patient's right to die is an argument based largely on grounds of personal autonomy. While those grounds appear attractive to some, there are particularly difficult problems associated with this argument: how far in advance should a decision not to have treatment be made? If it is made too far in advance, it will not be able to specify the conditions under which 'a living will' is to be put into effect. If, however, such a decision is made at a time of great distress, when a terminal illness is diagnosed, for example, can it be regarded as 'reasonable'? How should we evaluate the role of relatives and even of the state in encouraging people to end their lives, if looking after them is going to be an increasing emotional and financial burden?

If we affirm that the role of medical practitioners is not to kill but that neither is it "to keep officiously alive", what is 'officious' in the circumstances? Is it not to withdraw uncomfortable, even painful treatment when it is known that such treatment cannot help the patient? Is it to abstain from providing pain-killing drugs because they may cause death earlier (the so-called secondary effect), or is it to continue with nutrition when the practitioner knows there is no hope of the patient ever regaining consciousness?[14] There does seem a distinction between providing treatment judged necessary to relieve pain which may bring about death, and the deliberate administration of drugs to cause death, or even the withdrawal of nutrition and hydration knowing that death will result.

Much support for modern practices of euthanasia seems to be the result of the widespread view that terminal illness and serious pain go together and that the medical world needlessly prolongs life. I understand, however, that contemporary medicine can free most terminal patients of serious pain and it does not encourage the unnecessary prolongation of life.

Another difficult issue has to do with the 'harvesting of organs' of brain dead people who have either given prior consent or whose relatives have given consent. Published surveys show consistently that people are sympathetic to the use of their organs after death and that relatives usually respect the wishes of the deceased in this matter. They also show, however, unease about 'presumed consent', that is, people having actively to opt out if they do not wish to have their organs used after death. Various ways have been suggested of removing this unease, including giving relatives the right to object if they wish to do so, but the situation remains unclear.[15]

Respect for the dead is an important principle which involves some recognition of the continuity between the deceased person and the body. Such a body, at burial or cremation, should be, recognisably, the body of the person who has died. Any harvesting of organs should not be such as to violate this continuity or to cause unnecessary distress to the mourners.

Being clear about the point of death is also of crucial significance. If 'brain stem death' is generally accepted as such a point, we must be clear that this involves the irreversible loss of capacity for bodily integration, cognition and sentience. Moral theologians, of different views, have often warned about the dangers of pronouncing death too quickly and of moving the body with undue haste, especially when the use of organs is on the agenda.

In certain cases, individuals who are brain dead are kept 'alive' though mechanical and medical means so that their organs may not deteriorate before they are removed for transplantation. Questions have been raised as to whether 'elective ventilation' means that the point of death has been postponed; if so, is it moral, indeed legal, to harvest organs, for example while the heart is still beating? This process can also involve a 'stripping' of the body's parts. Is this consistent with the principle of respect for the dead? It is true that major medical and surgical procedures are rarely without their gruesome aspects but usually they are for the benefit of the person concerned. Elective ventilation is for the benefit of others and thus in a different category. Great care is needed, therefore, in its use and in the way bodies are treated.

At most, organ donation can be treated as a sort of 'intermediate technology' which may be acceptable to Christians whilst other, ethically acceptable, alternatives are being developed. From an ethical point of view, such alternatives should minimise harm and maximise respect for both the living and the dead. The generation of tissues and, eventually, organs from somatic (or 'adult') cells would certainly fulfil these conditions. If research goals for organ donation and transplantation, in addition to improving current procedures, could include the development of such alternatives, this would be an advantage.

Revolt against 'mere' utilitarianism

Because of the rapid advances in technology which we have noted, there is a temptation to argue in a crudely utilitarian way, particularly if it promotes scientific progress. If people's desires and preferences can be satisfied through scientific means, why should they not be? Why should parents not be able to select their children's sex if they wish to 'balance' their family? Why should research on embryonic stem cells not be allowed if it is going to help people with serious diseases and, logically, why should reproductive cloning be prohibited since, for some, it may be their only chance of having a child?

It is, perhaps, true to say that we can see the beginnings of a revolt against this kind of thinking. People are beginning to ask questions in terms of intrinsic value rather than use. Some sophisticated utilitarians incorporate such ideas into their thinking but, generally, utilitarianism is not associated with them. A transcendental basis for ethical thought and action may come to be more in demand. The end does not always justify the means and human beings, in particular, should never be treated merely as a means. The parents, for example, of a very sick child would not be justified in having another simply so that its organs, blood and marrow can be used for the benefit of the first. The birth of the second child may, indeed, have benefits for the first but that should not be the main reason for its existence.

Those responsible for welfare policies are having to ask whether we should always define them in materialistic terms such as housing, clothing, food and even physical safety, or whether our focus should, rather, be on the promotion of spiritual and social values which will contribute to the welfare of societies and individuals? A recent debate in Parliament on football hooliganism, for example, was dominated by demands for ensuring that ordinary football fans should be enabled to enjoy the game they had paid to watch, and that the general public should be protected from drunken and extremist violence. There was only one speech which asked basic questions about the socialisation of those who committed such crimes, their family background, what sort of education they had received and so on.

Again, there is renewed and growing awareness of the need to 'work with the grain of nature'. This is not all obscurantism; most recognise that human civilisation is built on intervention in the course of nature and this is illustrated particularly well by the worlds of medicine and of agriculture. There is concern, however, that some procedures are not so much about enhancing productivity or the natural qualities of plants, for instance, as about alteration of their basic structure which will affect the kind of thing they are, leading to unknown and possibly widespread environmental consequences.

Religion and morals

What is the relationship between religion and morals? We have seen already that moral awareness in relation to the world at large and, in particular within human communities, is widespread, and that the development of a common moral discourse, so crucial for our times, depends on this awareness. While such awareness is not necessarily linked to a religious worldview, historically the evidence must be overwhelming that moral discourse, if not awareness itself, is closely related to and often arises from such a worldview. The discipline of comparative religious ethics, for example, provides some support for this view, even if its very possibility has been questioned by those who would deny any kind of cross-cultural rationality. Then there is the question of motivation. It is true that there have been and are individuals who are motivated towards moral behaviour without having religious beliefs. On the other hand, religious traditions often form the ground for the formation of an educated conscience which, in turn, motivates action. It can, of course, readily be granted that non-religious people can act morally, indeed, altruistically and that they may be, in some cases, morally better informed. Still the question arises as to whether they can give an equally satisfactory account of certain moral principles, for example, the equal dignity of all human beings, the primacy of conscience and our sense of duty. As Kant saw, such an account can better be given by reference to a Supreme Being who is both the ground for such ideas and the one who makes them attainable, if not in this life, then in the next.[16]

Religion can, therefore, not only give an account of the moral and motivate us to act in particular ways, but it can provide a worldview within which moral discourse can be placed. It has been the gradual disappearance of such a worldview from our society which has led to widespread questioning of 'traditional morality' and to the sense that moral behaviour is free-standing and arbitrary, without any special relationship to ways of understanding the world and ourselves. The area of religion and morals is a large one, and there is room here only to mention in outline some of the issues at stake.

Morals and law

Another question which is often asked and which has enormous significance for the future is about the relationship of morality to the law of the land. It is, of course, a truism to say that what is morally desirable is not always appropriate for legislation. There is, nevertheless, a very real connection between morals and the law. Legislation must have sound moral underpinning and law must have moral, as well as coercive, force. The two principles underlying most recent legislation are those of liberty and the prevention of harm. Both have strong spiritual and moral connotations. Liberty is deeply rooted in Christian ideas of conscience and responsibility for our actions. As far as the criterion of 'harm' is concerned, it is far from clear that this applies only to other individuals. It is, in fact, widely acknowledged that it must include harm to society and to those institutions which it needs for its survival and prosperity. These certainly include marriage, the family and the essential dignity of the human person. Thus marriage and family law will not only make sure that the 'goods' of these institutions are not harmed, but that people within them are never treated merely as a means; hence the safe-guarding of monogamy and the life-long nature of marriage, even in the secular realm. It must be for reasons such as these that the European Convention on Human Rights, recently incorporated into domestic law, exempts states from, or limits the application of, some of its articles on grounds of morality.[17]

Finally

We have considered then how we arrive at moral decisions and the basis for them. We have looked at the ways in which morality is universal but also at ways in which it could be relative to a particular situation or culture. We have considered briefly the roots of the Anglican moral tradition and whether it can be used today. We have examined some contemporary moral dilemmas, including questions about personhood in the context of the very beginnings of life and its ending. We have attempted to both relate morals to religion and law and to make necessary distinctions between them. Finally, we have asked how we can give an account of moral awareness and behaviour, and have sought to do this in terms of our response to the reality which confronts us, most of all, to the reality of God himself. As Richard Hooker has said, "the being of God is a kind of law to his own working: for that perfection which God is, giveth perfection to that he doth".

Notes

[1] Hans Küng, *Global Responsibility in Search of a New World Ethic*, London, SCM, 1991, and in *Christianity and the World Religions*, London, SCM, 1993, especially pp12f and pp 441f.

[2] Samuel P. Huntingdon, *The Clash of Civilisations and the Remaking of World Order*, New York, Simon and Schuster, 1996, p320.

[3] See further Oliver O'Donovan, *Resurrection and Moral Order*, Leicester, IVP, 1986, pp31ff.

[4] James Ward, *The Realm of Ends: Pluralism and Theism*, CUP, 1912, esp. pp97ff.

[5] See further *Life in Christ: Morals, Communion and the Church*, Anglican-Roman Catholic International Commission, CHP, CTS, 1994, pp3ff, and *The Family Way*, in the Cambridge Alumni Magazine (CAM) Lent, 2000, No 29, pp19f.

[6] On this issue see Michael Banner *Christian Ethics and Contemporary Moral Problems*, CUP, 1999, pp270ff.

[7] Richard Hooker, *The Laws of Ecclesiastical Polity*, Arthur Pollard (ed), Manchester, Fyfield, 1990, Book I, pp34ff.

[8] On this see Richard Baxter, *Richard Baxter's Catholick Theologie: Plain, Pure, Peaceable: For Pacification of the Dogmatical Word-warriors*, London, R. White for N. Simmons, 1675.

[9] Gerhard von Rad, *Genesis*, London, SCM, 1972, pp59f.

[10] Lahore, Ashraf, 1969, p132.

[11] W R Sorley and G F Stout (eds), *Essays in Philosophy*, CUP, 1927, pp204ff.

[12] See further *Personal Origins, The Report of a Working Party on Human Fertilisation and Embryology*, BSR, London, CHP, 2nd Edition, 1996, pp32f.

[13] Pete Moore, *Babel's Shadow: Genetic Technologies in a Fracturing Society*, Oxford, Lion, 1999, pp154f. On the 'developmental' view of personhood, see John Habgood, *Being a Person: Where Faith and Science Meet*, London, Hodder, 1998.

[14] Michael Banner identifies the two opposite kinds of abuse in relation to terminally ill patients: benign neglect arising from a denial of the patient's condition or, on the other hand, overtreatment which can be painful, humiliating and unnecessary. He advocates the 'good death' of the hospice movement where the patient is as free of pain as possible and is provided with a high quality of life. In *Christian Ethics* and *Contemporary Moral Problems*, op. cit., pp 68ff.

[15] Based on results presented at the Symposium on Organ Donation and Transplantation, *The Multi-Faith Perspective*, Bradford, March 2000.

[16] In *Religion Within the Limits of Reason Alone*, Harper, New York, 1960, pp6, 131, 170f.

[17] See, in particular, articles 8,10 and 11.

27

A 'DUMBED-DOWN' CHRISTENING: CULTURE AND THE CHURCH OF ENGLAND

Since at least the 1970s there has been a fashion in the Church of England to minimise depth and mystery in its worship because of the alleged need to make its services 'accessible'. The new alternative service for baptism, which has now been approved, continues this trend.[1] Instead of explaining what baptism means and what the various parts of the service signify, its solution is to do away with key elements of the service altogether! It may be said, "It is only an alternative!" but the Church has a track record of 'alternatives' becoming the norm.

From ancient times, the structure of the service has included the renunciation of sin, the world and the devil and the turning to Christ as Lord and Saviour.[2] The new wording is designed to be easier to understand but critics are stunned at such a fundamental change to a cornerstone of their faith, saying the new 'dumbed-down' version strikes at the heart of what baptism means. If a child is being baptised, it is on the basis of the faith of the parents and the godparents, as well as the faith of the community. There is, finally, a commission both to hear and to proclaim the Gospel. Instead, bishops, responsible for the service, say that 'sin' now means eating too much cake and the 'devil' is an ambivalent figure. He must be delighted to hear this!

In all aspects, the new service falls short of what has usually been required. At a time of high interest in supernatural evil, the traditional renunciation of the devil and all his works has been replaced with an anodyne rejection of evil in its many forms. The very first baptisms of the Church took place after St Peter's call at Pentecost to "repent and be baptised ... for the forgiveness of sins" (Acts 2:38). The Church has always regarded repentance as necessary for beginning the Christian life and, for children, a cleansing, if not from actual sin, then certainly from the sinfulness in which the whole race has been implicated since the original sin.

Because of its anxiety to make everyone feel welcome and its desire not to offend anyone, the new service, almost entirely, does away with sin and the need to repent from its personal and social manifestations and consequences. The whole thrust of the service of deliverance from sin, protection from the devil and regeneration by water and the Holy Spirit, based on the teaching of Jesus himself, has been set aside and replaced by a 'welcome' which seems to have no basis in the promises of God, the faith of the parents and godparents, or of the Church as a whole.

Indeed, there seems to be ambivalence about the Church itself with such circumlocutions as 'God's family' being used. We are not told anything about the Christ in whom we are to put our trust. There is no acknowledgement of him as Lord and Saviour. In general, there is a reluctance to declare that the Bible sees the world as having gone wrong and needing to be put right. This is done by the coming of Christ. Baptism is nothing less than taking part in this story of salvation, no part of which can be sold short. Rather than the constant dumbing-down of Christian teaching, whether for baptism, marriage or death, we should be spending time preparing people for these great rites of passage. When it comes to the service itself, the need is not to eliminate crucial areas of teaching but to explain them. It is best to call a halt to these perhaps well-meant efforts before they further reduce the fullness of the Church's faith to easily swallowed soundbites which are unlikely to convince anyone or to meet their deep needs.

The Church's language, worship, pastoral care and evangelism, rather than simply accommodating to this or that culture, need to be prepared to be vigorously counter-cultural so that eyes may truly be opened to the human predicament and to God's way out of it. They have to show that the Christian worldview is not only credible but the most believable explanation of the world and of ourselves. We must keep commending the plausibility of Christian views on human dignity, equality and liberty rather than just capitulating to whatever is fashionable.[3]

This is a choice for the Church of England either to become simply an attenuated version of whatever the English people happen to believe and to value, or to be full bloodedly a manifestation of the 'one, holy, catholic and apostolic church' it still continues to confess in the creeds. Which way will it choose?

Notes

[1] See The Church of England's *Common Worship Christian Initiation: Additional Baptism Texts in Accessible Language,* Church House Publishing, London, 2015.

[2] See *Baptism,* in J. G. Davies (ed.), *A New Dictionary of Liturgy and Worship,* London, SCM, 1986, pp55ff for a convenient summary.

[3] On this see further Peter L. Berger, *A Rumour of Angels: Modern Society and the Rediscovery of the Supernatural,* Harmondsworth, Middlesex, Penguin, 1971, pp43ff, and Lesslie Newbigin, *The Gospel in a Pluralist Society,* SPCK, 1989, pp8ff.

EPILOGUE

WORKING IN THE LIGHT OF THE GOSPEL

Like people anywhere, and at any time, 21st century folk need to hear the story of how Jesus Christ frees us from our anxiety and guilt. How he draws us into friendship with him, as well as into friendship with others like us who have felt his healing touch. The circle of those touched by the story of Jesus know that it is *this* story which makes sense of all the other stories, even the most difficult ones. This story makes sense not just of our personal stories, or even that of our communities and nations, but of the universe as a whole.

This is why we have to retrieve Christianity from being 'just another faith' and recognise that it is a way of looking at the world. It has something to say (in affirming, questioning or judging) about every aspect of human knowledge. It will seek significance, meaning and depth, for example, in art or literature, but then also seek to relate what it has discovered to that touchstone of authentic discovery: that which we have seen and heard and touched with our hands, concerning the Word of Life (1 John 1:1). It is the same with the sciences. The *Logos,* who becomes incarnate in Jesus of Nazareth, is that principle of rationality who makes possible an ordered world which can be studied by rational minds.

Whilst always seeking to draw people into the ever-expanding and ever-deepening circle of reconciliation, the Church is always, because of the nature of the Gospel, also driven into the public sphere to bear witness there to God's love and his purposes for humanity and for the whole of creation. From the very beginning, the Bible tells us that the human story is the story of community and not just of individuals, whether noble or savage. A large part of the story of the Bible is about people, God's ways with them and theirs with God. But it is also about the peoples, near and far, around them. There is good news for them too, as well as the same judgement as for Israel when she strays from the path set out before her (see, for example, Amos chapters 1-2). God's providential care extends to them too (Amos 9:7) and, conversely, God can use them both to bring judgement on his people (as in Jeremiah) or to save them (as in the second part of Isaiah). Even in the most difficult conditions of exile, God's people are called on into the political and social arena to bear witness, without compromise, to a faithful God (the Book of Daniel and Jeremiah 29:1-14 are examples of how, in different ways, there can be faithful involvement in public life).

The initial aim of both extremist Islamism and aggressive secularism is to confine Christians to their church buildings where, it is hoped, they will atrophy and die. Against this, fidelity to the story by which they live will impel Christians and church to affirm the inalienable dignity of human beings, man or woman, old or young, poor or rich, black, white, brown or yellow, because they have been made in God's image. It will lead them to advocacy of freedom of expression and of belief. They will fight for the integrity of, and support for, the natural family and they will be deeply involved not just in helping the poor but in seeking justice for them.

As ever, in this century also, the Church and Christians should have an 'interior' agenda which is about the nurturing of people's spiritual and moral lives. It is about a firmer grasp of God's story and a deepening in our souls as a result. Contrary to popular opinion, the Church has the riches of contemplation, meditation, reflection and moral thinking in its armoury to assist with this task, not to speak of the variety of ways in which to give reverent attention to the Word of God.

There is then a social agenda which is about a patterning of our communities according to the justice and love of God, revealed in the Bible and modelled in faithful Christian communities in different ways and in different places: whether it is that *stabilitas* and hospitality which is Benedictine, or the sacrificial welcome of L'Arche to people of differing abilities and disabilities or the ministry to disadvantaged women in agencies like *Divya Shanti* in India or ECREST in Pakistan. All of these, and many more, have a relevance beyond their immediate tasks to society at large. They need to be emulated and multiplied for the sake of the Kingdom.

There is also a political agenda which is not necessarily party political but which seems to bear witness to the world view of the Bible, to its analysis of the human situation and to its spiritual and moral instruction in the public square. This is what many Christians shy away from. They wish to lead a quiet life of personal holiness, of service to neighbours and the building up of their church. These are laudable desires but if we are to transform cultures, institutions and nations, we also have to take the path of campaigning, advocacy and education on public issues. We need to persuade by the quality of our arguments and our love for those whom we seek to influence.

There is a very big job awaiting the Church and Christians in this century. We have been able to point to only a small part of it in this book. Even from that we can tell there is no time to waste:

> Then give us courage, Father God,
> to choose again the pilgrim way,
> And help us to accept with joy
> the challenge of tomorrow's day.

Fred Kaan

BIBLIOGRAPHY

Abbas Amanat, *Apocalyptic Islam and Iranian Shi'ism*, London, IB Tauris, 2009.

Ahdar, Rex and Nicholas Aroney, *Shari'a in the West*, Oxford, OUP, 2010.

Ahmad, Mirza Tahir, *Murder in the Name of Allah*, Cambridge, Lutherwork, 1989.

Allen Jr., John L., *The Global War on Christians*, New York, Image, 2013.

Almond, Brenda, *Fragmenting Families*, Oxford, Clarendon Press, 2006.

Ateek, Naim, *Justice, and only Justice: A Palestinian Theology of Liberation*, Maryknoll, NY, Orbis, 1989.

Avis, Paul, *Anglicanism and the Christian Church*, Edinburgh, T & T Clark, 1989.

Bailey, Kenneth E., *Jesus Through Middle Eastern Eyes: Cultural Studies in the Gospels*, London, SPCK, 2008.

— — —, *Poet and Peasant and through Peasant Eyes: A Literary Cultural Approach to the Parables of Luke*, Grand Rapids, Eerdmans, 1976.

Banner, Michael, *Christian Ethics and Contemporary Moral Problems*, Cambridge, CUP, 1999.

Barrett, David and John Padwick, *Rise up and Walk! Conciliation and the African Indigenous Churches, 1815-1987*, Nairobi, OUP, 1989.

Bebbington, David, *Evangelicalism in Modern Britain: A History from the 1730s to the 1980s*, London, Unwin Hyman, 1989.

Bede, *The Ecclesiastical History of the English People*, Oxford, OUP, 2008.

Benedict XVI, *Paul of Tarsus*, London, Catholic Truth Society, 2009.

Berger, Peter L., *A Rumour of Angels: Modern Society and the Rediscovery of the Supernatural*, Harmondsworth, Middlesex, Penguin, 1971.

Biggar, Nigel, *Aiming to Kill: The Ethics of Suicide and Euthanasia*, London, Darton, Longman and Todd, 2004.

Brown, Callum, *The Death of Christian Britain*, London, Routledge, 2001.

Buber, Martin, *Between Man and Man*, London, Collins, 1971.

Burke, S.M, (and S. Quraishi), *Quaid-i-Azam: His Personality and Politics*, Karachi, OUP, 1997.

Cahill, Thomas, *The Gifts of the Jews*, Oxford, Lion, 1998.

Campbell, R., *The Elders: Seniority within Earliest Christianity*, Edinburgh, T & T Clark, 1994.

Chadwick, Henry, *The Early Church*, London, Penguin, 1967.

Chadwick, Owen, *The Reformation*, London, Penguin, 1990.

Chapman, Colin, *Islam and the West*, Carlisle, Paternoster, 1998.

Church of England report, *The Search for Faith and the Witness of the Church*, London, CHP, 1996.

CIVITAS, *How Fathers fit into the Family*, Institute for the Study of Civil Society, London, 2001.

Cowling, Maurice, *Religion and Public Doctrine in Modern England*, Vol I, Cambridge, CUP, 2003.

Cox, Lynda Rose (et al.), *Magna Carta Unravelled*, London, Wilberforce Publications, 2015.

Cragg, Kenneth, *The Arab Christian: A History in the Middle East*, London, Mowbrays, 1992.

Denaux, A. and N. Sagovsky (eds), *Studying Mary: The Virgin Mary in Anglican and Roman Catholic Theology and Devotion*, London, T & T Clark, 2007.

Dillistone, F.W., *The Christian Understanding of Atonement*, Welwyn, Nisbet, 1968.

Dixon, Peter, *Peacemakers: Building Stability in a Complex World*, Nottingham, IVP, 2009.

Eberstadt, Mary, *How the West Really Lost God*, Conshohocken, PA, Templeton Press, 2013.

El-Masry, Iris H., *Introduction to the Coptic Church*, Cairo, Dar El Alam El Arabi, 1977.

Eno, Robert B., SS, *Teaching Authority in the Early Church: Message of the Fathers of the Church*, Wilmington, Del, Michael Glazier, 1984.

Evans, Gillian and Robert Wright (eds), *The Anglican Tradition: A Handbook of Sources*, London, SPCK, 1991.

Felix, George, *Quaid-i-Azam's Vision*, Salford, Agape Press, 2001.

Frisch, Morten and Anders Hviid, *Childhood Family Correlations of Heterosexual and Homosexual marriages: A National Cohort Study of Two Million Danes*, Dept. of Epidemiology Research, Danish Epidemiology Science Centre, Copenhagen, 2006.

Gaudeul, J. M., *Encounters & Clashes: Islam and Christianity in History*, 2 Vols, Rome, Pontifical Institute for Study of Arabic and Islam, 1984.

Glass, Catherine and David Abbott, *Share the Inheritance*, Shawford, Hants, Inheritance Press, 2010.

Gregorios, Paulos, W.H. Lazareth and N.A. Nissiotis (eds), *Does Chalcedon Divide or Unite?*, Geneva, WCC, 1981.

Hallaq, Wael B., *Authority, Continuity and Change in Islamic Law*, Cambridge, CUP, 2001.

Hannam, James, *God's Philosophers: How the Medieval World Laid the Foundations of Modern Science*, London, ICON, 2009.

Harris, Elizabeth, *What Buddhists Believe*, Oxford, One World, 1998.

Harris, John, *One Blood: 200 years of Aboriginal Encounter with Christianity*, Sutherland, NSW, 1990.

Herzog, J. M., *Father Hunger: Explorations with Adults and Children*, Analytic Press, Hillsdale, NJ, 2001.

Hewitt, Gordon, *The Problems of Success: A History of the Church Missionary Society, 1919-1942*, London, SCM, 1971.

Hill, Henry (ed), *Light from the East: A Symposium on the Oriental Orthodox and Assyrian Churches*, Toronto, Anglican Book Centre, 1988.

Hill, Mark (ed) *Religious Liberty and Human Rights*, Cardiff, University of Wales Press, 2002.

Hitchens, Peter, *The Rage against God*, London, Continuum, 2010.

Hooker, Richard, *The Laws of Ecclesiastical Polity*, (ed) Arthur Pollard, Manchester, Fyfield, 1990.

Huntingdon, Samuel P., *The Clash of Civilisations and the Remaking of World Order*, New York, Simon and Schuster, 1996.

Huntington, William Reed, *The Church-Idea: An Essay towards Unity*, 4th Edn, New York, Charles Scribner's Sons, 1899.

Iqbal, Muhammad, T*he Development of Metaphysics in Persia*, Lahore, Bazim-i-Iqbal, 1964.

Iqbāl, Muhammad, T*he Reconstruction of Religious Thought in Islam*, Lahore, 1930.

Ishaq, Ibn, Sirat Rasul Allah, *The Life of Muhammad*, (trans) A. Guillaume, Oxford, OUP, 1955.

Jackson, Emily, and John Keown, *Debating Euthanasia*, Oxford, Hart Publishing, 2012.

Jalal, Ayesha, *Partisans of Allah: Jihad in South Asia*, Lahore, Sang-E-Meel, 2008.

Jones, Peter, *The Other World View*, Bellingham, WA, Kirkdale Press, 2015.

Karas, Shawky F., *The Copts since the Arab Invasion: Strangers in their Land*, Jersey City, NJ, 1983.

Keller, Tim, *Counterfeit Gods*, London, Hodder, 2010.

Khalidi, Tarif, The Muslim Jesus, Cambridge, MA, Harvard University Press, 2001.

Kilner, John F. et al. (eds), *Cutting-Edge Bioethics*, Grand Rapids, Eerdmans, 2002.

Küng, Hans, *Global Responsibility in Search of a New World Ethic*, London, SCM, 1991.

Ling, John L., *Bioethical Issues*, Leominster, Day One Publications, 2014.

London, Herbert, *America's Secular Challenge: the Rise of a New National Religion*, New York, Encounter, 2008.

MacIntyre, Alasdair, *After Virtue: A Study in Moral Theory*, London, Duckworth, 2000.

Mar Thoma, Alexander, *The Mar Thoma Church: Heritage and Mission*, Kottayam, 1986.

Martin, David, *Pentecostalism: The World Their Parish*, Oxford, Biblelands, 2002.

Moore, Pete, *Babel's Shadow: Genetic Technologies in a Fracturing Society*, Oxford, Lion, 1999.

Murphy, Francis, CSSR, *The Christian Way of Life: Message of the Fathers of the Church*, Vol.18, Wilmington, Delaware, Michael Glazier, 1986.

Neill, Stephen, *Anglicanism*, Harmondsworth, Penguin, 1960.

Newbigin, Lesslie, *The Gospel in a Pluralist Society*, London, SPCK, 1989.

Newman, J. H., *An Essay on the Development of Christian Doctrine*, Notre Dame, Indiana, University of Notre Dame Press, 2010.

O'Donovan, Oliver, *Resurrection and Moral Order*, Leicester, IVP, 1986.

Parke, Ross, *Fatherhood*, Harvard, Cambridge, MA, 1996.

Phan, Peter, *Social Thought: Message of the Fathers of the Church*, Vol.20, Wilmington, Delaware, Michael Glazier, 1984.

Piper, John, *The Future of Justification: A Response to N.T. Wright, Nottingham*, IVP, 2008.

Platten, Stephen (ed), *Anglicanism and the Western Christian Tradition*, Norwich, Canterbury Press, 2003.

Polkinghorne, John, *One World, The Interaction of Science and Theology*, London, SPCK, 1986.

— — —, *Science and Providence*, London, SPCK, 1989.

— — —, *Searching for Truth: A Scientist looks at the Bible*, Oxford, BRF, 1996.

Radner, Ephraim and Philip Turner, *The Fate of Communion, the Agony of Anglicanism and the Future of a Global Church*, Grand Rapids, Eerdmans, 2006.

Regnerus, Mark, *How different are the adult children of parents who have same-sex relationships?*, Social Science Research 41, 2012.

Robinson, John, *Wrestling with Romans*, London, SCM, 1979.

Runciman, Steven, *A History of the Crusades*, London, Penguin, 1991.

Russell, Gerard, *Heirs to Forgotten Kingdoms*, London, Simon & Schuster, 2014.

Ruthven, Malise, *A Fury for God: The Islamist Attack on America*, London, Granta, 2002.

Samuel, Vinay and Chris Sugden (eds), *Sharing Jesus in the Two-Thirds World*, Bangalore, Partnership in Mission, Asia, 1983.

Sanneh, Lamin, *Translating the Message: The Missionary Impact on Culture*, Maryknoll, NY, Orbis, 1989 and 2009.

Schimmel, Annemarie, *Gabriel's Wing*, Leiden, 1963.

Shortt, Rupert, *Christianophobia: A Faith under Attack*, London, Rider Press, 2012.

Sider, Robert D., *The Gospel and its Proclamation: Message of the Fathers of the Church*, Washington, Delaware, 1983.

Smith, Margaret, *Studies in Early Mysticism in the Near and Middle East*, UK, Kessinger, 2003.

Stambaugh, John and David Balch, *The Social World of the First Christians*, London, SPCK, 1986.

Stark, Rodney, *The Triumph of Christianity*, New York, Harper Collins, 2011.

Stein, Peter, *Roman Law in European History*, Cambridge, CUP, 2005.

Stott, John, et al. (eds), T*he Anglican Communion and Scripture*, Oxford, Regnum/EFAC, 1996.

Swan, Laura, *The Forgotten Desert Mothers*, New York, Paulist Press, 2001.

Thomas, M.M., *The Acknowledged Christ of The Indian Renaissance*, London, SCM, 1969.

Toolan, John (ed), *Medieval Christian Perceptions of Islam*, New York, Routledge, 2000.

Toon, Peter, *Justification and Sanctification*, London, Marshall, Morgan & Scott, 1983.

Tyndale, William, *The Obedience of the Christian Man*, London, Penguin, 2000.

Ward, Benedicta (ed), *The Sayings of the Desert Fathers*, London, SLG, 1981.

Ward, James, *The Realm of Ends: Pluralism and Theism*, CUP, 1912.

Ware, T., *The Orthodox Church*, Middlesex, UK, Penguin, 1973.

Wessels, Anton, *Europe: Was it ever really Christian?*, London, SCM, 1994.

Womack, Sarah, *What Makes a Good Childhood in Britain Today*, Economic and Social Research Council, Swindon, 2003.

Wright, N.T., J*ustification: God's Plan and Paul's Vision*, London, SPCK, 2009.

Ye'or, Bat, *The Dhimmi: Jesus and Christians under Islam*, London, Associated University Presses, 1985.

Young, William, *Patriarch, Shah and Caliph*, Rawalpindi, 1974.

A

Abacha, Sani, 69
Abbasides, 201f
Abbott, David, 65, 107
Aboriginals, 51
Abortion Act 1967, 89, 104, 182
Abortion, 75, 276
Abraham, 16
Acts of the Apostles, 51, 75
Addiction, 22, 39, 70
Adoption, 22
Adultery, 26, 121
Advocacy, 172f, 189, 292f
Affection, 120
Afghanistan, 157, 168, 173, 177
Aflak, Michel, 205
Africa, 215f, 249, 261
African Independent Churches, 261
Agriculture, 281
Ahdar, Rex, 184
Aheb, 25
Ahl Al-Kitāb, 161, 167, 177
Ahmadiyya, 165, 168, 176, 185f
Aid, 176f.
Alawites, 160
Alcohol, 39
Alexandria School of Theology, 209
Alexandria, 155, 169, 196f, 250
Alfred, King, 81, 96
Alienation, 21f, 37f, 70, 158, 206
Alistair Hardy Research Institute, 44
Allen, John L., 108, 168
Al-Mahdi, 201
Almond, Brenda, 123, 125f, 180
Al-Qaeda, 153, 159
Altruism, 143
Amanat, Abbas, 184
Americas, 171, 179, 222
Ancient Oriental Churches, 72f, 251f
Andrewes, Lancelot, 243
Anglican Consultative Council (ACC), 220, 239, 248
Anglican- Orthodox Dialogue, 245, 250f, 258
Anglican-Roman Catholic Dialogue, 18, 245, 250, 254f
Anglicans, 162, 215f, 232, 236f, 243f, 255f
Anglo-Catholics, 260
Anglo-Saxons, 97
Animals, 141f

Anointing, 82f, 107
Anselm, St., 97
Anthony of Sourozh, 27
Anthropology, 215
Antinomianism, 17
Antioch, 198, 205, 218, 252f
Anxiety, 22, 38f, 70f, 291
Apologetics, 187, 196, 200
Apostasy, 156, 171, 185f
Apostles, 72, 231, 241
Apostolic Teaching, 222f, 231f, 249
Appeal to All Christian People, 238, 246, 250, 260, 262f
Aquila, 217, 233
Aquinas, Thomas St., 276
Arab Spring, 101, 153, 158
Arabic, 97, 160, 201f, 221
Arabs, 169, 199, 205
Aramaic, 160, 220
Archbishop of Canterbury, 220, 228, 248, 253, 255
Architecture, 170, 203
Arians, 197
Aristotle, 97f, 114
Armageddon, 39,
Armenia (ns), 160, 162, 170, 221, 253
Aroney, Nicholas, 184
Articles of Religion, 85, 222, 234, 236, 243f, 263
Arts, 93, 170, 275, 291
Asceticism, 202
Ascetics, 72
Ashám, 13
Ashoka, 95
Asia Bibi, 186f
Asia, 218f, 235, 249, 261
Assad Bashar, 159f
Assad, Hafez Al-, 159
Assisted Dying, 75, 146f, 180
Assurance, doctrine of, 21
Assyria (ns), 60f
Astrologers, 46, 68
Ateek, Naim, 208
Athanasius, Mar, 253
Athanasius, St., 197, 228
Athenagoras I, 250
Athens, 51, 57
Atkins, Peter, 46
Atonement, 13
Augsburg Confession, 247

Augustine of Canterbury, St., 68
Augustine of Hippo, St., 17f, 26, 43, 62, 115f
Australia, 51, 171
Authority, 78, 255
Autonomy, 128,146, 158, 182, 263, 273, 276f
Averroes (Ibn Rushd), 203,
Avicenna (Ibn Sīnā), 28, 203,
Avis, Paul, 264, 267

B
Ba'ath Party, 159f, 205
Babylon, 61
Badawi, Raif, 186
Badger, George, 253
Baghdad, 197, 208
Bahá'í, 151, 163, 168, 190
Bahrain, 178
Bailey, Kenneth, 204, 207, 211
Balch, David, 66
Balkans, 171
Bangladesh, 197
Banner, Michael, 53, 123, 284f
Baptism, 16, 246, 287f
Baqā, 29
Barrett, David, 261, 267
Basil, St., 243
Baxter, Richard, 284
Bebbington, David, 66, 245, 264f
Bede, The Venerable, 65, 79
Belief, 8, 57, 67, 77, 87, 93, 98, 104f, 156, 167, 171, 174, 177, 179f, 186, 189f, 292
Belonging, 67
Benedict XVI, Pope, 18, 20, 68, 77, 197, 221, 227f
Benedictines, 293
Bentham, Jeremy, 105
Berger, Peter, 289
Berhane, Helen, 108
Bethany, Sisters of, 253
Bible (Scripture), 8, 13f, 25, 30, 45, 47f, 61, 76, 81f, 97f, 97f, 147, 162, 182, 198f, 201, 204f, 215, 219f, 244f, 260, 273f, 288, 292f
Bible Churchmen's Missionary Society (BCMS, now Crosslinks), 253
'Big Bang', 41f
Biggar, Nigel, 148
Bill of Rights, 101f, 157
Bishops, 73, 75f, 199, 239f, 243f, 253, 257f, 263
Blasphemy, 156, 165, 170, 176, 185f

Body, the, 139f, 279
Boniface, St., 68
Bonino, Jose, 266
Book of Common Prayer, 81, 87, 117, 221f, 243, 248, 263
Bosnia, 174
Bouteneff, Peter, 79, 265
Boys, 125f, 131
Brain Stem Death, 140, 279
Brandon, James, 194
Brazil, 261
BRICS Countries, 155
Britain, 59f, 69, 77, 88, 95, 102f, 131, 137, 160, 187, 192, 218, 253, 261
British and Foreign Bible Society, 245
Brown, Callum, 42, 53, 218
Bruce, Fiona, 136
Buber, Martin, 53
Bucer, Martin, 243
Buchanan, Colin, 265f
Buddism, 44, 50, 95f
Buerk, Michael, 46
Burke, S.M., 168
Burma (Myanmar), 96, 100
Burman, Thomas, 211
Burqa', 110
Business, 41
Byrd, A. Dean, 130
Byzantium, 200f

C
Caesar, 61, 82
Cahill, Thomas, 53
Cairo Declaration, 187
Cairo, 155
Caliph, Caliphate, 161, 174, 201f
Calne, R. Y., 143
Cambridge Group for the History of Population and Social Structure, 113
Cambridge, 47, 125f, 187, 275
Campbell, R., 228
Canada, 256
Canon Law, 182
Caribbean, 261
Caroline Divines, 17, 244
Carthage, 169
Caste, 51, 219
Catholic Adoption Agencies, 104
Catholics (Eastern & Roman), 18f, 160, 243, 254, 257, 261
Celibacy, 257

INDEX

Celts, 97

Central Asia, 209

Chadwick, Henry, 210

Chadwick, Owen, 66, 107, 265

Chapman, Colin, 108

Charlie Hebdo, 185f, 191

Charter of Liberties, 82, 97

Chechnya, 174

Chesterton, G. K., 269

Chicago-Lambeth Quadrilateral, 225, 246f

Children, 114f, 125f, 131f, 136, 139, 155, 179, 183, 197, 287f.

China, 47, 99, 178f

Chishti, Rehman, 100

Chloe, 233

Christendom, 57

Christianity, 10, 25, 87, 101, 174, 177, 196f, 201, 218f, 243, 259, 275, 291

Christians, 8, 23, 31, 44, 57, 59, 77, 87, 96, 98f, 142f, 151, 161f, 176f, 181, 180f, 195f, 219, 221f, 246, 249, 252, 280, 292f

Chrysostom, John, 198, 243

Church Mission Society (CMS), 51, 228, 252

Church of England, 63f, 74f, 219, 234, 241, 243, 246, 251f, 258, 260, 287f

Church Planting, 240

Church, the, 19f, 23, 57, 62, 68, 70f, 93, 106, 114, 116, 129, 179, 182, 198, 217f, 231f, 244f, 255, 288, 292f

Churches, 136, 155, 161f, 167, 170, 181, 195f, 206, 217f, 246f, 258

Church's Ministry Among The Jewish People (CMJ), 253

Citizenship, 52, 102, 156f, 166f, 176f, 183, 193, 200

Civil Partnerships, 106, 118

Civil Rights Act, 105

Civilisation, 203, 271, 281

CIVITAS Think Tank, 88, 130, 184

Clement of Alexandria, 196, 198

Clergy, 72, 75, 77f, 97, 117, 119f, 161f, 203, 206, 209, 244f, 253, 257, 262

Cloning, 75, 136, 141f, 280

Cognition, 140

Coleman, Paul, 108

Coleman, R., 267

Comity, 249

Common good, the, 57

Common Law, 81, 96

Common Origin, 51

Communication, 220

Communion of Saints, 244

Communion, 224, 245, 253, 258f

Community, 60, 68, 71f, 78, 93, 104, 131, 156f, 177f, 182, 185f, 193, 195f, 204, 218, 234, 251f, 262, 276, 281, 287, 291f

Compassion, 139, 145, 147, 166, 274

Complementary, 126f
Confessors, 45, 72
Conflict, 224f
Congregation for the Doctrine of the Faith (CDF), 255
Congregations, 74, 78, 234
Conscience, 7, 57, 64, 77, 87f, 98, 103f, 148, 156f, 179, 182f, 186, 260, 271, 274, 282
Consent, 139f, 278
Conservative Party, 122
Constantine the Great, 96
Constitution of Medina, 96
Constitution, 81f, 167
Constitutions of States, 157
Contemplation, 145, 292
Contextualisation, 206f
Converts, 167
Cook, E. David, 143
Copenhagen, 185f
Copts, 169, 196, 205f
Corinth, 218, 233f
Coronation Service, 74, 81, 107
Council of Jerusalem, 75
Councils, 219, 225f, 248, 263
Counselling, 121
Counsellors, 73, 76
Covenant Marriage, 121
Covenant, 16
Covenant, the Anglican, 248
Cowling, Maurice, 108
Cragg, K, 34, 101, 172, 205, 210
Cranfield, C.E.B., 34
Cranmer, Thomas, 243
Creation, 47, 51, 59, 63, 182, 236, 272f, 292
Creeds, 225, 246f, 289
Cross, the, 40, 82, 157, 200
Crown, 88
Culture, 32f, 57, 67f, 70, 74f, 114, 125f, 170, 192, 205f, 215f, 251, 269f, 287f, 293
Custom, 188
Cybrids, 136
Cylinder of Cyrus, 95
Cyprian, St., 219
Cyprus, 250
Cyrus the Great, 95f, 164

D
Dalai Lama, 50

Damascus, 169, 199, 201
Danes, 60
Daniel, 292
Daniell, David, 54
David, King, 97
Davies, J. G., 289
Deaconesses, 72
Deacons, 72, 243
Decision, 238f
Decree of Ecumenism, 255
Delinquency, 132
Democracy, 78, 98, 101, 153f, 164, 167, 170, 174f,
Demography, 122f
Denaux, Adelbert, 264
Denmark, 88
Depression, 147
Desertion, 121
Designer Babies, 131
Desire, 31
Destiny, 45, 236
Development of Doctrine, 222f
Development, 199f
Development, moral, 273
Devil, 287f
Dhimma, Dhimmi, 102, 156, 169f, 176f, 184, 189f, 252
Dialogue, 52
Dickens, Charles, 76
Dignity, 50, 67, 69, 107, 147f, 179f, 271, 282, 289, 292
Dikaioō (and cognates), 15, 18
Dillistone F. W., 13
Direction, 45
Discipline, 238f
Discipling, 57, 71, 139
Discrimination, 104, 156, 176f, 189
Disease, 141, 147, 180, 216
Disestablishment, 74f
Divine Positive Law, 273f
Divorce, 116f, 125f, 156, 183
Divya Shanti, 293
Dixon, Peter, 172
Dobson, James, 130
Dolly the Sheep, 141
Donne, John, 221
Donors of Organs, 139f
Donors of Sperm, 132
Drugs, 39
Druze, 160

Dunstan, St., 82
Duty, 272f

E
Early Christians, 62
East India Company, 252
Easter, 46, 77
Ebadi, Shirin, 162
Eberstadt, Mary, 42, 53
Economy, 154f, 175, 261
ECREST, 293
Ecumenism, 224, 243f, 259f
Edessa (Urfa), 169, 199
Edict of Milan, 96
Edinburgh Missionary Conference (1910), 260
Education, 78, 127f, 131, 156, 177, 180, 193, 198, 252f, 271, 281, 293
Eggs, human, 135, 142
Egypt, 27, 60f, 100f, 154, 166f, 174, 177, 196f, 202f, 227
Egyptians, 60f, 155
Ekklēsia, 234
Elders (Presbyters), 241
Elective Ventilation, 140, 279
Elizabeth I, 254
Elizabethan Settlement, 246
El-Masry, Iris H., 210
Embassy, 76
Embryo, 68, 75, 135f, 142, 180, 222, 276f
Employment, 156, 176, 183, 271
Engagement, 52, 57
Engineer, Asghar Ali, 173
English, 221
Eniffiss, J., 266
Enlightenment, 98, 115f, 179, 183
Eno, Robert B., 210, 228
Ensoulment, 276
Environment, 93, 181, 272, 281
Ephesus, 218, 233f
Epigenesis, 272
Episcopal Church, 259
Episcopē, 240f
Equality, 50, 67, 72, 87, 102f, 126, 157, 166, 174f, 205, 271, 289
Erasmus, 18
Eritrea, 98f
Eschatology, 178
Establishment, 74f, 259
Ethics, 135f, 142, 282

Ethiopia, 221, 253
Eucharist, Holy Communion, the Lord's Supper etc., 16, 82, 218, 237, 244, 246, 255
Eucharistia, 75
Eugenics, 276
Europe, 47, 81, 113, 123, 161, 179, 197, 200, 218, 221, 227, 258f
European Convention, 87, 283
European Court of Human Rights, 106
Euthanasia, 75, 146f, 270, 278f
Evangelical Lutheran Church of America, 259
Evangelicals, 59, 63, 73, 98f, 162, 245, 255, 260
Evangelism, 57, 103, 197, 209, 288
Evangelists, 72, 99
Evans, Gillian, 229, 266f
Evil, 287
Exile, 61, 75
Exodus, 208
Experience, 93
Extremism, 151, 158, 161, 165f, 173, 177, 185f, 192f

F
Faith and Order Commission (WCC), 250, 260
Faith, 9f, 16f, 67, 76f, 82f, 87f, 100, 107, 183, 192, 215, 220, 228, 242, 255f, 272, 287f, 291
Faithfulness, 41f
Family, 8, 37, 41f, 68, 72, 75, 93, 102, 107, 109, 113f, 125f, 131f, 147, 179f, 217f, 237, 283, 292
Fanā, 29
Farah Autun, 205
Farshid Fathi, 162
Farsi, 162
Fathers, 88, 113, 120f, 125f, 131f, 180, 219
Feeding, 146
Felix, George, 168
Fellowship, 241f
Feminism, 109, 132
Fertility Technology, 68
Field, Richard, 244
Finland, Church of, 258
First Amendment of the US Constitution, 105
FitzGerald, Thomas, 79, 265
Forgiveness, 39f, 71
France, 122
Freedom, 7f, 51, 57, 63, 67, 89, 93f, 110f, 151f, 156f, 159, 162f, 167f, 171f, 183, 185f, 193, 200, 236, 289, 292
Fresh Expressions of Church, 233f
Friendship, 40, 71, 182, 291

Fundamentalists, 215
Fuqaha, 202

G
GAFCON (Global Anglican Futures Conference), 217f, 240, 242, 248
Galatia, 218
Gallicans, 254
Gaudeul, Jean-Marie, 200, 211
Gaza, 168
Gbonigi, Emmanuel, 69
Gender, 73, 126f
Genetic Engineering, 135
Genetics, 276
Genocide, 171
Gentiles, 16
Germ Line Therapy, 135f, 142
Germans, 68
Gertz, Steven, 184
Ghali, Boutros, 205
Ghazzālī, Abū- Hāmid, 30
Gifford, Zerbanoo, 66
Girls, 126f, 177
Gitari, David, 69
Glass, Catherine, 65, 107
Global Ethic, 271f
Global South, 217f, 240, 248
Glorious Revolution, 244
God, 10
Goldingay, John, 65
Gomez, Drexel, 264
Gospel, the, 22, 37f, 65f, 70f, 81, 107, 216, 221f, 235f, 244, 287, 291
Government, 87, 129, 135, 157, 164f, 176, 187, 203
Grace, 10, 16, 20, 22, 27, 73, 93, 235, 245
Graham, Billy, 77
Grandparents, 129
Greed, 42
Greek, 97, 203f, 220, 232
Greeks, 51, 98, 114, 170, 234
Gregorios, Paulos, 265
Gregory the Great, St., 68
Guillaume, A., 107
Guilt, 38, 291
Gulf, 151

H
Habba, 25
Habgood, John, 285

INDEX

Halabja, 197
Hallāj, al- Manṣūr, 28
Hallaq, Wael B., 35
Hannam, James, 48, 53
Haqqani Group, 164
Harm, 283
Harris, Elizabeth, 54, 107
Harris, John, 54
Harris, Robert, 194
Harrison, D., 264
Harrison, R. K., 34
Harūn Al-Rashīd, 201
Harvard, 127
Hate Speech, 103, 187
Hattá't, 13
Hay, David, 44
Hebrew, 220
Hegel, G. W. F., 38, 116, 120
Henry I, 82, 97
Hermeneutics, 215
Herzog, James, 127f, 133
Heteronomy, 273
Hewitt, Gordon, 264
Hilarion Alfeyer, Metropolitan, 251
Hill, Christopher, 265f
Hill, Henry, 210, 265
Hill, Mark, 54, 65
Hinduism, 44, 51, 100, 165
Hindutva, 100
History, 113, 115, 170, 175, 181, 192, 198, 205f, 271
Hitchens, Peter, 179, 184
Hizbullah, 39
Hobbes, Thomas, 65
Holocaust, 208
Holy Land, 39, 49, 167
Home-Start, 121
Homilies, Book of, 238
Hooker, R., 16f, 21, 243f, 284
Hope, 9
Hospice Movement, 145f, 180
Hospitality, 52, 76, 84, 208, 293
Hospitals, 146
House Churches, 162, 217f
House of Commons, 136
House of Lords, 102f, 118, 187
House of Love (Dār Al- Mahabba), 197
Human Fertilisation and Embryology Act, 89, 132f, 222, 277

Human Rights Act, 87
Human Rights, 162
Humility, 83
Hunayn Ibn Ishaq, 203
Hunt, Kate, 44
Hunt, Pauline, 123, 130
Huntington, Samuel, 271, 284
Huntington, William Reed, 224f, 229, 245f, 264
Hussain, Saddam, 160, 176, 197
Hydration, 146

I
'Ishq, 27f
Iberia, 97
Ibn Al- Tayyib, 204
Ibn Al'Assāl, 204
Ibn Ishaq, 107, 190
Ibrahim, Anwar, 173
Icons, 244
Identity, 127f, 131f, 136, 192, 225, 247, 263
Ideology, 179f, 192
Ijmā', 33
Ijtihād, 33
Imago Dei, 43, 50, 59, 63, 72, 98, 126, 147, 247, 292
Imam, 178
Imams, 191
Immigration, 123, 178
Immune System, 141
Impartation, 19
Imputation, 16f
In Vitro Fertilisation, 135
Incarnation, the, 201
Inculturation, 206f, 223f
Indaba, 248
India, 100, 163, 165, 168, 173, 178f, 190, 197, 225, 247, 249, 252f
Indigensation, 206f,
Indonesia, 173
Industrial Revolution, 97
Instruments of Communion, 220f, 248
Integration, 70, 119, 140, 156, 181, 272
Interdependence, 263
Inter-faith Dialogue, 177, 199f, 227, 271
Intermediate Technology, 142, 280
International Covenant on Civil and Political Rights, 156, 189
Intimacy, 200
Iqbāl, Muhammad, 27f, 202, 211, 275
Iran (Persia), 39, 95f, 159f, 170f, 178, 199, 209

Iraq, 158f, 160f, 170f, 176, 178, 197
Ireland, 261
Ishaq Ibn Hunayn, 203
Islam, 25f, 44, 60, 100, 155, 166, 168f, 173f, 184f, 185f, 191f, 200f, 220f, 275
Islamic State of Iraq and al-Shām (ISIS), 191f
Islamic State, 96, 159f, 175
Islamisation, 155
Islamism, 8, 23, 100f, 151f, 159f, 166f, 173f, 184, 191f, 205, 292
Ismā'ilis, 151
Israel, 60f, 82, 160, 164, 167f, 170, 174, 195f, 292
Istanbul (Constantinople), 72, 169, 199, 250
Istighrāq, 28
Istiḥsān, 33
Istiṣḥāb, 33
Istiṣlāḥ, 33
Italy, 122

J
Jackson, Emily, 148, 184
Jakobovits, Lord, 14
Jalal, Ayesha, 184
James II, 244
James, St., 234, 243
Jeremiah, 61
Jerusalem Declaration, 241
Jerusalem, 196, 199f, 200, 218, 233f, 250
Jesus Christ, 10, 14, 16f, 21, 26, 37, 40, 42, 44, 46, 61, 69, 71, 76, 78, 82f, 116, 139, 189, 200f, 216, 220f, 231f, 244, 256, 258, 273, 287f
Jews, 8, 16, 87, 96f, 114, 151, 160, 163, 167, 170, 176f, 196, 199f, 208, 218, 234
'Jihadi John', 191
Jizya, 199f
John of Damascus, St., 201f
Johnson, Boris, 42
Jones, Peter, 184
Josiah, 25
Judea, 218, 235
Judge, E. A., 66
Judiciary, 157, 164, 175, 186
Just War, 75
Justice, 14, 62f, 72, 110, 122, 158, 166, 176, 183, 186, 208, 249, 253, 271f, 291, 292f
Justificare, 18
Justification, 15f, 21f, 245, 255f
Justin Martyr, 196

K

Ka'b Ibn al-Ashraf, 188
Kaan, Fred, 293
Kabul, 165
Kant, Immanuel, 116, 282
Karachi, 165
Karas, Shawky, 210
Kashmir, 165, 168, 174
Keller, Tim, 39, 53
Kenya, 69, 249
Keown, John, 148, 184
Khalidi, Tarif, 211
Khalifah, 275
Khamanei, Ayatollah, 163
Khatami, Mohammad, 162
Kikuyu Conference, 249
Kilner, John F., 143
Kingdom of God, 293
Kitchen, Kenneth, 65
Kleinfeld, Judith, 129f
Korea, 261
Kosovo, 174
Kraft, Charles, 68f
Küng, Hans, 19, 271, 284
Kurdish, 160
Kurdistan Regional Government, 158
Kurds, 160f, 171, 176
Kuwait, 170

L

Lambeth Conference, 220, 226, 229, 237f, 246, 248, 250, 255, 259f, 263
Laodicea, 233f
Laos (Laity), 99, 206, 248, 262
L'Arche, 293
Larkin, Philip, 77
Laslett, Peter, 125
Latin, 204
Law, 25f, 105f, 128, 157, 171, 175, 177, 182f, 188, 191f, 204f, 270, 283f
Lazareth, W. H., 265
Lebanon, 178
Legislation, 75, 104f, 128, 283
Leo XIII, Pope, 254
Leonard, Graham, 266
Lesbians, 131
Liberation, 208, 222
Libya, 170, 176
Life and Work, 260

Life, 141
Lima Text, 247
Ling, John L., 137, 143
Literature, 203, 291
Liturgy, 226, 243f, 253f
Living wills, 278
Locke, John, 115f
Logic, 201
Logidzomai, 16
Logos, 47, 291
London Missionary Society, 245
Lord Chancellor, 87
Lord Chief Justice, 87
Lossky, Nicholas, 266
Love, 9, 18, 20, 25f, 31f, 40, 71, 292f
Lucar, Cyril, 245
Lusitanian Church, 204
Luther, Martin, 20
Lutheran- Catholic Declaration on Justification, 20f, 245, 256
Lutherans, 196, 247
Lydia, 217, 233

M
Macedonia, 218, 221, 235
MacEoin, Denis, 184
MacIntyre, Alasdair, 66
Madrassas, 177, 179
Magna Carta, 82, 97, 193
Mahabba, 27
Mahdi, 178
Malayalam, 252
Malines Conversations, 255
Mallouhi Mazhar, 207
Malta Report, 255
Mā'mūn Al-Rashīd, 201
Mandaeans, 161, 176
Marriage Preparation, 119, 121
Marriage, 8, 43, 75, 87, 113f, 139, 156, 180, 183, 273, 283, 288
Marsh Arabs, 176
Marshall, W. J., 229
Mar Thoma Christians, 252, 260
Martin, David, 261, 267
Marturia, 196f
Martyrs, 14, 72, 178, 196
Marx, K., 38
Marxism, 99, 192
Mary Tudor, 19

Mary, The Blessed Virgin, 244, 263
Mascall, E. L., 265f
Massignon, Louis, 27f
Mazzafar, Chandra, 173
Meaning, 45
Media, 77, 151, 166, 185, 193, 195
Medical Ethics, 270f
Medical Technology, 8, 281
Meditation, 292
Meitosen, D., 266
Meliorism, 63
Mellitus, St., 68
Men, 72f, 102, 114, 119f, 126f, 131f, 218
Mentoring, 127f, 209f
Mercy, 62, 139, 208, 258
Mesopotamia, 198, 227
Methodists, 249, 259f
Middle East, 60, 101, 155, 157, 168f, 177, 195f
Millet, 96
Milton, John, 221
Mind, 46
Mindanao, 178
Ministry, 71f, 78, 235f, 255, 259f
Miracles, 145
Mission Theological Advisory Group, 79
Mission, 23, 43, 59, 72f, 114, 126f, 227f, 231f, 241, 245, 249, 251f
Missionaries, 73
Missisauga, 256
Mitochondrial Disease, 135
Mohammed, 189, 191, 202
Monarchy, 60, 81f, 97
Monasticism, 27, 169, 197f, 202f, 227f
Monism, 28
Monogamy, 271, 283
Moore, Peter, 285
Moral Awareness, 93, 269f
Moral Judgements, 270
Moral Law, 271f
Moral Relativism, 270
Moral Rules, 270
Moral Theologians, 140
Morals, 215, 269f, 281f, 292f
Morgan, Patricia, 123, 130
Morsi, Muhammad, 154f
Moses, 189
Mosques, 163, 170, 179, 186
Mothers' Union, 224

Mothers, 88, 113, 120f, 126f, 131f, 136
Moule, CFD, 123, 242
Movements, 241f
Moynahan, Brian, 228
Mozarab (*Musta'rab*), 204
Mubarak, Hosni, 154
Muddiman, John, 242
Mullahs, 162
Multiculturalism, 52, 180, 193
Multi-Faith, 83
Munib, Younan, 196
Murder, 26
Murphy, Francis, 66
Music, 78
Muslim Brotherhood (Ikhwān Al-Muslimīn), 100f, 153f, 166, 174
Muslims, 31f, 61, 87, 96, 100, 102f, 151, 165f, 174f, 181, 183, 185f, 191f, 199f, 221, 227

N
Nablus, 196
Nahḍ a, 205
Nahḍ at, Al-'Ulema, 173
Nation State, 218
National Church, 218f
National Council of Churches of Kenya (NCCK), 249
National Socialism, 192
Nationalists, 154, 157, 170, 205
Natural Law, 97f, 269f
Natural Rights, 98
Nature, 136, 273f
Needham, Joseph, 47
Neill, Stephen, 264f
Neo-Platonism, 28
Nestorians (Assyrian Church of the East), 203, 250, 253f
Netherlands, 68, 147
New Age, 46, 68
New Delhi Statement, 225, 246
New World, 98
Newbigin, Lesslie, 66, 289
Newman, John Henry, Cardinal, 19, 223, 229
Niebuhr, Richard, 69
Nigeria, 69
Nikāh, 119
Nikean Club, 251
Nineham, D. E., 34
Niqāb (veil), 109f
Nissiotis, N.A., 265

Non-Conformists, 245
Non-Jurors, 244
Norman Conquest, 81
North Africa, 169f,
Nuns, 72, 109, 197
Nurture, 120
Nympha, 217, 233

O
Oath of Allegiance, 244
Oath of Supremacy, 244
O'Donovan, Oliver, 284
Old Catholic Churches, 260
Orb, 82
Ordinal, 248
Ordinariates, 257
Organ Donation, 139f, 278f
Organ Transplantation, 139f, 278f
Organisation of the Islamic Conference (now Organisation of Islamic
Cooperation), 187f
Origen, 198
Orthodox Churches, 72f, 99, 160, 244f, 250f, 261
Otto, Rudolf, 29
Ottomans, Empire, 160, 170, 200, 204, 251
Oxford, 203

P
Packer, J. I., 266
Padwick, John, 261, 267
Pagans, 196
Page, Richard, 87
Pakistan, 163f, 170, 176f, 185f, 199, 209, 225, 241, 247
Palestine, 174, 195f, 206f
Palliative Medicine, 146, 180
Parenting, 120, 181
Paris, 185f
Parish Church, 218, 234
Parke, Ross, 130, 133
Parliament, 59, 155, 157
Partnership, 74, 78f
Pastoral Counselling, 45
Pastors, 45, 117, 155, 209f
Paul VI, Pope, 255, 257, 262
Paul, St., 16, 22, 26, 51, 57, 61f, 83, 146, 218, 221, 233f
Peace, 96, 190, 271
Pentecost, 288

Pentecostals, 215, 261
Perfection, Doctrine of, 260, 284
Persecution, 98f, 158, 176, 178
Persian Empire, 203, 221
Person, 8, 115, 142, 145, 179f, 276f, 283
Peter III, 253
Peter, St., 288
Phan, Peter, 66
Phenomenology of Religion, 128
Philippines Independent Catholic Church, 260
Philippines, 178
Phillips, David, 60
Philosophy, 97, 169, 198, 236
Physiology, 141
Piper, John, 15, 21
Pius V, Pope, 254
Plato, 114
Platten, Stephen, 263
Plērōma, 232
Pobee, J. S., 266
Poetry, 203
Pole, Cardinal, 19
Police, 186f
Policy, 75, 104
Politics, 293
Polkinghorne, John, 47
Polygamy, 271
Pontifical Council for Promoting Christian Unity, 265
Poor, the, 62, 153, 292
Portugal, 204
Porvoo Declaration, 258f
Power, 101
Prayer, 75, 237, 241f
Pre-Nuptials, 121
Preparatio Evangelica, 10
Presbyterians, 247, 257
President's Council on Bioethics, 137
Press, 157, 164, 167, 175, 187
Priesthood, 60, 71, 73
Priests, 155, 243
Primates Meeting, 220, 239, 241, 248, 263
Primum non nocere (first, do no harm), 139f
Principalities & Powers, 232
Principled Comprehensiveness, 224
Prior, Michael, 195f
Prisca (Priscilla), 217, 233
Prison, 179, 192f

Prophets, 14, 26, 32, 231
Protestants, 18, 21, 99, 219, 246, 252, 258, 261
Province, the, 219
Psychiatry, 38, 45
Psychology, 120
Psychotherapy, 38
Public Life, 50, 59f, 105
Public Opinion, 269, 276
Public Preaching, 103, 187
Pure Relationships, 117, 126
Purpose, 236

Q
Qatar, 159
Qibla, 31
Quaid-i-Azam, M. A. Jinnah, 168
Queen, the, 81
Qur'ān, 27f, 173, 188f, 201f, 221, 275

R
Rābi'a Al-'Adawiyya, 30
Radicalisation, 192
Radner, Ephraim, 228
Rahner, Karl, 20
Raiwind, 101
Ramsey, Michael, 250, 255
Reason, 46f, 236, 273
Reasonable Accommodation, 57, 77, 89, 105f, 157
Reception, (doctrine of), 73, 255
Recreation, 72
Reformation, 218f
Reformation, the, 18f, 21f, 62f, 235f, 243, 247
Reformers, the, 19f, 22, 51, 62
Refugees, 61, 75, 161, 207
Regensburg Agreement, 19
Regensburg Lecture, 221
Regnerus, Mark, 88
Relationships, 118, 125f, 148
Religion, 173, 186f, 270, 273, 281f
Religious Education, 128
Remission, 145
Renaissance, 97
Repentance, 70, 288
Reproduction, 142
Reproductive Medicine, 269f, 276
Respect for the Dead, 140f
Responsibility, 7, 93

Revelation, 198, 236, 269, 273
Revolution, 153, 162f, 177
Richards, Peter, 123, 130
Righteousness, 19f
Rihbany, Abraham, 207
Robinson, J. A. T., 40, 53
Rochester Cathedral, 76
Roman Catholic Church, 73, 99, 117, 244f, 249, 252, 254, 255f
Roman Empire, 96, 114, 196, 221
Roman Law, 182
Romania, 250
Rome, 218f, 233f, 244f, 256
Root, Michael, 259, 266
Rose, Lynda, 194
Roslin Institute, 141
Rouhani, Hassan, 162f, 171
Rousseau, Jean-Jacques, 65
Rūmī, Jalāluddīn, 27f
Runcie, Robert, 251, 263
Runciman, Steven, 53
Russel, Gerald, 168
Russia, 178f, 251
Ruston, Roger, 54, 108
Ruthven, Malise, 184
Ryle, J. C., 16f

S
Sabeel Ecumenical Centre, 208
Sacraments, 16, 43, 73, 82, 115, 225, 234f, 246, 260
Sacred Space, 49f
Sacrifice, 13f, 143
Safety, 110f
Sahas, D. J., 211
Salafī, 153f, 160, 165f, 173
Salvation History, 15, 288
Salvation, 198, 245
Samuel, Prophet, 97
Samuel, Vinay, 53
Sanctification, 17f
Sanctions, 172
Sanneh, Lamin, 69, 220, 228
Saracco, Norberto, 53
Sasovsky, Nicholas, 263
Saul, King, 97
Saunders, Cicely, 145
Saunders, Peter, 137
Saudi Arabia, 159, 178, 186

Sax, Leonard, 130

Schimmel, A., 35

Schmaus, Michael, 20

Science, 47f, 67, 93, 97, 135f, 169, 236, 272f, 280, 291

Scott, Richard, 66, 108

Ṣdq, 15f

Secularism, 10, 46, 67f, 75, 107, 179f, 187, 227, 292

Security, 110f, 159

Sedition, 188

Segregation, 52

Sentience, 140

Septuagint, 232

Seripando, Cardinal, 19

Service, 83, 186, 226f, 293

Sexuality, 237, 254, 259

Shah, 153

Shah, Rebecca Samuel, 261

Shah, Timothy, 261

Shakespeare, William, 221

Sharī'a, 23, 32, 101f, 151, 157, 171, 176f, 178, 183, 185f, 191f, 205, 208

Shenouda, Pope, 102

Shī'a, 151, 160f, 165, 173, 177f, 184, 192

Shiraz, 163

Shirk, 201

Shortt, Rupert, 108, 168

Siblings, 129, 133

Sider, Robert D., 210

Simul justus et peccator, 19

Sin, 16, 23, 29, 287f

Sinai, 155

Sinclair, Maurice, 264

Sirhindī, Shaykh Ahmad, 28

Sisi, Abdel Fattah, 166

Slavery, 62f, 98

Smith, Margaret, 27, 34f, 202, 211

Social Cohesion, 190

Social Contract, 60

Social Science, 70

Society for the Propagation of the Gospel, 252

Society, 34, 57, 62, 70, 93, 97, 115, 129, 156f, 164, 168, 175f, 192, 261, 273, 282, 293

Sociology of the Family, 114

Sociology of The New Testament, 62

Son of Man (the), 14

Sookhdeo, Patrick, 194

Sorley, W. R., 284

South Africa, 69

South America, 221, 261
South Asia, 173f, 178, 249, 253
South India, Church of, 258
Soviet Union, 164
Sperm Bank, 131
Spirit (the Holy), 8, 17f, 21f, 231f, 288
Spiritual Direction, 45, 293
Spirituality, 44, 67, 128f, 198, 205, 254, 261, 292
Sri Lanka, 96, 100, 225
Stabilitas, 293
Stambaugh, John, 66
Stark, Rodney, 53
State, the, 74, 78, 132, 171, 179f, 246, 278, 283
Stein, Peter, 184
Stem Cells, 142
Stephenson, Alan, 265
Stewardship, 126, 182, 274
Stott, John, 224, 264
Stout, G. F., 284
Stransky, T. F., 266
Stuart, Hannah, 194
Substitution, 16f
Suffering Servant, 14
Ṣūfīs, 27f, 151, 165, 173, 192, 202, 207
Sugden, C. M.N., 53
Suicide, 147f, 180
Sunday Trading Bill, 49, 103
Sunnah, 188f
Sunnis, 159f, 173, 177, 178, 192
Supreme Governor, 83
Swan, Laura, 210
Sweden, Church of, 258
Synagogues, 102
Synods, 75, 239, 248
Syria, 27, 154, 159f, 170, 178, 198, 202, 208, 227, 252f
Syriac, 203, 220, 252
Syrians, 60, 260

T
Tablīghī Jamā'at, 100f, 174, 184
Tahir Ahmad, Mirza, 190
Taliban, 164, 177
Tamils, 100
Tanzimāt, 200, 205
Taqiya, 178
'Teaching of Hate', 157, 166, 177, 190, 191f

Technology, 135f, 269, 276f
Tehran, 95, 153, 162, 171
Teleology, 48, 272f
Terrorism, 151, 164, 173, 185, 193
Texas, University of, 88
Theocracy, 153, 166, 174
Theodore Abu Qurra, 201
Theodore of Mopsuestia, 198
Theological Education by Extension, 208
Theology, 198, 206, 252, 262
Theotokos, 244
Thomas, M. M., 53
Thompson, Martin, 130
Thorne, John, 194
Tillich, Paul, 21
Time, 48f
Timothy of Baghdad, 201f
Toolan, John, 211
Toon, Peter, 15, 19f, 22
Totalitarianism, 179
Tractarians, 254
Tradition, 78f, 128, 181f, 193, 199, 202, 205, 235, 244, 249, 255, 262, 269
Transformation, 70
Translatability, 69, 220
Travancore, 252
Trent, Council of, 19f, 219
Trinity, 201
Troas, 217
Tunisia, 167
Turkey, 167, 170, 178, 253
Turkoman, 160
Turner, Philip, 228
Tyndale, William, 21, 51, 221
Tyranny, 98, 101, 175, 274

U
Ummah, 174, 192
United Churches, 249f, 262
United Nations Human Rights Committee, 156
United Nations, 161, 176
United States of America, 63, 88, 105, 137, 155, 160
Universal Declaration of Human Rights, 87, 98, 101, 156, 167, 171, 175, 177, 186
Universe, the, 45f, 67f, 71, 272f, 291
University, 179, 192f, 203
Utilitarianism, 68, 272, 280

V
Values, 271f, 280
Vatican II, 19, 249, 255
Vietnam, 99,
Vikings, 60
Violence, 174f, 189f, 192f, 281
Virgin Birth, 201
Vision of God, 25
Vision, 75, 205
Vocation, 41, 71f,
Voluntary Principle, 241f
Von Rad, Gerhand, 284

W
Wahdat Al-Shuhūd, 28
Wahdat Al-Wujūd, 28
Wahhābī, 160, 165f, 173
Wainwright, G., 266
Wake, William, 254
Wales, 249
Walīullāh, Shah, 32, 35
Ward, Benedicta, 35, 210
Ward, James, 272, 275, 284
Ware, Kallistos, 250, 264f
Webb, Pauline, 266
Welcome, 77
Wessels, Anton, 79
West (the), 8f, 65, 97, 151, 154f, 164f, 169f, 178f, 187, 197f, 203f, 209f, 215f, 227, 235, 247
West Africa, 76, 173, 182
West Bank, 168, 196
Westermann, Claus, 107
Westminster Confession, 247
William and Mary, 244
William Wilberforce, 62f
Williams, Pharrell, 163
Willibrord, St., 68
Windsor Report, 248, 263
Winston, Robert, Lord, 136
Winter, Tim (aka Shaykh Abdul Hakim Murad), 187, 190
Wisdom, 232
Womack, Sarah, 130
Women, 72f, 102, 114, 120 126f, 131f, 136, 151, 156f, 166, 175f, 183, 217f, 222, 251, 253f, 271
Word of God, 201, 234f, 255, 292
Work, 38, 41, 72, 76, 93, 157
World Council of Churches, 225, 246f, 254, 261f

World View, 48, 68, 75, 107, 289, 293
World War II, 104
Worship, 32, 57, 74, 76f, 81, 99, 156f, 165, 167, 175f, 186, 202, 206, 221, 242, 287f
Wrath, 40
Wright, N. T., 15f, 21
Wright, Robert, 229, 264f

X
Xenotransplantation, 141f, 276

Y
Yarnold, Edward, 265f
Yazdigard, Emperor, 96, 164
Yazidis, 8, 151, 160f, 176, 190
Yemen, 178, 208
Ye'or, Bat, 210
Young, William, 107, 211, 228
Youth, 178f

Z
Zoroastrians, 31, 163, 199
Zargaran, Maryam, 162

ACKNOWLEDGEMENTS

The author and the publishers gratefully acknowledge that materials included in this book first appeared in articles published in newspapers, magazines and journals, as set out below and reproduced with permission:

- Chapter 1.1 is adapted from my Latimer Briefing 13, *Justification by Faith: Orienting the Church's Teaching and Practice to Christ –* A lecture in honour of the Revd Dr Peter Toon (London, Latimer Trust, 2013).
- Chapter 1.2 was first published in *A Faithful Presence; Essays for Kenneth Cragg* (Melisende, 2003).
- Chapters 2.2, 3.1, 3.3, 4.1, 4.2, 4.4, and 4.5 were first published by Standpoint Magazine in January 2013, June 2013, May 2012, October 2012, September 2014, May 2011, and March 2015 respectively.
- Some material from chapter 2.3 was published in my article *The Sacramental Significance of the Coronation* (2013) 15 Ecc LJ 71-74 and is reproduced here with permission.
- Material from Chapters 2.4, 3.5 and 5.5 were previously published by the Mail on Sunday in January 2015 and the Daily Mail in August 2014 and January 2014 respectively.
- Chapters 3.2 and 3.8 have been adapted from my previous articles published by The Telegraph in September 2013 and February 2010.
- Chapter 4.3 is adapted from my earlier article that was first published by the Spectator in December 2013 under the title, 'Act now to save the Middle East's Christians'.
- Chapter 5.3 was first published as *The Anglican Communion and Ecumenical Relations* in The Wiley-Blackwell Companion to the Anglican Communion, ed. Ian Markham, etc. (Oxford, 2013) and is reproduced here with permission.
- Chapter 5.4 was first published in the October 2002 edition of the Crucible Magazine.

The author and the publishers are grateful to these publications, as well as to The Catholic Herald for permission to reproduce material that they had first published in March 2015.